THE HEATHENS

WILLIAM HOWELLS is presently Professor of Anthropology, Curator of Somatology, and a member of the faculty of the Peabody Museum at Harvard University. Born in 1908, he attended St. Paul's School before attending Harvard, where he received his S.B. and Ph.D. degrees. He has taught at the University of Wisconsin (1939–54) where he was Chairman of the Department of Sociology and Anthropology (1953–54). In 1954, he became Professor of Anthropology at Harvard University, and is now Chairman of the Department.

Professor Howells is a past president of the American Anthropological Association (1951). He has edited the *American Journal of Physical Anthropology* (1949–54) and served on the Advisory Panel for Anthropological and Related Sciences of the National Science Foundation (1954–55).

In addition to THE HEATHENS, Professor Howells has written *Back of History, Mankind So Far,* and *Mankind in the Making.*

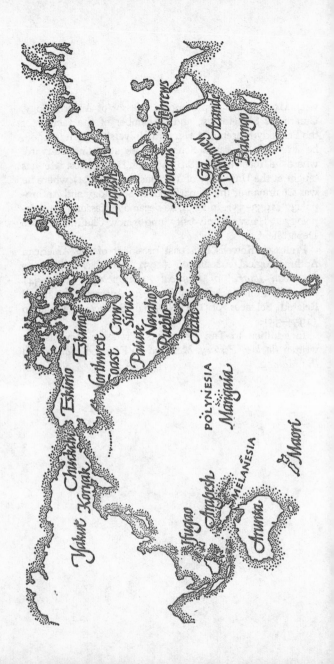

THE HEATHENS
Primitive Man and His Religions

WILLIAM HOWELLS

ILLUSTRATED WITH PHOTOGRAPHS

PUBLISHED IN CO-OPERATION WITH
THE AMERICAN MUSEUM OF NATURAL HISTORY

THE NATURAL HISTORY LIBRARY
ANCHOR BOOKS
DOUBLEDAY & COMPANY, INC.
GARDEN CITY, NEW YORK

The Heathens was originally published by Doubleday & Company, Inc. The Natural History Library edition is published by arrangement with Doubleday & Company, Inc.

Natural History Library edition: 1962

TO MY WIFE WITH MY LOVE

FOREWORD

During the nineteenth century, anthropologists kindled the fire of imagination in the mind of the public with their colorful accounts of primitive society and with their interpretation of "savage" and "barbaric" customs. Above all, it was the magic and religion of these societies that stood out over other aspects as truly strange and exotic. But the early anthropologists had to rely mainly on reports of adventurers and explorers and missionaries; there was not the body of detailed, impartial, and accurate information that there is today.

Even when Frazer wrote his monumental *The Golden Bough*, anthropology had not developed the technique of field work to the science it now is. As the science grew, it eschewed the more distasteful aspects of its past, such as the use of derogatory terms like "savage" and "barbaric"; and it equally eschewed generalizations about the "childlike nature" of primitive peoples and their propensity for cannibalism. In the process of establishing itself as a true science, anthropology also came to concentrate on hard facts rather than intangibles.

In this way the performance of magical and religious ritual received attention, but the innermost feelings and emotions of man's religious life were generally left alone as more proper to the disciplines of psychology, philosophy, and theology. But these feelings and emotions are nonetheless social facts, and have to be dealt with somehow, particularly if we are dealing with religion rather than with the abstract form of society, or social structure. This is not an easy field, as even scientists have feelings and emotions and must try to overcome them in order to deal impartially with those of others.

Since the first publication of Professor Howell's THE HEATHENS, there have been significant additions by leading social anthropologists to the available literature, such as Evans Pritchard's notable monograph, *Nuer Religion*. On the same lines we have been given equally penetrating and detailed studies by S. F. Nadel (*Nupe Religion*), Robert Bellah (*Tokugawa Religion*), and John Middleton (*Lugbara Religion*), among others. Within a more general frame of reference there was the 1952 posthumous publication of A. M. Hocart's *The Life-Giving Myth*, and of very great importance is a recent book by Edward Norbeck, *Religion in Primitive Society*, in which he deals with the origins of religion, concepts of the supernatural, ritual, priesthood, and with the role of religion as an agent of social control. But THE HEATHENS remains a popular classic in presenting primitive religion (in its non-derogatory sense) which, in light of modern anthropological knowledge and theory, removes it once and for all from the aura of "savage" superstition, colorful but barbaric, with which it was for so long surrounded.

The strangest and most exotic customs appear in the following pages as logical, necessary, even commendable contributions to moral behavior amongst people not yet subjected to the influence of any of the great formal religions. The most bizarre magical practices are shown to be closely related to the exigencies of everyday life, providing, in default of scientific knowledge, the comforting illusion that man is able to cope effectively with any situation that might arise. Even with our advanced technological development, scientists and laymen alike preserve similar illusions in our own society today.

In explaining the sociological function of religion, Professor Howells in no way detracts from its spiritual essence. To primitive man, magic—that is, the performance of certain physical actions—is effective in itself. The driving of a nail into a wooden effigy in the prescribed manner will automatically produce pain or death in the human counterpart, without the intervention of any genii or spirits. But there are some situations that cannot be dealt with in this way. Here we cross the tenuous border between magic and religion and enter the world of belief—the world of spirits, of ancestors, and of gods.

In THE HEATHENS the whole fascinating magico-religious complex emerges neither as a fuzzy mystique, nor as mere cold scientific fact, but as a pillar of societies throughout the world; as essential to the smooth running of each society as it is to the inner peace and stability of the individuals that comprise it. We not only begin to understand why other people do not live and think as we do, but we see that their ways are often better fitted to their circumstances than ours would be.

And Professor Howells finally brings us to the realization, both humbling and inspiring, that we are, after all, basically not so very different from those whom we yesterday called barbaric and savage.

COLIN M. TURNBULL
*Assistant Curator of
African Ethnology*

April 1961
*The American Museum
of Natural History*

CONTENTS

THE HEATHENS

The Idols of the Tribe have their foundation in human nature itself, and in the tribe or race of men. For it is a false assertion that the sense of man is the measure of things. . . . And the human understanding is like a false mirror, which, receiving rays irregularly, distorts and discolours the nature of things by mingling its own nature with it. . . . The human understanding is unquiet; it cannot stop or rest, and still presses onward, but in vain. Therefore it is that we cannot conceive of any end or limit to the world, but always as of necessity it occurs to us that there is something beyond.

FRANCIS BACON, *Novum Organum*

1

RELIGION, PRIMITIVE AND CIVILIZED

Scholars were cocking horn-rimmed spectacles at primitive religion for a long time before they saw much of its real nature. Naïve in the beginning, the anthropologists collected curios: along with fetishes, kachina dolls, and the like, they brought home stories of bloody funeral rites, or of human sacrifices, or of naughty orgies held on the disarming pretext that they did something good for the crops.

In these days, however, the science of man is less simple. The museums are pretty full, and the students are experienced enough now to grasp some of the meaning of what they have found. They have come to see the social and religious practices of an uncivilized people, not as a disorderly set of superstitious habits (which might be straightened out in a hurry by anyone with a white skin), but rather as a framework of dovetailing institutions, which are clung to for the solid reason that they comfort and strengthen their possessors. This is as profoundly true of religion as it is of government and law: religious ideas help in the struggle for existence as verily as a bow and arrow, or a fish trap. Here we have a point of great importance both in our knowledge of supposedly primitive people and in our understanding of religion itself. That is one of the things anthropology has discovered.

Do you remember the Wild Man of Borneo? The men of Borneo are not really wild. They hunt heads, it is true, but they do it from carefulness, not wildness; it is a social and religious necessity, and they—the tribe which does the hunting, you understand—get a certain good from it. Primitive religion, in spite of appearances, is not a name for childish tumult and bestial abandon. It is careful, thoughtful, purposeful; and it is good medicine.

The Wild Man was put with the freaks in the side show, but he might as well have paid his own quarter and looked at the rest of us. American citizens live in an advanced and comfortable nation, yet great numbers of them feel insecure and uncertain, either individually or in groups, to the point of bitter unhappiness. By good reports, your chances of being psychotic would be less in many primitive tribes than right where you are, surrounded though you may be by sanitation, law, psychiatry, uplifting literature, and good advice on every hand. Primitive people have long ago put into practical religious forms many things that your countrymen are trying to find for themselves in lectures and books on the good society, or on how to find happiness, or on what is wrong with them. This is not because the Noble Savage is so exceedingly noble; it is just that his religions are meaningful, and we can learn something from them.

Certainly it is not hard to see the significance of religion in the study of mankind generally. There is probably nothing that touches man's interest more acutely, and so his religious acts make up a most revealing part of his whole behavior. Therefore a study of religion tells not only about religion itself but also about man and his special psychological and social nature, seen in his most earnest moments.

There are various approaches to the study. Philosophy, for one, looks for the meaning and the moral in religion. Psychology tries to find why man is religious. Or rather psychology once did, under William James and his followers, but the psychologists some time ago vacated the field in favor of the theologians, who tend to merge it with philosophy. History studies the past of a given religion, to trace its growth and changes, comparing it with others for similarities, relationships, and differences. This field now belongs to the sociologists as much as to the historians, the former having combined all three of the above attacks and broadened out the inquiry to include the connections between religious and cultural development.

Finally there is the anthropological approach, which is more like natural history: anthropologists go about like bird watchers, with notebooks, studying actual, living communities of all kinds, making careful records of how they worship, and trying to discover why. It is not after meaning that the students seek, nor any absolute values; they desire only to know what is actually being done, and what human reasons lie behind it. That is the method, essentially, although of course anthropologists, like sensible scientists, have not hesitated to plunder the goods of the sociologists, historians, psychologists, and philosophers.

Somewhat to their annoyance, workers in this field have been ticketed as people who prefer to associate with savages. At a dinner party somebody three places away will lean toward you and shout: "I understand you are an anthropologist. Where have you been?" This is a demand bid, and if you cannot instantly answer that you have spent eighteen months among the Ibobio, or point to the ravages of some tropical disease that was absolutely new to science when you discovered it by getting it, the conversation will humiliatingly shift to another subject. It is true nevertheless that anthropology's first duty is toward unliterate people—those who, lacking writing, are unable to keep their own history, and thus to hoist themselves up into the realm of self-criticism. Anthropology must do this for them; it must take them at one moment, the present, and put them on paper in the most intelligent manner it has learned, trying to make some honest interpretation without neglecting to gather up all the information which might allow some different interpretation later on.

Working with relatively simple societies has certain important advantages. One is that of standing outside such a society, and being able to see all around it because of its small size, and so to see all parts of it at once, the first requisite for finding out how these parts fit together. This, of course, is valuable in the study of religion. Equally valuable, and perhaps more interesting for us, ourselves, is the advantage of being able to see the gaps between two different societies; I mean by this, to compare several societies, each in good working order, to observe the different ways in which they fulfill their religious needs; to see, therefore, in what ways religious needs may be fulfilled. And the only people who can show us that are heathens and pagans.

The reasons are these. Christianity, like the other major world religions, is not a good object for the anthropological study of religion, because it is too old and too big. It covers all of Western civilization. It is not a simple, aboriginal, native cult; its dogma and philosophy have come from the hands of sixty generations of the Church's scholars, being added to, purified, generalized, and adapted, until it has gathered together people of every color, speaking every language. (It is of course not the only such religion: Islam has sat in the saddle of history in the Arab world, from westernmost Africa to the Philippines; and Buddhism, Judaism, and Confucianism have had similar natures.) Therefore it is rather the tribal cults, from Shinto down to the simplest deferences of the Hottentots, which provide us with what we need, because they are geared to the life of a single people. They have not been deliberately broadened out. In them it is easier to see the direct springs of religious behavior inside a society, without the interposition of great teachers and high ideals or ethics. For they grow up naturally, to satisfy religious necessities; they need no sophisticated philosophy, and ethics are entirely secondary.

Christianity, furthermore, in spite of its towering position in history, is only one religious manifestation, so that to base a study of all religion on Christianity alone would be as unscientific as to write a comparative anatomy of the mammals after dissecting one elephant. For other religious beliefs and conventions are possible, no matter how heathenish, and they actually exist in the uncivilized world in great variety. So, in order to know of what man's religious nature is capable, we must see everything he does in the name of religion, the whole range of his piety from the most benighted to the most enlightened.

There is no special name for primitive religions and churches, but I should be inclined to call them "native cults," meaning that they are indigenous, like plants or animals, and have in most instances grown up among the very tribes they serve.[1] They differ from the higher religions in several ways, other than the ones I mentioned.

The great faiths are messianic, being founded on historical figures of great personal force, like Jesus or Mohammed. Secondly, they are strongly ethical. Thirdly, they might be called world religions, because they have a missionary character allied to their messianic one. They see no boundaries, each considering itself the one true creed; they are imperialistic, going out to bring into the fold others than those people among whom they grew up, so that Christianity, Islam, and Buddhism now have the vast majority of their adherents beyond the borders of the nation where their messiahs first preached.

So each has a message and sufficient vitality to carry it abroad. In order to succeed, they have still another trait, which is a great exclusiveness in belief; a jealousy of their own doctrines and an intolerance of others, which they relentlessly seek to blot out. Each is basically a sufficient philosophy, propounded by the messiah and worked upon by his followers in the endeavor to make the whole thing into a single logical and ethical structure. Not so the wide-eyed native cults, which are open to any suggestion and will accept any idea that seems appealing or useful, sometimes even if it opposes a prevailing one. And although they may look on the gods of other people as enemies, they are quite

[1] They have often been called "nature" or "natural" religions, but these words imply something special: that the sources of a cult are found invariably in "nature" or that there is something more artificial about the others.

willing to recognize their existence and do not try to grind them out by denying them belief.

This purification of the higher religions has given birth to a label you will recognize at once: "superstition." Little of this snobbery exists in native cults, where, provided it works, anything goes. Christianity, however, must draw the line between superstition and religion. It has no place for horoscopes or for knocking on wood, because these attempts to tamper with the future cannot possibly be reconciled with Christian doctrines of the acceptance of God's will. So they are put beyond the pale and called superstitions. But does that end them? No; just as in native cults, they remain notions which compel our attention. Or have you never knocked wood? It is estimated—I do not know by whom—that the yearly income of the country's fortune-tellers is a hundred and fifty million dollars. That is big business.

In order to get at their salient features, I have, of course, been generalizing to some extent about native cults—in opposition to what we are most familiar with in religion—and I do not mean to put all these cults on the same plane, by any means. Some aboriginal religions are most unorganized and informal, belonging very much to the people and the individual worshiper, while others approach the great sects in the development of doctrine and ritual, even to reaching the point of feeling that certain popular practices are unorthodox and superstitious. What I have been saying is in the hope of conveying the typical undiscriminating, heterogeneous, and varied nature of native cults, which may be difficult to grasp for anyone used only to the differences between Christian denominations.

So, compared with the tidier aspect of Christianity, primitive religion looks like a regular junkyard of the supernatural. There is now another aspect, however, to understand about native cults. This is the fact of their perfect legitimacy. It is quite true that we know their gods do not exist and their magic is hollow, but this book will be without point if we go back to Wordsworth and talk about a pagan suckled in a creed outworn, for the usefulness of religious belief has no relation to its accuracy or absurdity in physics, geology, or astronomy.

I do not mean only to repeat that these religions do the social job for which they are intended; I have said that, and I think it will come out often enough in the book. I desire here to implant the realization that primitive devotees are not people of another planet, but are essentially exactly like us, and are engaged with precisely the same kind of religious appetite as the civilized. And that appetite is fed and stilled by their own religions. This is very important; it is why we are taking those religions seriously. They are not toys. They are what we might be doing ourselves; and they are what most of our ancestors were indeed doing, two thousand years ago today.

This is a point that passes by too easily, so I propose to belabor it for another paragraph or so. Look at your newborn babe. What is his religion? Let us borrow the Tarzan motif and imagine a group of American babies somehow growing up in the wild to fend for themselves. Is there any reason to think that they might mature with a better grasp of the world around them, or a finer, more moral set of religious ideas, than a similarly abandoned batch of little Crows, Crees, or Krus? No; there would be nothing whatever to tell them that the sun is not a god and does not go around the earth. Look now at the practitioners of heathenism: Eskimos, Apaches, Basutos, Yaghans, Botocudos, Dravidians, Igorots, Truk Islanders. Our brains and theirs have the same structure, are fed by the same amount and kind of blood, are conditioned by the same hormones and titillated by the same senses; that is all well known, and nothing in their performance has ever been discovered to point the contrary. I see I am cribbing from Shylock, but I am not making any special plea for other people— I am just clearing ground. I mean that it is nothing but pompous preening if we ourselves, as individuals, as Christians, or as Occidentals, take any special credit for the great civilization, system of knowledge, and religion which have gradually accumulated in thirty or forty centuries on the continent of Europe and in the Near East.

I do not mean, certainly, that we should not take immense pride in it and be endlessly loyal to it. I only mean that we are lucky. It is evident from ancient European skeletons that, physically and mentally, we have not changed essentially in perhaps fifty to a hundred thousand years, and yet it is only three or four thousand since the mushrooming of knowledge and commerce shoved the Occident ahead of the rest of mankind. This has been the result of fortunate historical and geographical incidents. If we (the European Whites) could provide the mental soil for that tremendous growth, then so might other races have done the same thing in the same place; for they have readily partaken of it when they received it, sometimes absorbing it with unnerving speed, as did the Japanese.

Doubtless the practice of religion is very old. We are certain that Neanderthal man had it, because he put weapons in the graves of his dead, obviously so that the latter should not find themselves surrounded by ghostly game and have nothing to hunt it with; and in a cave in Switzerland he also made a shrine containing bears' skulls. But this was fairly late in the Stone Age, and man is much older than that. The more recent past abounds in decaying religious monuments. And if we had good records of all the primitive people, and their cults, who lasted into modern times, these records would be the very Alps for volume and variety.

Actually a sifting of our knowledge of living primitives —the only knowledge safe to use—has shown two things: that there is hardly a limit to what the human mind can fancy, but also that there are certain typical forms in religion, certain particular notions, which the mind seems to find especially interesting and important; high points in the mental landscape to which attention turns again and again, or perhaps channels into which the imagination easily slips and runs. Everywhere people believe in souls, for example, and in magic, and generally in certain other things like witches. These ideas, probably old and seemingly as natural and universal as speech itself, cannot be meaningless and haphazard. Only when civilization has made possible the appreciation of higher religions do these simpler cults appear to us as delusions, and it is easy, in our skepticism, to underestimate them.

I have now descanted at some length on what I am going to talk about and what I am not going to talk about. My purpose is to forget our own familiar religious ideas and look through sympathetic eyes, from a little distance, at some different ones. My point is this: a savage tribe searching for an earthly salvation in its own religious resources usually finds it; poor people are not necessarily unhappy, and neither are rain makers and ancestor worshipers.

There is really nothing new in this or in what follows. I am giving the reader little that he could not find out himself by going to the right library in the right frame of mind.[2] Indeed, I should apologize for writing the book at all[3]—I am a physical anthropologist, not the other kind. And, finally, if the reader is avid for blood rites, or snake cults, or maidens being tossed off cliffs, or stuff about the secrets of the ancients, I am afraid he will be disappointed. In fact I know he will. It is not that sort of book.

[2] Since this book was first published, there has appeared a *Reader in Comparative Religion* (1958), edited by William A. Lessa and Evon Z. Vogt. This contains sizable extracts taken from many of the sources I have used herein, and numerous others: the interested reader who wants more detail and information will find it excellent for browsing or for study.

[3] I probably never would have written it if it were not for Professor Alfred Tozzer, who first taught me this subject at Harvard, and to whom I wish to proclaim my debt.

2

THE NATURE OF RELIGION

Whatever religion may be, the human material for it is probably similar in all men and all tribes of men. There may be differences in its expression. One group may appear more religious, another less. Or one tribe may go in for the appeasement of local ghosts, another for the worship of remote high gods, and a third for magic to open the rain clouds and lure the game. But all give signs of satisfaction with their own observances, and primitive societies without religion have never been found.

As to the people themselves, there are those who are pious and those who are not. And there are those who may have doubts about what they are told, and those who may be extra gullible about witches and demons. But such individual notions matter little; most people get their beliefs straight out of the public pool and accept them implicitly. These are the ideas that have social force and do the work; they are the ones that people talk about and act upon together. They are the things I shall deal with, and what I say hereafter is meant to apply to public religion rather than private.

This does not let the individual out entirely, of course, because we have to look at society through him—it is the individual, not society, who acts religiously, though society tells him how to do it. When we consider religions we must first consider man, because religion is rooted in man and would of course not exist without him. It is a human manifestation. It is made by man. This is something different from the old epigram: "Man made God in his own image." It is not a question of the existence or non-existence of supernatural beings, for there could be no religion connected with them if man himself did not exist and feel the need of it.

It is, instead, a question of what there is in man, or about him, which makes him religious. I do not mean a quality of religion, like a phrenologist's head bump, something which might almost be dressed up and put in an allegory. There has in the past been brisk discussion of a religious emotion, or "instinct," as the one responsible factor, and such a thing has been accepted and sought for in other supposed emotions, or derivations or combinations of them: awe, love, fear, shame, conscience, as well as diverted sexual or social longings, and so forth and so on. Now of course the things signified by such terms may have strong connections with religious behavior, in different individuals and to different degrees, but this is a far cry from supposing that there may be found a particular, recognizable instinct, drive, or type of reaction which might be isolated like a bacillus and accepted as the one thing explaining why societies inevitably turn to religion like a flower to the sun. The quest for some such factor has not succeeded. In any event it is a subject for the psychologists, if they care to have it. What I am leading up to is different; it is a matter of certain palpable facts about man and his past which tend to show that it is not one lone element within him, but rather his whole organism and life which predispose him to "religious" behavior—which cause him to produce religious ideas and then to respond so readily to them.

First of all there are some important characteristics of man himself. We are fearfully and wonderfully made, and we can get a better idea of how fearfully and wonderfully by comparing ourselves with some of Noah's other passengers. Among all animals, the warm-blooded mammals are the most active, with the most intricate organization and the best-developed nervous systems. Among these, in turn, it is the Primates (especially the monkeys, the anthropoid apes, and men) which have, on the whole, the largest brains and the most refined and acute set of senses, so that their awareness of the world around them is increased beyond that of all living things. The highest of these animals not only possess good hearing, sensitive hands, and excellent muscular control, but have undoubtedly the best eyes in all of nature; they see stereoscopically (focusing on the same object from different points), so that they judge size and distance most accurately. Only men, apes, and monkeys completely enjoy this ability, and only these same animals are able to see so full a range of colors. With this fullness of vision we (and our low-brow relatives) absorb more of our surroundings than all other creatures—without realizing quite how well endowed we are, we nevertheless experience great pleasure in gazing at landscapes and living things. Lacking his range of senses and muscular refinement, think how handicapped an animal man would be. Compare yourself with a dog. He sees a grayish world tinged only with blue and brown, and he can feel and understand very little through the use of his paws, let alone accomplish anything with them, like playing billiards. There is only one thing he can do better than you: starting from scratch, he can smell you before you can smell him.

So man, approached only by his zoological next of kin, is constructed in such a way as to feel the impact of the physical world much more forcibly than any of the beasts. Thus far we have considered only the nature of what his senses receive, and how they receive it, like currency coming into a cash register. How is the money used? This, of course, is a question of brain, and here again man has no peers, for in relative size and complexity his brain outclasses all others. This is so obvious that I need not go on about it, except to remark that the only animals who can be induced to proceed any distance in reasoning along human patterns are the apes and monkeys. Accordingly, although they fall woefully short, they resemble us in this as in other things, and represent a stage from which we ourselves must have arisen.

For a purely animal existence, our large brains are a luxury rather than a necessity. While other creatures can retain sensory and motor nervous patterns—i.e., do a certain amount of remembering—the plenteousness of our own brains not only makes them act as much vaster storehouses but also allows us to think about things we have never actually experienced—to imagine. Therefore, if what our senses receive is a multiplication of what most mammals can take in, and if what our brain can then make of it is also a great multiplication of what a simpler brain can do, then it is easy to see that the final effect of beholding a lake, a bolt of lightning, or a dead man can be infinitely greater on us than on any of our four-footed friends.

Even so, the effect would be naught if we were stolid creatures, unroused by such a wealth of sensation. But we are not. Our nervous organization is matched by, and related to, a highly excitable temperament or emotional nature. You might say that any species of mammal which had evolved into a man, and had come to experience so much, had every right to an excitable disposition and a parlous insanity rate. Probably there is justice in this; however, by referring to some of the other Primates again I think it is possible to see that this keyed-up temperament is, partly at least, an organic inheritance, belonging to the monkeys and apes generally. While temperament is something which cannot be measured properly, it can be said that all the apes appear to be subject to temper tantrums like a child's. Chimpanzees seem to have a normal excitability much like ours, though somewhat higher, while gorillas, outwardly more placid and contented, may really be inhibiting their natural emotionalism more than chimps, being actually capable of marked emotional disturbances. To make an analogy, it is rather as though among the higher Primates and ourselves the emotional motors idled at a high rate, capable of quick acceleration.

There are other important qualities in which our relatives

resemble us, indicating that they are old traits and that we did not acquire them only on becoming human beings. One such quality is gregariousness. All men live in societies, or at least families, a hermit being very much of an exception. Of the higher Primates, the orangutan apparently often lives in solitude, but the others are typically extremely clannish; they either live in close family groups, like gibbons, or go about in sizable bands, which are not chance groupings but solidly knit affairs which will admit an occasional stranger only after he has hung around at a respectful distance long enough to become familiar. This cohesiveness is based on the fact that the individuals of a group are all socially or psychologically adjusted to one another, and it may show itself in a number of ways. One way is the above hostility to strangers, or meanness to a new colleague in the zoo. Another is the misery some animals will show if they are separated from their accustomed fellows, and the sympathy and affection of which they are capable toward one another, much more marked than, for example, among dogs. Yet others are the sensitivity they have for the moods of their companions, and the susceptibility to suggestions from one another or from human overlords, and the adaptability to the general mood of the group, or to demands made upon them by students putting them through tests. All this responsiveness and malleability is a sign of a rich and flexible nervous organization, capable of a great range of adjustment and not, as in lower animals, limited and hampered by a lot of ready-formed patterns, popularly known as instinctive behavior.

What I have said about human and Primate nature is based on serious investigation of matters of fact, and not on my own assumptions. I have been trying to hold up man's own physique and psyche as things legitimately founded in his evolutionary past; in other words, to show man not as an inexplicable what-is-it in the scheme of things but rather as the culmination of a trend producing creatures capable in the highest degree of receiving, and reflecting on, stimuli from their surroundings, and of great sensitiveness in reacting personally and adjusting themselves thereto. I do not think, however, that I need appeal to fact in order to state that this trend has not yet produced a sublimely happy animal, but only one capable of variable internal weather and of uncomfortable awareness of his difficulties. Nonetheless, in order to preserve the scientific tone of this dissertation, I will introduce one exhibit.

The Grant Study of Harvard University, in an attempt to reverse the field of medicine, has been studying the characteristics of "normal" young men[1] by selecting suitable Harvard sophomores over a period of four years up to a total of 259 students. These men were not meant to be unusual; on the contrary, they were meant to be as usual as possible, with the following qualifications. They were Harvard boys, of course, and Harvard is not the easiest college to enter. They were passed by the Hygiene Department as having no marked physical disabilities such as diabetes, infantile paralysis, deformities, and so on, and no psychological abnormalities; and all were doing satisfactorily in college, none having fallen afoul of the dean by day or by night. "Actually, some attempt was made to enlist those whose adjustments were superior. That the group was superior, in various categorizations, to the population at large and to the average college undergraduate, should be obvious."[2] Nevertheless, of these 259 normal or better-than-average students, 232 had at least one personal problem that either bothered them sufficiently to make them ask advice of the Grant Study staff, or made itself obvious to the staff members themselves. Only a small proportion of problems was acute (17 per cent of cases), but none of them was frivolous and all were disquieting, and most of

---

[1] See Clark W. Heath, *What People Are: A Study of Normal Young Men* (1945); Earnest Hooton, *Young Man, You Are Normal* (1945); C. W. Heath and Lewise W. Gregory, "Problems of Normal College Students and Their Families," *School and Society*, Vol. 63 (1946).

[2] Heath, *What People Are . . .* , p. 12.

the boys had more than one problem apiece. Remark now that 232 out of 259 is, to the nearest figure, 90 per cent. Who, then, is "normal"? If you were one of the 10 per cent, out of a generally superior physical and intellectual group, to whom life is all serene, you could count yourself lucky, since it seems more "normal" to have at least one fly in your ointment. It is true, of course, that these boys had not reached the Age of Discretion, and were still floundering in the adolescent Age of Worry; but this does not change the fact of man's great capacity for apprehensiveness. What does it batten on? This brings us from human nature to human history.

Man's life is hard, very hard. And he knows it, poor soul; that is the vital thing. He knows that he is forever confronted with the Four Horsemen—death, famine, disease, and the malice of other men. And because he can speak and so frame ideas for himself and his mercurial imagination, he is nature's great and only worrier; he can worry alone and he can worry in unison, always with justice. It is among people living a primitive existence, however, that this should be particularly true.

Man is distinguished from all other animals by culture. Culture, which largely is made possible by language, comprises everything which one generation can tell or teach the next; in other words, its non-physical inheritance. The complexity of our own culture shows what man is capable of, but the most primitive of surviving tribes, small bands of wandering hunters, show the kind of culture in which man has lived for perhaps a million years, including, for many thousands of years, some of our own ancestors in Europe, who must have had brains as good as our own. This was a bitterly harsh existence made harsher because, as I have said, he knew the worst; unlike animals, he was aware of the precariousness of his life and of the fact of death.

We today have some recompenses: our expectancy of life is long and we can make false teeth. Truly primitive people may keep only one jump ahead of nature, instead of our two or three. We can fetch our food from far away;

they must depend on the weather and the game in one small region. We can cure disease or prevent it; they can only palliate it. We may still have nightmares of being chased by bears or lions; they may encounter the real thing, armed only with a stone-headed spear or ax. For primitive or ancient men, therefore, culture has been a thin shield indeed, so that they have been forced to use their resources to the utmost. And religion is related to all this because religion is one of their resources.

Taking two of the Four Freedoms will make this a little clearer. Freedom of speech and freedom of religion are of no concern to the compact society of a savage people. They are solely preoccupied with freedom from want and freedom from fear, and I will seize on this to make a somewhat exaggerated distinction. Freedom from want they achieve by their own practical efforts, while freedom from fear they achieve by religion. That is to say, they feed and clothe themselves, and also protect their goods, by everyday material tools and techniques which they have invented and which they understand perfectly: they will use a bow made partly of bone to strengthen it, to shoot an arrow expertly tipped and feathered, and perhaps poisoned, and will accompany this with delicate tricks to quiet the quarry's fears, or call it to the hunter; and they make their clothes and houses in perfectly practical ways, according to climate and material. It is all hard work but it is satisfying because it is direct and dependable. Freedom from fear (including, note well, the fear of want) is something else, however, because it can seldom be attained directly. Want is a physical hazard; fear is a mental hazard.

Now by "fear," I should like to say clearly, I do not mean simply fright: that funk induced by something in the dark, or by the threat of pain, or by a terrible mistake. I use "fear" because I need a short Anglo-Saxon word to stand for a number of longer Latin words like anxiety, insecurity, frustration, maladjustment, apprehensiveness, inadequacy, dissatisfaction, disappointment, vulnerability, and so on—all those lesser cares which rot the apple of content and keep life from its fullness. Such corrosive feelings may exist for some clear reason which cannot be removed. Or they may come from a dimmer consciousness of accumulating wrongs and ills. Or they may arise in small common neuroses, with no direct cause at all. But, though it may seem so unnecessary, this kind of heckling is constant, and a natural part of existence, the debit side of the ledger.

We have managed to compress our fears into a much smaller compass, because we have spread such a wide scientific control over many of the things, such as pestilence, which might threaten our security, but a backward society has so little that can be called science at its disposal that it is left with no certain answer to a great many of its urgent necessities, let alone its minor complaints. And an answer it must have, to forestall fear, or even panic. (This is true even of ourselves.) The principal answer is religion, which is thus used to piece out the ground between what man can attend to himself and what his imagination tells him must be attended to. It is the extension of his wishes and beliefs beyond the edges of what his senses grant him; it is what lies outside the light of the campfire. It is the notions he feels he must accept if life is to be satisfactory, or even safe. In other words, religion is composed of all the serious things man feels obliged to take for granted.

Religion therefore may be said to complement science. The latter has been defined best, I think, as a system of knowledge which admits of no internal contradictions. It is a body of facts which continually grows but does so only by adding new facts which are acceptable in the light of those already known. If two apparent facts are in conflict, then one of them is wrong or else the principle used in relating them is in error. For anthropological purposes, however, I should define science simply as the understanding of the correct explanation or principle for anything at all. If this is so, then the simplest technical exercise, like baiting a hook so that a fish will want to bite it, is scientific, while putting a spell on the same hook and bait to make the fish bite, regardless of his appetite, is religious. Thus people solve their problems either by science or by religion, since, if science hasn't an answer, religion has.

This is only a preliminary characterization of religion, and is not meant to be a full-fledged definition. It introduces the anthropological view; it attempts to say what religion does, without necessarily saying what it is. The fact is that no satisfactory definition of religion has ever been made. One good reason for this is that each definition has depended on the approach of the person making it, which takes us back to the six blind men and the elephant. A philosopher says, "Religion is x." But then a psychologist says: "What about y?" And an anthropologist says, "Yes, and what about z?" If you then lamely concede that "Religion is $x + y + z$," you are surrounding it, not defining it. I say this in the hope that I may sound less awkward when I shortly begin to talk in a circle myself.

E. B. Tylor[3] defined religion simply as the belief in spiritual beings, of any kind, and called this belief "animism." Marrett[4] simplified it further, to a feeling compounded of awe, fear, and wonder, aroused by the supernatural, and called this "pre-animism." But in these there appears no idea of action on this belief or feeling; this was inserted by Sir James Frazer and William James. Said the latter: ". . . the religious life consists of the belief that there is an unseen order and that our supreme good lies in harmoniously adjusting ourselves thereto."[5] This, however, is callous; respectful as it sounds, it is much like H. L. Mencken's disparaging dictum: "Its single function is to give man access to the powers which seem to control his destiny, and its single purpose is to induce those powers to be friendly to him. . . . Nothing else is essential."[6] Frazer,[7] however, insisted not only on the necessity of both belief and practice,

---

[3] *Primitive Culture* (1871).

[4] R. R. Marrett, *The Threshold of Religion* (1909).

[5] William James, *The Varieties of Religious Experience* (1902).

[6] *Treatise on the Gods* (1930).

[7] J. G. Frazer, *The Golden Bough* (1890; abridged edition, 1922).

but also that of religious feeling, or humility; but Frazer, in so doing, chose to exclude magic (sorcery, the use of spells, etc.) from religion.

These men put forward the original anthropological idea, but, as Marrett pointed out, they were concerned with religion in the individual, and neglected the social nature of religion, which was stressed by the French sociologist Durkheim.[8] The latter was also led by his argument to exclude magic from religion, like Frazer. According to his definition, a sense of the sacredness of certain things gives rise to beliefs and practices which become a communal affair, i.e., a church, and he considered this last element indispensable.

Other definitions have been coined in plenty. The first recent philosophers who had the nerve to define religion at all spoke of it as man perceiving the infinite, or something of the sort; Kant called it the recognition of our duties as divine commands. The opposite extreme, the most detached view, is that of Reinach, who termed religion "a sum of scruples which impede the free exercise of our faculties."[9] To paraphrase him, religion is inhibitions. This sounds cynical, but it has the sense of the compulsive nature of religion in it; it is better as an epigram, however, than as a definition. On the whole, the anthropological efforts remain much the best, and modern students take the same line, usually rewording the older definitions so carefully and fulsomely that they sound as though they had been written by a lawyer. They do not satisfy, however, because religion needs a description rather than a definition. It has too rounded a nature to be expressed as a single idea or to be delimited by means of a single characteristic.

For example, the best attempted definitions have included as necessary elements belief, practice, emotional attitude, and the social nature of religion. But these things themselves need further qualification. Belief, in religion, is typically not simply the acceptance of an idea, like the

[8] E. Durkheim, *The Elementary Forms of the Religious Life, a Study in Religious Psychology* (1915).

[9] S. Reinach, *Orpheus*, English translation (1909).

moon being made of green cheese; it is more intense, it is an attitude, and need not even be formulated very clearly. It is the strong sense that there is more power in the universe than is present on the surface, and that such power may have a personal interest in you; and this strong sense acts as a compulsion, not simply as an argument. It is a matter beyond experience and does not require to be known by any of the ordinary means of perception. Practice or ritual also has a strong feeling of compulsion in it; it often contains the force of a wish, and it is accompanied by the conviction that there is more in your action than is put there by your mind and your arm. Furthermore, whether it is prayer, spell, or any other form, ritual is something established and accepted, so that in this sense it is always ceremonial. And the social aspect of religion means more than popular enthusiasm for the cult; it means that it serves some positive function for society itself, usually highly beneficent. Note, however, that none of this includes ethical ideas, or a belief in gods, or even a clear notion of what the power in the background may be.

If I were to try a definition here, I should say that a religion is a set of earnest policies which a group of people adopts under an unconscious compulsion in order to tidy up their distraught relationships with one another and with the universe as they perceive it, without the aid of science. In man's own eyes, perhaps, religion is a diplomatic conspiracy against the invisible, and since he keeps the score himself he usually manages to be satisfied with the results. But I would go completely around behind him and define it still again, as the normal psychological adjustment by which human societies build a barrier of fantasy against fear. And since, like any psychological adjustment, it is born in stress, it is therefore a source of emotion.

I am not particularly pleased with the above attempts, especially as I have just finished saying that it seems impractical to define religion at all. As a matter of fact, I should prefer to abandon the word "religion" entirely, for my purposes, and substitute "religious behavior" through-out; but of course it is too clumsy. And I am certainly not the first to conclude the futility of a definition; William James, among others, did so, in his *Varieties of Religious Experience*. Religion will not stand compressing; you must either try to grasp it as completely as possible or leave it alone. I think that, in addition to what I have already said, the reason for this is what follows.

Religious belief is an expansion of the whole world of reality. It is an imaginative improvement, or enlargement, on the people themselves, their rulers, their abilities and techniques, and also on the animals and the face of nature around them. This enlargement is semilogical in the lines it follows, and it is not mere make-believe. (Notice that it is therefore different from ordinary drama, from fairy tales, and from sleight of hand.) Accordingly, since the mind of man is capable of so much, it seems to me impossible to take religion as a phenomenon and to classify it or limit it, since after all it has the same limits as man's imagination. If we can find the boundaries of imagination, or can grasp some natural arrangement within it, then we can do the same for religion, but not otherwise. And if we cannot find some one key to its internal order, we lack a central idea on which to frame a definition.

This seems to mean that there is no good in trying to classify the outward forms of religion, because it is a sterile exercise; the things that should be classified are within man. That is true, strictly speaking. Nevertheless it is only the outward forms that show religion at work, and if they can be sorted out into what seem to be the most significant groups, they should indicate the most usual or important religious needs, and what most deeply stirs human imaginations.

Such a survey I will attempt forthwith. In the latter part of the book I shall deal with native cults of various types and various degrees of simplicity or complexity. Before get-ting to these, however, I shall describe some other things so simple that they can hardly be called "cults" at all, because they are more the actions of individuals than of groups, though they are group beliefs: I mean magic, the belief in witches, and so on. In any case, cult or no cult, I shall not pretend to treat any of these phenomena completely, pursuing it in all its forms and everywhere it exists, because there are whole shelves of books on each one of them. I will do no more than sample them, to show in the case of a few particular societies how they are related to the whole life of the people.

What follows, in other words, is the concrete evidence as to religious behavior and what it does. What I have tried to say so far is this. Man is a supremely sensitive and excitable animal, whose fancies and fears leap up around him like flames. He is also imaginative, ingenious, and highly adaptable, socially and emotionally. As far as he is able, he gains his ends by direct methods, using his eyes, his hands, and his tongue: "scientifically," he brings changes in the world around him (such as making a live animal into an edible one). Where this does not suffice to meet what he feels, consciously or unconsciously, to be his necessities, he is apt to make the adjustment not by changing his surroundings but by changing himself. And the main medium whereby he changes himself is religion.

3

MANA AND TABU: A FORCE
AND A DANGER

There is probably no better example of how a basic religious feeling—a sense of the special, the supernatural—takes form as a religious belief than in the idea of mana. The word itself is from the Pacific, being common to many of the languages of Melanesia and Polynesia, but it has other names in other places. Mana means a kind of force or power which can be in anything, and which makes that thing better in its own special qualities, such as they are, perhaps to the point of being marvelous.

A man who has mana is stronger, or smarter, or more graceful, though mana is not strength or brains or agility. That man's spear or, if he has been civilized, his tennis racket, has mana if it does what is expected of it with particular sureness; but mana is something different from the niceness of balance or the workmanship which has gone into it. At the same time, if the pro who made the spear or the racket consistently turns out first-class spears and rackets, then he obviously has mana of his own, or else he has ways of inducing mana into whatever (spears or rackets) he makes. And there is no difference in the mana which is in the tool, or its owner, or its maker; it simply causes each one to excel in his special way.

Mana, therefore, is an explanation for whatever is powerful, or excellent, or just right. Cole Porter's "You're the Top" reels off a list of things which, if you think of it that way, have mana (Mahatma Gandhi, Napoleon brandy, and cellophane). I need hardly say that if you ever took pains to use a special pen or pencil whenever you wrote a college examination you were thinking along the same lines.

Typically, mana is a sort of essence of nature; it is not a spirit, and it has no will or purpose of its own. It can very well be compared with electricity, which is impersonal but powerful, and which flows from one thing to another, and can be made to do a variety of things, although in itself it remains the same flowing force. In the beliefs of different cults, mana may be supplied by various sources: it may come from gods or spirits, or it may be instilled by the correct ritual, or it may simply exist naturally where it is. But this is only a question of making it conform to other ideas of a cult, and is of no special significance. The one important matter is whether it works. For example, a Melanesian may find a stone; it may have a strange shape, or obtrude itself on his notice in a peculiar way, and he will decide that possibly it has mana. He will take it home and bury it in his garden, and if he gets a particularly fine vegetable crop he will know that he was right, because the stone has transmitted mana (which is far better than fertilizer) to the plot.

In spite of such uses, mana would hardly deserve to be called more than a superstitious explanation of luck, or of other people's successes, if it did not in some cases engender a strongly respectful attitude—if it did not give rise to what can be called a religious sensation and belief, because, though unseen, it influences man to regulate his behavior by it. Among certain tribes, that is what it does.

The Iroquois Indians conceived of a potency, inherent in all kinds of natural objects, called orenda, which word they also used to signify "extraordinary," "wonderful," "ancient," and so on. The manitou of the Algonquins was a good deal the same, and did not mean a personified spirit so much as something in nature which caused a sense of wonder or a momentary thrill. Among the Sioux, wakan or wakonda stood for a better-defined idea, quite like mana as I have described it, although wakan also meant spirits.

An Oglala said that wakan meant many things, and would have to be understood from the things that are considered wakan. "When a priest uses any object in performing a ceremony that object becomes endowed with a spirit, not exactly a spirit, but something like one, the priests call it tonwan or ton. Now anything that thus acquires ton is wakan, because it is the power of the spirit or quality that has been put into it. . . . The roots of certain plants are wakan because they are poisonous. . . . Again, some birds are wakan because they do very strange things. . . . In other words, anything may be wakan if a wakan spirit goes into it. . . . Again, if a person does something that cannot be understood, that is also wakan. Drinks that make one drunk are wakan because they make one crazy. . . . Wakan comes from the wakan beings. These beings are greater than mankind in the same way that mankind is greater than animals."[1] Thus wakan, though it is impersonal, can be a power for evil, as well as good.

How the idea of wakan fits into the religious life of the people has been studied in another tribe, the Crows.[2] Typical Indians of the Plains, the Crows lived a nomadic life, normally in small bands, hunting the buffalo; and those actually hunting or fighting did so in even smaller groups. The social structure was loose and informal, and life for each man was intensely personal, with a certain loneliness in it. He had little feeling of acting with a group, and all his rewards and satisfactions were for what he accomplished strictly as an individual. There was in fact only one kind of glory: prestige from his personal feats as a warrior. War was not of our brand, but was composed of chance skirmishes and deliberate raids against traditional enemies,

[1] J. R. Walker, "The Sun Dance and Other Ceremonies of the Oglala Division of the Teton Dakota," *Anthropological Papers of the American Museum of Natural History*, Vol. 16 (1917).
[2] R. H. Lowie, "The Religion of the Crow Indians," *Anthropological Papers of the American Museum of Natural History*, Vol. 25 (1922). Also *Primitive Religion* (1924).

ostensibly to get horses but actually simply to expose one-self to danger, for the greatest achievement was the most foolhardy one. To ride into an enemy camp and cut out and drive off some of its horses was splendid; to do it alone was more splendid; and to do it alone on foot was most splendid. Many of the Plains tribes had an established scale of bravado (the system of "counting coup"), in which each stunt increased the informal "rank" of a warrior by a given degree and was signalized by an eagle feather cut or painted in a distinguishing way, to be worn on his head. A man with many horses and a history of hairbreadth adventures was a contented and respected personage, and his opposite smarted under public pity, not to say ridicule; the Crows would concede to the latter, however, that it was not his fault, and was due to the fact that he had not been favored with visions.

For visions were the key to all success, and were what every Crow longed for, and thought constantly of, because they brought power. This the Crows called maxpe, which was their word for wakan, and their idea of mana. It was certainly vague and indefinite. Maxpe was given by supernatural beings, who appeared in a vision and awarded it; when a man had it, he was fortunate and powerful thereafter. The spirits might tell him to sing a certain song which they taught him, or to wear something special on his head, when he went out, and if this were so, the power might become associated with that object. But this was not necessary; the power was simply there, at his disposal, because of the vision.

Nor was it a question of the spirit being present to help him; the spirit came in the vision, but it left the rest up to the Crow. The worth of the maxpe, or the vision, could be found only by putting it to the test. It might turn out to be false, and the visionary might lose his life. Or the vision, and subsequent visions, might sustain him throughout his career, so that other men followed him, and perhaps wanted to borrow and use his songs and his vision objects.

For the vision, if it were good, would give him power quite out of the ordinary.

One of the Crows, Gray-bull, had a grandfather in the old days who as a younger man had never been to war, and this had been joked about by the other men. Then one afternoon as Gray-bull's grandfather was sitting in his tent, two white-headed birds hopped in through the entrance and changed into a man and a woman. Gray-bull's grandfather saw that the man's face was painted in a particular way. The man told the woman to sing to Gray-bull's grandfather, and he listened. Then the man said: "Look at me," and Gray-bull's grandfather saw that he had a bird skin tied to his head. "Whenever I want to use this bird on my head," said the man, "I let a woman tie it, and think at the same time that the enemy cannot shoot me." The woman said, "I have plenty of things and horses and whenever I meet enemies they are easily captured." Then the two of them changed back into birds and went out.

Gray-bull's grandfather asked the chiefs about his vision. They said it sounded all right, and that he should follow it; he made himself a bird skin of the kind the man had showed him, and wore it, and he sang the song that the woman had taught him. After this, once, there was an encounter with the enemy, and forty of them were hiding in a gully. Gray-bull's grandfather painted his face like the man in the vision and went out to the gully. One of the enemy shot at him with a gun, but Gray-bull's grandfather took the gun and threw it away. Another man drew a bow at him, but the bowstring broke, and Gray-bull's grandfather took the bow away from him. Gray-bull's grandfather then came back in safety, but many times after that he did other things of the same kind, and was a great warrior.

Gray-bull's grandfather had no idea who the birds in the vision were. The Crows knew about a number of supernatural beings, who were generally responsible for giving visions; the most important of them were the Sun, Old Man Coyote, the Morning Star, and the Dipper (who was actually seven brothers). There were others as well, but about none of them were the Crows very precise. It was believed, for example, that the Sun made the land and the Indians, but not everything. But there was no standard idea about the various beings, such as a strong cult might insist on; individualism ruled in religious conceptions as in other things. For a Crow would believe something about a deity that he had seen in a vision far more firmly than something he had been told about that deity by another Indian. And, although there were tribal rituals connected with some of these beings, especially the Sun, the main interest in them was because they gave visions and power. That was why a Crow prayed personally to them.

Even so, when a vision was given, it might be by a different being from the one prayed to, and although the visionary might have a conviction as to the identity of his vision-giver, he might on the other hand not know who the being was. Mostly they were simply men, of the kind you see in dreams: people you never saw before. Lone-tree saw a man who gave him human flesh to eat; Lone-tree knew that he was the Dipper, but there was no sign of it until he turned away, and Lone-tree saw seven stars in his hair braid. One man got visions from little dogs. Medicine-Crow had an excellent vision of a handsome white man who said: "You are poor and I have known about you for a long time. You will be famous and a chief." The white man spoke in Crow—lamentably, because if he had spoken English Medicine-Crow would then have been able to speak English himself. Then the white man yawned, and Medicine-Crow saw—wonderful sign!—that all his teeth were gold. He told Medicine-Crow that there were a great many white men in the East, and that Medicine-Crow would go there four times. Medicine-Crow had been taken East once, and although he was an old man when Lowie spoke to him, he still expected to go there three times more.

Visions were quite different from dreams. Although, as I have said, the proof of the pudding was in the eating, a vision somehow had a convincing quality that stamped it with certainty and truth, even though it seemed like little enough in itself. One Crow dreamed of an Indian on horse-back wearing a chicken-hawk feather. That was all; but it impressed the man so forcibly as being a vision rather than an ordinary dream that he painted his face like the phantom's, and wore a chicken-hawk feather himself; he also named one of his children Chicken-hawk-woman, and another Wraps-up-his-tail, because the rider's horse had a wrapped tail. He was always lucky.

Sometimes visions simply came, unsought and unexpected, like the one above, or like that of Gray-bull's grandfather, who was sitting in his tent when the birds called. But in the typical case a man so hungered for a vision to help him—and this is significant—that he would mortify himself to call it down. There were several ways of doing this, like going to the mountains to fast in the cold, or even cutting off a finger. If he were praying to a being for a vision, this self-inflicted misery of course exaggerated and drew attention to his unhappiness. So he said and believed, but it is also easy to see that his powerful desire, and his treatment of himself, by reducing him to exhaustion and the point of delirium, rendered him far more susceptible to a "vision," or a hallucination. Gray-bull wanted a vision, and was helped by a famous warrior, who put a skewer through the skin over one of Gray-bull's shoulder blades and hung a shield from it, and in the same way tied a horse to the other shoulder. All day long Gray-bull followed the band on foot, leading the horse, which was getting hungry and thirsty and jerking its head against the lead rein. Toward the end of the day, Gray-bull looked at the horse and noticed a stripe on its leg. Taking this for a sign, he freed the horse and spent the night on the spot. In the night he saw a gray horse with a stripe on its leg, and heard an unseen person say: "This horse belongs to the Dakotas." Gray-bull went to war against the Dakotas, took a gray horse, and on it did the deeds necessary to become a great warrior.

The religious nature of all this lies in the intensity of feeling and the importance attached to visions, together with the idea of a special power, which is outside strength or skill or wisdom, because the Crows were quite able to appreciate and make allowance for the last-named qualities. They also believed, of course, in the beings who gave the visions, and in the objects which became valuable because of a vision. But in this complex the main thing was the visions themselves, and the essence of power they contained. Fame and glory in war were the focus of Crow life, the one source of glamor and zest; and the key to this kind of success, or to any other, was the power of visions.

Moslems, particularly North Africans, believe in a power of the same kind, called baraka (holiness).[3] It is a power for many kinds of good, and is quite general: mountains have it, the sea has it; it lives in the sun, moon, and stars, in animals—especially horses—plants, and magic squares. It tends, however, to be personal, associated with such as brides and bridegrooms, the new mothers of twins and triplets, and children generally. And it is sensitive to pollution and destruction by uncleanness of various kinds, or by unrighteousness; and, generally speaking, women and Christians are bad for it, as is fighting or breaking religious laws. The welfare of a country depends on the baraka of the sultan, who may lose it, perhaps to people who kiss his hand.

It is above all the property of two special kinds of people: descendants of the Prophet (not the most unusual distinction in the Moslem world) and "saints"—holy men who get it through being pious, or by luck, or by being not quite right in the head. One such saint lives, or lived recently, in the Rif. When he was a boy he was a servant in the house of a rich woman. On a cold morning he was ordered to fetch water, which caused him to make the wish that the spring would dry up. It did, giving him a reputation which has been supported ever since by other marvels which his baraka has brought about. He will cure a wounded man by sitting at his side and refusing to eat until the patient is out of danger. His favorite recreation is chas-

[3] Edward Westermarck, *Ritual and Belief in Morocco* (1926). C. S. Coon, "Tribes of the Rif," *Harvard African Studies*, Vol. IX (1931).

ing women in the market place, to hit them with a stick; this apparently does not come under the head of fighting, and has had no ill effects upon his baraka. Other saints use their power mainly for curing, and baraka will remain around a saint's tomb, where its influence will also cure, or bestow other benefits. If you do your practicing near one such tomb, you can learn to play the flute in a week.

The Pacific Ocean, as I have said, is the real home of mana. Mana was first brought to the attention of anthropologists by the distinguished missionary-ethnologist Codrington,[4] who studied and described it in Melanesia (New Guinea to the Fiji Islands). The Melanesians see mana in its most general form: a force, as Codrington says, "which acts in all ways for good and evil; and which it is of the greatest importance to possess or control." Much of Melanesia is ghost-ridden; everywhere, in the woods, the streams, the beaches, live the ghosts of the dead, and spirits of a slightly higher order, who are never remote and always near at hand. All of them are full of mana, and act as reservoirs of mana, and act through it. Therefore, if ghosts and spirits can be propitiated, their mana can be controlled. Better yet, however, is mana which has come to reside in a man or an object; the Melanesians are much interested in its tangible aspects because it can be handled directly. If mana exists in a stone or a bone, good; it can be put in the garden or laid on a new canoe; for mana can be conveyed from one object to another, just by keeping them together. The lively interest in ghosts and spirits has an ulterior aim; Codrington says that the basis of Melanesian religion is the pursuit of mana.

It was, however, in Polynesia (the islands from New Zealand to Hawaii) that the idea of mana reached its most refined state, even though it did not overshadow other aspects of religion, as it did in Melanesia or among the Crows. The Polynesians, beyond any other people who lacked writ-

[4] R. H. Codrington, *The Melanesians, Studies on Their Anthropology and Folk-Lore* (1891).

ing, through the philosophical efforts of their priestly caste
made a fully ordered system out of their religious cosmos,
so that their theology was comparable to that of the Greeks
or the Hindus. A hierarchy ran from the creator of the universe down through later gods to the living chiefs and on
to the commoners, and all through this skein was distributed mana, with the greatest amount at the top. It was
the basic force of nature through which everything was
done, for the gods made weather, and the chiefs provided
for their people through the preservation and exercise of
mana.[5]

The comparison of mana with electricity, or physical energy, is here inescapable. The Polynesian conception of it
was not scientific, of course, but it was otherwise completely logical. Mana was believed to be indestructible, although it might be dissipated by improper practices. It
came originally from the gods; nevertheless it was not possessed by them any more than by any other being or substance, but was independent of them all. It flowed continually from one thing to another and, since the cosmos was
built on a dualistic idea, it flowed from heavenly things to
earthbound things, just as though from a positive to a negative pole. It came to the people through the chiefs, who
were the direct descendants of the gods, and the chiefs kept
it and conducted it to whatever function needed it: ceremony, war, or agriculture. It was not a privilege of the chief
that he had so much mana. It was, rather, his function in
the scheme of things to serve as reservoir and transmitter
of it.

Mana could be contained in any person or thing; however, a man's potential capacity depended on his position
in the whole hierarchy. Chiefs were the main vessels, acting
as contact between god and man. Priests, or people of high
birth, stood next in relative capacity, with commoners low
in the scale, and women, who were of the dark, or earthly,
half of nature, lowest of all. And, since mana flowed from

[5] E. S. Craighill Handy, "Polynesian Religion," *Bernice P.
Bishop Museum Bulletin*, No. 34 (1927).

high to low, an unguarded contact between a chief and a commoner was therefore an evil thing; the chief suffered a loss of mana, which he should preserve for the good of the people, and the commoner, with his limited capacity for mana, might be blown out like a fuse. So contact was avoided, not through any fear of disrespect, but in the public interest, so that the mana of the chief, the tribe's vessel, should not be lowered.

A man's capacity for mana could be increased, however, by study or the acquisition of skill. If he became a master, a tuhuna, in any field, such as canoe building, house building, or knowledge of sacred lore, he acquired mana which helped him in his profession and which did not come via the chief. Mana could also be generated ritually, and so ceremony could increase the mana of a canoe, or of a tuhuna, or of a chief himself, and such ceremonies were important. Handy believes, in fact, that ritual performed for the gods was basically for the purpose of regenerating or increasing the mana of the gods themselves, so that, while they depended on the gods, the people were also able to strengthen the gods by their own exertions.

Tabu is another idea which, like mana, the Polynesians thought out carefully, and from which they have given us the word (properly tapu) for our own use. We have taken it to mean something forbidden not by statute but by convention. Obviously there is nothing religious about such an incidental interpretation as this. Among primitive peoples where it has any importance, however, tabu stands for the threat of a powerful evil influence. "Thou shalt do no murder" is both civil and moral law, but is not a tabu in the best sense. "Don't eat mashed potato with your fingers" might be our kind of tabu. But "Keep away from the third rail," to someone who lacks a scientific idea of electricity, is a tabu of the original kind.

Tabu was, in Polynesian philosophy, an upset, or anything that caused an upset, in the proper balance of mana, which of course resided in everyone. As Handy says: "Any disturbance of this equilibrium in an individual, either by a surcharge of mana or by a loss of his natural endowment of mana, affected him disastrously."[6] So a commoner was tabu to a chief and a chief was tabu to a commoner, since contact between them would drain off mana from the chief and overload the other. Everyday living for ordinary people was therefore hedged by tabu on either side: above by chiefs and those of royal blood, and below by women or worse—i.e., such things as the evil spirits who were responsible for sickness and death, and who hovered ever ready to take advantage of someone in a delicate or dangerous situation, like a woman in childbirth. To quote Handy again, "What is spoken of as the 'common' needing protection from both divine and corrupt represents the middle ground between the superior and inferior aspects of nature, the common ground of human beings and natural objects, where superior and inferior united in a balanced equilibrium." The effect of tabu on general behavior was very noticeable, especially in the etiquette surrounding a chief.

Everyone had mana in one degree or another; it was located especially in the head, the hair, and the spine. Chiefs, having a tremendous amount by virtue of their close kinship with the gods, constituted an involuntary menace to others, who had to follow strict rules in order not to get an accidental overdose. His barbers necessarily touched the chief's hair, whereat their hands became extremely tabu, to the extent that they could not touch their own heads, or feed themselves, or carry out ordinary actions, until they had been purified and relieved of the tabu by the right ritual. In the same way, a chief's mana ran into everything he used, so that all this became dangerous too. Nobody else could use his furniture, sit in his place, or sleep on his mat; and it was deadly to use his fire to cook with, or even to step over it, or to eat any of his leftover food, or drink out of a castaway cup, no matter how unwittingly any of these things might have been done. This is not theoretical,

[6] Ibid.

for there are cases on record from recent times in which a Polynesian had died of dread, and of no other visible cause, simply on discovering that he had inadvertently done one of these things.

In some places the chief was even carried about on a litter, because if he trod a path with his own feet, that path became forever dangerous to commoners. It is clear that without this precaution a chief might make an island of moderate size practically unusable in a short time, so that his only choice was to forgo exercise and keep his feet up. Wherever the tabu idea reached such extremes as this the chief, in spite of his necessary presence as the scion of the gods, must have been an appalling nuisance to everybody, including himself. In fact, in the early nineteenth century, life in Hawaii became so nearly not worth living that Kamehameha II and his people bravely decided to put everything at stake, and all sat down together at one meal, transgressing every tabu. They survived, amid general rejoicing. This seems fatuous enough to us, but to them it was rather like testing an atom bomb in the back yard, in hopes it was a dud.

A chief was not the only source of tabu to a commoner, who could contaminate himself in various other ways. An obvious one was by touching a corpse, since the presence of ghosts and spirits made it highly tabu and dangerous; consequently those who were forced to handle the dead acquired tabu of the hands like the royal barbers, and had to be purified in the same way (ritually, and usually by the use of heat and water). Warriors who returned after killing enemies also had to be purified similarly. Mana and tabu could flow from one person to another through food, so as a general thing men in Polynesia did not eat with women, or use the same fire, but had an eating house of their own.

In addition to all this tabu of the person, there were acts which might create tabu, just as there were those which might alleviate it. Anything consecrated by rite, to instill it with mana, or protect it, naturally became tabu. The chief might lay a special kind of tabu on crops, or fishing grounds, as a conservation measure or to make sure there would be a good supply for a feast; this would make them inviolable to trespassers; he might do it by naming the object after his own head, or by hanging a piece of his clothing in the field. Finally there were tabus on first fruits, because the gods had made crops grow by their own mana, and their tabu therefore lay upon the harvest, or the catch of fish, until a portion of it had been given back to them, an act which lifted the tabu and made the rest available to mortals.

Out of the Polynesian refinement of tabu there protrudes a strange idea: that holy and unholy things are dangerous for the same reason. They are two sides of the same coin, being only relative, and their common nature is their danger, their tabu quality. Consider this example. To all people, primitive or otherwise, the idea of incest is shocking and the act a sin—in Polynesia, a tabu thing. An ordinary Hawaiian who committed incest with his sister would have polluted himself so completely, and rendered himself so enormously tabu, that there could be no hope at all of purifying him ritually, and he could therefore only be put to death. A Hawaiian chief, however, married his sister, because of their mutual divine descent, and this was held to be quite proper. Why? Because the capacity of the chief for mana and tabu was equal to the danger, the tabu quality, and so he simply became more tabu than ever. What defiled the commoner consecrated the chief.[7]

This same general idea was familiar to the ancients. The Hebrews had it. They had not worked it out upon an expressed belief in mana, which in their case would be merged with the power of Jehovah itself (although the Old Testament suggests such a notion time and again, and a Polynesian would not hesitate to say that Moses was a great tuhuna, palpably suffused with mana). The Hebrews, however, did think and speak of things which were unclean and things which were holy in the same way, as being sacred

[7] A. R. Radcliffe-Brown, *Taboo*, The Frazer Lecture (1939).

and untouchable. "Sacred," to us, signifies only the things which are raised up and perfect, the things of heaven, but it first meant those things which are not for human beings to touch. The Hebrews were warned not to go too close when a heathen rite was being held, because they themselves might be "sanctified," i.e., made tabu. Other Hebrew ideas of tabu objects ran close to the Polynesian: dead bodies, mothers after childbirth, most manifestations of sex, warriors, and of course things connected with Jehovah. Any tabu-breaking made the sinner unclean until he could be purified, and tabu objects like new mothers or warriors also called for purification.

Leviticus and Deuteronomy of course teem with tabus, and there can be nobody who has not realized that many of them have no reason for existence in morals or ethics, as we understand them. That is an essential feature of a tabu; it is not, as I said, a matter of moral law at all, although naturally the two can mingle. To the Hebrews, the pig was an unclean animal, and they could not eat it. What was the sense of this? In constructing Solomon's temple, they could use no tools of iron. What was the sense of that? There probably are reasons, but not moral ones. The Hebrews, in their tribal origins, were not swineherds, and so perhaps the pig was enemy food, and not for them. And iron may have been prohibited for religious purposes among them, as among some other peoples, because iron was something newfangled; when custom had become fixed they were using bronze or stone tools, and that was the way it should be. Such things gradually became a code of religious laws with the force of tabu.

The classic example of tabu in the Old Testament is the case of the unfortunate Uzzah, the son of Abinadab. Jehovah had ordained that, after it was consecrated, only Aaron and his sons might touch the Ark of the Covenant or the things associated with it. But once, as the Ark was being moved, it was shaken by the oxen and Uzzah put out his hand to steady it, and that was the end of him. Now, except that Jehovah had indicated that the Ark was sacred, and therefore dangerous, there was nothing that we can find wrong in what Uzzah did; by every ethical or moral standard in our own philosophy or that of any other people, Uzzah was doing the right thing; he was trying to keep the Ark from harm. Yet he had forgotten the tabu. He touched the tabued object and got the full voltage. It sounds, altogether, as though Jehovah were issuing not a command, but rather a warning, not to touch the Ark. (The idea of its being charged with something like mana is very clear in the Bible.) It is a question whether, in the original viewpoint which the story represents, Jehovah could have helped this anyway; whether He could have saved Uzzah after the Ark had been sanctified (although, as it actually reads, "the anger of the Lord was kindled against Uzzah"). This was not the only time somebody suffered through inability to handle the holiness of the Ark; the Philistines once got hold of it, in one of their innumerable military entanglements with the Israelites, and it caused them an epidemic of the most unpleasant kind. They were then only too glad to return it to the people who had a ritual to cope with it.

Tabu, as an idea, is widespread, though few cultures have rendered it into so well formed a doctrine as that of the Hebrews and the Polynesians. It attaches, in one tribe or another, to all sorts of things. At crises of life people are surrounded by an aura: at birth, adolescence, often at marriage, and of course at death. Varying reasons may be supplied; usually they are occasions when spirits are likely to take an interest in human affairs, an intrusion which is always unwelcome. But the basic feeling is probably simpler. It is a feeling of apprehension at a change, a feeling that the time is out of joint, that the course of everyday life has been deflected and that the situation is delicate and everyone should be careful. Consider birth. Women are forever having babies, but the fact remains that it is a rather extraordinary thing for them to do, and it leaves everyone excited, nervous, and disturbed. If civilized folk continue to go all atwitter over it, it is easy to see why it makes the uncivilized tread warily. Marriage is similar; bride and groom are entering into a highly intimate relationship in which they can exchange all sorts of tabu influences—primitive people will agree with you that there are few things more mysterious or interesting than sex—and it is therefore natural to proceed with the proper ritual caution in joining them.

Here and there, many different kinds of things create this feeling of tabu. Categories of people do so: women, with their strange physiology; warriors, from their connection with blood and death; and strangers, who come in trailing unfamiliar influences after them, upsetting the local balance of such things. Chiefs or kings; blood; special times, places, or things—examples of tabus on these are endless. Tabu foods are a common idea, and the Hebrew type of prohibitions on certain meats, or certain ways of preparing them (not seething the kid in his mother's milk), is widely found in East Africa.

Finally, of course, various actions may be tabu, and it is here that many obvious moral laws come under tabu's cloak. I said before that the two are not necessarily connected, and cited the laws of Moses as containing many cases of tabu without morals. Naturally, however, there is no reason why they should be separate, and every reason why they should tend to coincide. Grossly faulty ethical behavior always revolts human beings, and of course makes them feel that it also revolts the natural order of things which tabu guards, and therefore such acts as killing and incest have become tabu almost everywhere that the conception of tabu has developed. Thus it is that the majority of the laws of Moses are indeed moral laws and show tabu and morals pulling side by side. I refrained from making this point before, in order to emphasize the essential nature of tabu by itself, but it is important and obvious that tabu should always tend to align itself with the social good.

To discount some of the theoretical embroidery of the Polynesians, the most general primitive idea of tabu is of

something that renders a person unclean, putting him in a
state of ritual badness, in which he is exposed to every kind
of worldly or ghostly evil.[8] His usual defenses are down and
he becomes liable to infect the people about him as well as
himself. The Polynesians have a word for this state: noa.
So has a Kikuyu of East Africa, who calls it thahu and gets
into it by stepping over a corpse, eating out of a cracked
plate, and various other acts. And you know yourself that
if you spill salt at the table you are thahu until you have
thrown some of it over your left shoulder. Also, even if you
contract a tabu involuntarily, you are nevertheless responsible for the consequences, just as if you take arsenic when
what you wanted was bicarbonate.

The Eskimos of Coronation Gulf have a clear and simple
understanding of the subject.[9] They have two brands of
tabu. Aglirktok is a private kind, which for some reason
belongs to one person in particular, and not to others. He
may pick it up because of something that happens, or because he reaches a certain age, or because he inherits it; it
may cause him to avoid certain foods, or dress in a certain
way, and so on. It is quite possible for him to come by it
unknowingly: if his father or uncle dies while he is far
away, and he thereupon inherits a tabu against eating seal's
liver, he may infringe upon the tabu and so bring evil to
himself and his family before he realizes what he has fallen
heir to. The other tabus are called aglernaktok, and are
general, pertaining to the thing itself. No one can eat the
marmot (of the woodchuck family). No one can start anything on Friday or Sunday. (They did not know about this
latter tabu until the whites arrived, and were much obliged
to be told of it; it explained the good fortune of the white
people, because they observed it, and must have been caus-

8 See Radcliffe-Brown, op. cit.

9 Vilhjálmur Stefánsson, "The Stefánsson-Anderson Arctic Expedition of the American Museum: Preliminary Ethnological Report," Anthropological Papers of the American Museum of Natural History, Vol. 14 (1914).

ing the Eskimos a lot of grief through unconscious tabu-breaking.)

Now people do not willingly break tabus. Furthermore the angakok, the native physician, can find out what particular tabu has been broken, and correct matters, if evil consequences appear. And it is the responsibility of everyone to avoid breaking tabus, or to confess if one has been broken, because the evil can come down on the family or the community as a whole; failure to confess is the dangerous thing, and hiding of a broken tabu will bring the most terrible of troubles. An Eskimo doing this is therefore a mortal danger to the whole group, and is liable to be killed. He is like a Typhoid Mary on the loose. Thus there is a strong communal duty in the matter.

Frazer believed that tabu was actually a sort of negative black magic, and that the reason for not doing something was because of a known consequence; i.e., do not eat the heart of a deer, because the deer is a timid animal, and eating his timid heart will make you timid also. There are many such rules to be found, and they are correctly called negative magic, but they are not tabus. For a tabu is something to be avoided because of an ineffable, unlimited danger, with no necessity for the logical connection in the foregoing.[10] It is true that people will generally say that a broken tabu will bring disease and even death, but that is the rational view talking, not the religious. Anything might happen, and the essence of tabu remains the state of danger and of maladjustment, and the inner compulsion to stay clear of it. It is in this light that Reinach's definition of religion—scruples invading the free exercise of our powers[11] —takes on meaning; in fact, by "scruple" Reinach specifically meant "tabu."

Tabu makes our first argument on behalf of primitive re-

[10] Marrett, op. cit. Hutton Webster, in *Taboo, a Sociological Study* (1942), agrees with Frazer's view. I am trying to describe the idea of tabu in its most extreme, essential form, and I admit it is not possible to say flatly what is a tabu and what is not.

[11] See p. 20.

ligion; the first chance to answer the question of why anyone should be devoted to such a baseless belief and what
earthly good could come of it. A minor reason is the personal one; it is the reassurance which individual people can
draw from an explanation which seems sound and is accepted by everyone else. It is a wonderful thing in this life
to know what to do and what not to do; especially the
latter, because it is less demanding to avoid doing something
than to accomplish something. Tabu shows everyone the
correct path to walk, and by marking out the pitfalls gives
a sense of safety. Not eating the flesh of the marmot, let
us say, and accepting a few limitations in dress or behavior,
is a small price to pay for the ability to look forward with
confidence, knowing that one is in tune with the universe
and that one's ills are not likely to be serious.

Furthermore, when misfortune does arrive, tabu will give
its believers the explanation for it and the sense of relief that
comes from at least knowing the source of trouble. Nobody
likes to have teeth pulled, but if a long siege of aches and
pains is finally traced to a bad tooth, the sufferer will rush
almost joyfully to the nearest painless dentist, glad to have
his general ill-health reduced to a particular single cause.
This is parallel with the idea of tabu, and tabu will often
work in the same way, by the power of suggestion. Of
course it may lead to an occasional catastrophe, as when
a Hawaiian gave himself over hopelessly to death because
he had made a fearful misstep, but even these cases acted to
replenish the faith of others in the system's efficacy.

Far greater is the social usefulness of tabu. Whether it
is forming a part of Eskimo religion, which is as informal
as a broken umbrella, or of the polished sphere of Polynesian philosophy, it is doing yeoman service for the community by constituting an ever present prop to morale and
by supporting the existing structure and knitting it always
more firmly together. It does this primarily by setting up a
code of behavior the reasons for which are not only accepted by all but profoundly believed in. It is the effects of
this in turn that bolster the body politic. For the actual be-

havior tabu dictates is not the essential thing; at bottom, it simply creates a sense of carefulness and discipline.

Radcliffe-Brown[12] suggests that tabus are an unconscious way of emphasizing certain important values, which are by themselves too intangible to make their importance duly and constantly felt. In order to exist, a society needs the good will and submissiveness of its members, and in a roundabout way tabu gives them the opportunity to feel that and to express it. For example, to a small tribe the birth of a new member, or the death of an older one, is a matter of importance. And birth and death tabus, which are temporary unusual behavior, make each person connected with the event feel its importance and realize that others are also impressed with it. So tabus act as a ritual confirmation of a tribe's community strength.

I should say that it is probably more general than this, and that tabu serves, where it is recognized, to give a common direction to a society and its ideas of conduct, along with a feeling of common responsibility among its members. It enables such a society gradually to mold a system of morals, lending to the latter the force of religious emotion. But over and above this there are tabus without moral need, and these act simply to ensure that everybody is socially in step and in sympathy, without the need of civil enforcement, like law. And they do act this way. It is obvious, of course, that in some cases Polynesian chiefs, being men of intelligence, used the system of tabu to strengthen their prerogatives, but apart from this they were as deeply in the web as everyone else, and they understood that, no matter how burdensome it was personally, they simply had the greatest share in the common responsibility.

We may not be too pleased at the spectacle of a society goose-stepping to a set of tabus. But it may be accepted that they are better than a vacuum. Values of some sort are necessary; we ourselves need our faith in our own law, our type of government, and our institutions in general;

[12] Op. cit.

these things support us more than we know. Tabus are a potent agent for a society's control of itself, and it would probably not be possible to organize a community of the complexity of, say, the Polynesians, without the aid of tabu or an equally powerful religious substitute. This is the sort of thing that shows religion to be a necessary social invention.

4

MAGIC, BLACK AND WHITE

Say "magic" to yourself, and in your mind you will probably see a man in evening clothes lifting a rabbit out of an opera hat. This is only a vestigial meaning of the word, however, and not even a particularly correct one, for it stood in the beginning for everything which we might call occult, and not simply for parlor miracles. You call it magic when the slip of paper with your name on it turns out to be inside the ball of string, but you do not call it magic when you break a wishbone and make a wish, yet it is this latter which is a better sense of the word.

In the Kei Islands, south of New Guinea, when a newly launched canoe is sent on its maiden trading voyage, the authorities of the village make four young girls sit in a row in a hut, quite motionless, while the boat is at sea; this will ensure that the canoe will travel steadily, on an even keel. Here are a wish and a spell put into magical action, but there is no question of fooling anyone, or even a sense of the miraculous connected with it. A Zande of the Belgian Congo may use menzere, a plant which is very strong medicine, for evil purposes. He can put it in a box and go by night outside of the house of his victim and call out his name. If the victim answers him, he can catch the words and shut them up in the box with the medicine, and the speaker will be taken with disease. This is not sleight of hand. It is not quite cricket, either, I should say.

For magic, properly, means all the formulas for doing

things which are beyond one's personal powers. It is not, however, complicated; it makes use of fairly simple things: medicines, which are the correct materials, and spells, which are the correct things to say or do as you use the materials. Magic is world-wide, by which I mean that it is the property not only of all primitive people but also of ourselves and all our ancestors, and it is the same thing precisely wherever it is found. In civilized circles magic is disreputable (to those who are able to recognize it), but it has no such odor among backward peoples; among them it is not looked on as "superstition" or "occultism," but is simply considered the right way of doing something. In short, magic is the whole system of primitive knowledge and technical art above what, so to speak, can be done by hand.

As a matter of fact, it would not be easy for an uncivilized person to define magic at all, or to see it as something by itself. One reason why we are able to do so is that we have developed a conception of science, which is an absolute insistence on knowing the physical reasons for anything, or on seeing the actual connection between two events. Science accepts no compromises, no contradictions, and no assumptions.[1] Because science expressly demands the physical, the natural, it must expressly avoid the supernatural. Now people use science and magic to gain the same ends, but the doctrines of magic are different; it does not make the same distinctions. Science wants to know whether a given method will work, and why; from knowing why, it will go on to devise other methods for other things. Magic also wants to know whether a thing will work, and is much interested in why; but it is willing to make assumptions as to why, and does not insist on digging out physical causes; it is content to let the causes remain invisible and so, possibly, supernatural. In magic, apparent conflicts of fact are not fought out but evaded, and if they seem serious, further explanation may be simply invented to reconcile them.

I am not implying that there is any mental difference be-

[1] See also p. 18.

tween practitioners of magic and of science. Primitive people are perfectly able to perceive physical causes when they are not difficult to see—Indian woodcraft shows that. What I do mean is that our understanding of the principles of science makes the limits of magic a little clearer for us. When we plant crops we put into the ground fertilizer of some sort, to furnish chemicals which we know the crops will need. The New England Indians put a fish in each hill of corn, a trick they taught the Pilgrims. They could not have given us equations in organic chemistry, but I dare say that their explanation for doing this would have been sound enough, and consequently scientific. A Zande, however, in planting grain, will put into the ground the juice of one of his medicine plants, which is quite ineffective. That is magic. But the distinction would be hard to explain to the Zande, thinking as he does. Magic is "scientific" to the user of it.

Magic does not, however, interfere with anybody's practical actions. Nobody ever tried to plant his garden entirely by magic. As I said before, magic is for what is above one's personal powers. A gardener will do everything he can by himself in the way of preparing the ground, planting, watering, keeping off the birds, and so on; he will spare no practical efforts. The magic is added to take care of the supernatural end, to increase the crop yield by this means, or to protect the garden from possible adverse magic or other evil influences. That is important about magic; as actually employed, it is largely used against other supernatural objects, which is, naturally enough, where it is most effective.

There is not much primitive theory behind the action of magic. Tribal myths may say that it has mana in it, or the power of the dead, or spirits which make it work. But, basically, magic is simply a set of formulas. It is the way things are, that is all. (Are you clear in your mind as to why you wish on a shooting star?) It is impersonal; it is as though invisible wires ran through the supernatural world from a piece of magic to the effect it produced, and the magic were like pressing a button. It is not controlled by spirits, in spite of any connection they may have with it. And it is something different from mana and its other face, tabu. Mana is a force, not a formula, and it affects qualities already existing; the same mana can make a man brave, a canoe fast, and a storm terrible. Magic, on the other hand, is always specific: the right magic should always have a certain effect, no greater, no less, and no other. If mana is something like electricity, then magic is something like gunpowder. You can pick it up and carry it where you want; you can put the right amount of it where you want it and set it off when you want to, and the explosion will be limited to what you have touched off.

If there is no good explanation for the power in magic, it does nevertheless tend to follow certain principles. Frazer devoted the first part of *The Golden Bough* to an analysis of magic, with a great many examples, and little can be added to this. One general law, he found, determined most magical formulas, the Law of Sympathy. That is to say, magic depends on the apparent association or agreement between things, and is firmly founded on two great misapprehensions: that things which are alike are the same, and that things which were once in contact continue to be connected. These two principles he called the Law of Similarity and the Law of Contagion. This takes in most of magic, except for one more stout fallacy, that of "post hoc, ergo propter hoc," which is the belief that since *b* happens after *a*, *b* was therefore caused by *a*. The finest magic you could have, of course, would be based on all three of these delusions.

The Law of Similarity gives rise to homeopathic magic, of which the most familar kind is image magic or, as it is known in the trade, envoûtement. This is the business of making an image to represent a living person, who can then be killed or injured by the sorcerer via the image. It is best if you make as good a likeness as possible (modern science enables you to paste a photograph over the face, a technique employed by Pennsylvania hexers) and formally name it after the person who is to undergo treatment. You may then stab it, or burn it, or shoot it, or chop it up, or bury it to rot slowly, as your pleasure dictates. There is no need to be precipitate, of course; you may begin by rubbing pepper all over it, and end by roasting it very slowly. It is not necessary to kill the victim at all. You can hold the effect down to shooting pains if you prefer. But there is the method; it is up to you.

This business goes on today in our own country and in Europe (I understand that the Balkans take most of the ribbons), and it also turns up in what is believed to be one of the oldest evidences of religious thinking in our past. Animals drawn on the walls of Paleolithic caves in Europe often have spears thrusting into their hearts in what seems plainly to be a magical attempt to wound the game, or perhaps to bring down an already wounded mammoth. This corresponds entirely with a fable current in the sixteenth century of a traveling magician who, to entertain a king, killed a pigeon sitting on the roof, by drawing a picture of the bird on the wall and stabbing the picture. The king applauded heartily, but on reflecting a little he told the magician that if he ever did such a thing again he would be hanged.[2]

In 1308 the Bishop of Troyes, Guichard by name, underwent a long trial for the murder of Queen Jeanne, wife of Philip IV of France. It is not known what finally became of him, but the testimony regarding his episcopal behavior should cause a raised eyebrow. He had, it developed, consulted a witch and invoked a demon, and this little company made a wax image which they baptized Jeanne, for the queen. Then they put needles into the head and other parts of the body. Jeanne fell duly ill and could not be cured; she did not, however, get worse. The bishop continued to stick needles into the image, until it looked like a pincushion. Jeanne still refused to die. The bishop, in a

---

[2] See G. L. Kittredge, *Witchcraft in Old and New England*, 1929, for this story and the two cases following.

fury, cried out, "How, devil; will this woman live forever?"; he knocked the limbs off the image and tore it into bits; he trampled on the pieces and threw them in the fire. The queen expired.

A more flagrant homicide took place in 1323, in Coventry, and was confessed in detail by one of the accused, Robert le Mareschal, who turned king's evidence against the other, John de Notingham, a known magician. Twenty or more citizens of Coventry came secretly to these two and made them an offer of thirty-five pounds if they would do away with the local prior, by whom they were being oppressed, and also with the local officials of the crown, and with the king himself! The citizens supplied the raw materials, wax and muslin, showing that the choice of method was theirs. After five months, Robert and John had made images of all the victims-to-be together with one extra one, representing an innocent bystander named Richard de Sowe; he was for purposes of testing or, in scientific parlance, the "control." To brush up on technique, they started in with Richard, sticking a sharp piece of lead into the head of his image. Robert then went around to call on the real Richard, to find out how things were going. To his great satisfaction, he found Richard running about his house crying, "Harrow!"—obviously out of his head. The experimenters kept Richard in his demented state for about a month, taking a reading now and again. Then they removed the piece of lead from the head of the image and put it into the heart, and Richard died forthwith. Robert and John must have been truly elated, but before they could proceed to the real objects of their machinations, they were arrested. John died in durance; Robert's end is not history.

I have cited these cases because they are so fully recorded, but every quarter of the globe could produce the same kind of thing. Furthermore this is black magic, and by no means the only kind of homeopathic magic in use. You might even be cured in much the same way; a doctor may take magical steps to catch your disease, and then cure it in himself, which will cure you along with him. It would be possible to compile long lists of things that should be done, or should not be done, because of their sympathetic effects. You are apt to get the qualities of the animals you eat, so you should give due regard to your diet and not, for example, eat a fighting cock which was the loser in a fight. This can be turned around: a South African Bushman who has wounded a game animal and is camping on its trail will eat only the flesh of slow-moving beasts, for the effect this will have on the animal being pursued. Plants may have "signatures" to show their properties: the mandrake, with its forked root, has so human a form that it must be a potent medicine indeed for human beings. And liverwort must be good for the liver. Then plants, like animals, may be influenced by men; orgiastic fertility rites are basically to stimulate the crops through the sympathetic magic of human procreation, and women who have had many children are good for sowing the grain while barren women are bad. Other actions without number follow the same principle: various South African Bantu bring rain by sprinkling water on the ground from a calabash, or make a wind by waving a hyena's tail.

Contagious magic, from the Law of Contagion, is equally popular. An example from Codrington shows the idea: if a Melanesian (island not stated) has been hit in battle by an arrow, his friends will bind up the wound and put a cool poultice on it, to keep the fever down and make him comfortable. And they will also put a poultice on the arrow which they have taken out of the wound, because it was connected with the wound, and this, too, will help the cure. The enemy who fired the arrow and saw it hit has other ideas, however; back in his camp he keeps the bow near the fire, and twangs the string from time to time, because the bow fired the arrow that made the wound, and through this connection he can send twinges of pain, and tetanus. Throwing in a little homeopathic magic, he increases the inflammation by drinking hot, spicy drinks himself.

Anything connected with the person can be used along the lines of image magic; if you can get a hair, or a nail cutting, or even a belonging, especially clothes, you may wreak your worst will on the one from whom it came. Quite usually something like this is added to an image being used in image black magic; in fact, a hair from your enemy's head is likely to be the first thing any sorcerer would ask you for before taking on a contract to liquidate him. When an East African Nandi has captured an enemy tribesman, he may cut off some of the captive's hair at once; it will then do the latter no good to escape, because deadly magic will be sent after him forthwith. Spitting is dangerous for the same general reason, since spit can be used as well as any other relic. A Chuckchi of Siberia will not spit in public, but this is not because he thinks it nasty. It is only because he knows it is unsafe, and so he goes off by himself and digs a little hole, and spits into that. I am not sure that a small venture in sorcery by the Board of Transportation would not do more to clean up the subway stations than a five-dollar fine.

Less tangible things will do as well for mischievous intent. You may attack a man through a footprint he has left, by putting black medicine in it, or broken glass. An Australian native will lame a kangaroo by putting embers from the fire in its tracks. A man's name, his shadow, or his reflection also has something of himself in it, and he is vulnerable through them. It is true that there is another belief involved in these, connected with the soul, of which more later. However, the notion of contagion is plainly present. A name can be put directly into a spell, and this may be all that is necessary to direct the magic. Partly for this reason there is a widespread dislike, or even abhorrence, of having one's name used freely, so that in many tribes a man's true name is kept absolutely secret, and he uses a different one. A photograph is another impression of a person, like a footprint or a shadow, and a great many primitive people take exception to a camera for this very reason, so that indiscriminate snapshooting has landed more than one explorer in hot water. Finally, what about mirrors? Would it not be

bad luck to break one, after all the personal images that
have been registered in it?

So much for the derivations of magic. A look at some
of its varieties will show its scope. Actually it can be, and is,
used in every kind of enterprise, although the more practical and down-to-earth the endeavor, the less likely it is that
magic will figure importantly in it. Black magic is of course
the most famous kind. Properly, this is evil magic, from that
for killing and wounding down to that for any slightly
shady or surreptitious desire; but with the growing disre-
pute of magic in our own culture we have come to speak
of all of it as the black art. Black magic looms large, but I
think this is more because of its sensational character than
because a whole population is busy grinding up bones and
stabbing images; among primitive people no doubt the far
greater amount of magic actually performed is for beneficial purposes, or for defense against *imagined* black magic.

In medieval Europe, black magic flourished in the turning about of Christian practices in order to reverse their effects. If the mass, said properly, is an influence for good,
then the mass said backward is an influence for evil. Frazer
cites the mass of St. Sécaire, once practiced (or said to
have been) in Gascony. The priest comes at night to a
ruined or deserted church, peopled by owls, bats, and
toads. At the first stroke of eleven he begins to mutter the
mass backward, finishing at the last stroke of midnight. The
host he uses is black, with three points, and instead of wine
he drinks water taken from a well into which an unbaptized
infant has been thrown. He makes the sign of the cross, not
in the air with his right hand but on the ground, with his
left foot; and so on, through a whole series of precisely in-
verted devotions. At the end he pronounces the name of a
victim who, under the onslaught of all this evil, withers and
dies. I once heard Mary Austin say that, when she was a
little girl, the cook had recklessly told her that the devil
could be raised by reciting the Lord's Prayer backward.
Mrs. Austin, who had a hardy spirit, went right out under

the apple tree and recited the Lord's Prayer backward, with the utmost care. No devil appeared, which daunted her considerably.

Mohammedans are equally given to this kind of knavery. In the Rif they prefer written spells to incantations; learned magicians study the Koran, and by reading between the lines they discover how spells should be constructed. Such writings make excellent booby traps; they can be put in the roof of a man's house, or tied in a tree, or buried under the path, or put in the fire so that they are inhaled with the smoke. Lunacy follows.

White magic combats black. The same North Africans who put black medicines around to injure others will wear on their own persons charms made in the same way to protect them against the same thing. And, on the principle that it takes a thief to catch a thief, the medicine will have been prepared by the same magician. Such a magician is not entirely respectable, because magic is frowned upon by the true religion anyhow; more primitive societies, however, have practitioners of good magic who are esteemed and necessary figures. Much of this kind of magic is for curing bodily ills. Much of this in turn is based on a knowledge of the magical properties of plants and animals, but on the other hand a great deal of it is a matter of neutralizing black magic, since the latter is responsible in large part for disease and death. When you have a pain and call in the magician doctor, he must determine whether black magic is the cause and, if so, how to defeat it. This makes a battle of magic. Because of the principle of contagion, the original evil magic makes a trail to the sorcerer, by which to trace him. It may even be possible to turn his own magic back along the trail, by superior white magic, so that it backfires on the sender. Such things show why great care and attention are used on magical practice; magic is not too safe for amateurs.

By and large, the remainder of the field of magic's application is devoid of malice and is either useful or harmless. Magic dictates a great many details and practices in hunting, fishing, or raising crops, or running the weather; all of these are connected with getting food. In the East Indies a fish trap will be made especially of wood from a tree which was particularly attractive to birds; a Cambodian trapper gets himself caught in his own nets in order to increase their efficiency; Australian blackfellows make a whole ceremony of emerging from a "chrysalis" which they make of boughs and leaves, this being a magical exhortation to the witchetty grubs to increase. Still another kind is love magic, which can be considered good or bad, depending. A Blackfoot man managed to get a hair from the head of his young lady, who was being obstinate, and this was put into a little bag of medicine which the medicine man then gave him to wear. The girl straightway began following the previously forlorn lover everywhere, until she became so tiresome that he gave the purloined hair back to her and called it quits. But if the object of magical wooing is already somebody else's wife, then the magic can fairly be called black.

There is something of a distinction, it should be noticed, between private and public magic. The former is apt to be disapproved of because it encourages individual research along lines that may be dangerous, and opens an easy avenue for mischief, even though a great deal of magic is necessary for everyday pursuits. Why trust a sorcerer? Public magic, however, is that which is done as a rite on behalf of the tribe, and it may elevate the magician to a position of importance. An outstanding example is the rain maker of East and South Africa, where rain is vital to raise grain and fodder for the cattle. Among various nations he is either one of the most important officials of the government or else the king himself, and his responsibility is great. In parts of South Africa, also, it is the king who is charged with ensuring the good quality of the seed grain, and at the planting season the people bring their stores to him to do the proper magic over. (Notice that the position of such people is like that of the Polynesian chiefs and tuhunas, who were also charged with procuring excellent crops, but who worked through mana.)

Another field of public magic is omen taking, which gave the augurs their importance in classical times. I will deal with this further on. Other such officials may direct ceremonies to make food animals increase (similar to the Australian example above), or to bring them near the tribe. But even where the magician or medicine man has no such definite office he may be one of the foremost members of society (in the absence of rival interests) because he will be called upon to deal with all sorts of difficulties which confront the group, such as catching a thief, providing a method of keeping tigers away, and so on, as well as treating the sick, a most necessary function.

Thus the magician stands as a distinctive figure, varying in importance, in native cultures. As a matter of definition, I should say that "magician" implies a professional worker in the kind of magic which is on the whole public and good, and who fills in a simple society the general role of doctor, lawyer, and even financial adviser, whereas "sorcerer" connotes one dealing, also professionally, in matters that his clients would rather have kept secret, and one whose work may be downright anti-social. "Medicine man" will do for magician. I have, however, been avoiding "witch doctor," "wizard," and "witch," because they are ambiguous and suggest witchcraft, which should be considered as something quite different from magic.

You will have seen, I hope, from this outline of magic, how universal is its appeal and how universal its application. It can be very simple, like refraining from a few gestures which might call up a wind. Or, among the Azande, who are usually most punctilious about their magic, a man may pick up a stone, say to it, "You are such-and-such a medicine; now keep the birds away," and put it in his garden, without further ado. In this case it may be that the Zande is only trying to fool the birds, and that he does not expect any more than if he pointed his finger at the birds and said, "Bang, you're dead." For in the main magic demands and gets great attentiveness from the performer, and exactness in following the prescription. The two elements of a formula are, as I have said, the medicine and the spell. The medicine is the material end of the formula and must be compounded without any departure from the directions; and it includes things powerful in their own right, like lion's claws, shark's teeth, seeds, moss from a skull, etc. The spell, the spoken or acted part, may have to be equally exact; it may be largely mumbo jumbo, but it is apt to contain a strong phrasing of what the spell is supposed to do, i.e., the will of the worker, to add punch to the magic.[3]

Medicine can be expensive. This is natural if the ingredients are scarce, like dragon's scales or unicorn's horns, and there was a flourishing luxury trade in such things in medieval Europe. Another and better reason is that the formula may be secret, or else very difficult to prepare and work, or both. This of course is no misfortune to the magician, because it is what gives him his professional standing and assures his clientele that they are getting their money's worth.[4] Complex medicine objects may become a well-recognized phenomenon, of which fetishes are probably the

[3] J. H. Leuba, in *A Psychological Study of Religion* (1912), wanted to add to Frazer's laws two more: a Law of Repetition, by which an arrow which has once found the mark will do so again, etc., and a Law of Effort of Will, by which a magician lends all his own oomph to the spell he is making. I think this causes a slight confusion with the idea of mana, and that, properly speaking, magic is believed to work automatically, needing no special qualities beyond the correct formula.

[4] As exhibits of the potent effects, and the drawing power, of such magic ingredients, let me cite the cases of two face creams, both of them advertised in print in a certain large tribe which shall be nameless, but whose initials are U.S.A.

"Unique, golden-jarred AMOR SKIN," says a mail ad, "contains the vital ingredient *vividerm*, taken from the glandular tissues of the long-lived tortoise." AMOR SKIN costs twenty dollars, plus tax. *Vividerm* is not otherwise described. The New York *Times Magazine* for Sunday, December 29, 1946, advertises ENDOCREME, which contains ACTIVOL, "an effective replacement for woman's own natural skin-beautifying substance." ACTIVOL is not otherwise described. Neither is woman's own natural skin-beautifying substance.

best example. These things are used all through West Africa and the Congo Basin, and the name is apparently derived from a French mispronunciation of the Portuguese word feitiço, for sorcery.

Fetishes come in different types, each having a particular function, but all the recognized ones are for good purposes. Each is supposed to have a spirit in it, generally a foreign ghost, but while this spirit is thought necessary, and lends force, it is not treated with, and the nature and the operation of a fetish are really purely magical. A fetish consists of a human or animal statuette, or a bag, or an animal's horn, and contains specific medicines and needs its own spell, performed by its rightful licensed owner. Let us look at Nkosi,[5] the lion, who actually consists of a male and female couple, the male being a human statue and the female a sack; each of these contains red and yellow clay, head and claws of an eagle, tails of a ferret and a wildcat, and the claws and hair of a lion, among other things. Its power is to seize a thief and squeeze him until the blood jumps out of his nose and mouth. If something worth the trouble has been stolen, the losers put the owner of a Nkosi to work. They go to the scene of the theft with the two parts of the fetish, of which the male half gets most of the attention; he is waked up with gunpowder set off under his nose, and people chew kola nuts and spit the juice all over his front, and then kill a goat and spatter the blood on him. He is given a terrific shaking, while everyone beats drums and sings, and his proprietor exhorts him to catch the thief. If anyone thereafter falls ill of a nosebleed he will, whether innocent or not, go to a doctor, who may diagnose the case as Nkosi sickness, because he or one of his relatives has been stealing. The patient then goes to the owner of a Nkosi, who orders Nkosi to let the man go, imposes some restrictions on the patient (don't eat chicken, caterpillars, or

[5] J. van Wing, S.J., "Etudes Bakongo. II. Religion et Magie," *Institut Royal Colonial Belge, Mémoires, Section des Sciences Morales et Politiques: Mémoires—Collection in 8⁰*, Vol. IX, Part 1 (1938).

spiders; don't go to a funeral), and collects a fee. If the man dies, he has disobeyed orders. If he gets well, the Nkosi owner gradually removes the restrictions and collects more fees. If a village plantation or coco palm grove has been given the Nkosi treatment, and this has been noised all over the countryside, it is clear that there is likely to be little plundering, even by men from other villages.

It should be said that these people are not "fetishists" or "fetish worshipers," terms which have been used in the past by writers on religion, but which anthropologists do not countenance. The Bakongo of the Congo Basin, whom I have been describing above, have a completely different cult of ancestor worship, which is their real religion and which I will describe later. Furthermore, they do not worship fetishes. They simply use them for magic. Fetishes are like other highly formalized medicine objects found elsewhere in the world. The medicine bundles of many Plains Indian tribes are made up, owned, and used in much the same way.

It would be possible to go on exploring the subject of magic in general almost endlessly, puttering about with types and examples. Yet in the end it is all the same; it comes down to a suppositious, misguided philosophy, a pseudo science. Then why, if it is so false, does it not fall down of its own weight? Human nature, I should say; and that is a two-edged answer because, on the one hand, human nature cannot see through it, and on the other, human nature really wants it.

Magic seems logical. It is obviously a track that our minds like to follow, and so it will not give itself away easily. Why should an ordinary intellect which has invented a piece of magic, and which feels it to be right, be bothered to check it scientifically? You can feel superior only if you have never formed an opinion in this way yourself. Or if you have never taken over somebody else's opinion or explanation without testing it; for that is another cloak which magic wears: everybody else believes in it, and if it has religious respect attached to it, and perhaps even a legend to explain its origin, then only a strong-minded person would suspect it. It is hard for you to feel, without a qualm, that there is nothing wrong with the number 13, when all the weight of other people's opinions is against you. Men are believers, not doubters, and furthermore they prefer the beliefs they heard first; very few Methodists turn Catholic, and vice versa.

Even if you were a born skeptic, and given to examining magic in a casually scientific light, the chances are largely in magic's favor. Things happen anyhow: hunting magic is made and the game is duly killed; rain magic is made and sooner or later it rains. If something goes wrong, it is not the magic which is blamed, but the magician. He has slipped up in his spells, or something has been left out, or else the magic has run into some countermagic, or else the client has not followed instructions. This is doubly sure to be the explanation because most magic is carried out in this magical realm, against other magic or witchcraft. You use magic to protect yourself, your house, or your garden against witchcraft. Nothing happens. That proves the magic was good.

But in any case human memory would favor magic, because people are impressed with successes and forget the failures. They remember for years that Babe Ruth pointed to the very place in the bleachers where he was going to hit the next pitch, and did it, and they forget the endless prophecies, made from 1933 on, that Hitler would die within a month. We know that the Bishop of Troyes killed an image of Queen Jeanne, and that the queen died, but I think it is likely that plenty of people made images of, let us say, the Bishop of Troyes without getting in the public eye for it, because they did not manage to kill him. But above all this, magic can actually work. Men have died (in Polynesia and elsewhere) because they were aware that they were being attacked by a sorcerer. And, on a lower note, if you can keep wandering thieves out of your plantation by publicly putting it under the magic of Nkosi, what more can you ask of magic?

So there is little that can be put against magic on the debit side, apart from the sin of stultifying real logic and investigation. Mark Twain had some harsh and funny things to say about magic in *A Connecticut Yankee,* but when you have agreed with all this, there remains a great deal to be put to its credit. Human nature, as I said, really wants magic, and gets true good out of it. It is not comforting for man, especially primitive man, to realize how helpless he can be, and magic enables him to avoid realizing it; it gives him a soothing conviction that he can take care of himself, because nature can be bossed around by pulling imaginary wires. It is another form of religion which acts to quiet the nerves of individuals and of society, and to allay the urges of panic and disunion. It gives people something to do in situations where there is really nothing to do; it is the practical answer to the feminine cry of "Don't just stand there! Do something!" If, in a thunderstorm, you do not see how you can fail to be hit by lightning, there are three things you can do: (a) fold your hands and sit still, (b) pray, and (c) work magic (even if it is only crossing your fingers). These alternatives would all be equally efficacious, I should say, but there can be no doubt that (b) and (c) are the more comforting. In some ways magic is the most comforting of all. A prayer to the gods is all right, but it is a request only, and it might even get into the wrong incoming basket, whereas magic, if it is done right, is guaranteed. Man can put his best foot forward with magic; he can act on his own behalf, without delay. Finally, if you have magic there is always hope at the bottom of the box. Somewhere there must be an explanation and a formula.

A whole community can get the same benefit and sense of protection from public magic. And even black magic may work in the public good, because it makes a harmless outlet for spite and envy, and allows quarrels among men or families to peter out in magical skirmishes rather than in real physical or legal encounters of which the whole group would have to take cognizance, with the consequent upsetting of the peace. A man with a grudge may try to deal out sickness to the object of his hate—he is not likely to go so far as to try to kill a fellow villager, because murder by magic is still murder—and he will then take the credit if his enemy splits a toenail or gets the flu; he will feel avenged and the trouble is over. If he used civilized, direct methods of revenge like setting fire to his adversary's barn, or going in and punching his face in his own front hall, the whole community would be embarrassed and have to intervene, and the thing would rankle. Far better the most gruesome dismembering of images than homemade bombs wired to the ignition of an automobile.

But much of magic's usefulness is to individuals, simply because it tends to be an individual concern. To this degree its services to humanity differ from those of tabu, which emphasize community responsibility. In fact, around the turn of the century writers wished to distinguish magic broadly from the rest of "religion," particularly from worship addressed to gods and spirits. The difference between the two, said Frazer, is the question of whether the forces which govern the world are conscious and personal (i.e., gods) or unconscious and impersonal. Churchly religion looks to gods who, if supplicated, may interfere in your favor and change the situation, perhaps by a miracle; in magic, however, no such attitude of piety is necessary, and there is nothing miraculous in it, because magic is simply the proper manipulation of things as they are (to primitive man). Magic has no supernatural patrons. Magic takes a cold-blooded view of things; magic can compel things to happen, whereas prayer to a god can only attempt to persuade. Durkheim noted that "religion" is social while magic is personal, and in defining religion he required that its possessors must be united in a church, by which he expressly meant to exclude magic. Marrett dwelt on magic's antisocial possibilities and indicated how religion is always approved by the group while magic tends in the long run to be disapproved (by public opinion, but not by the underlying popular will). Others wished to reconcile the two things, arguing that magic and religion both recognize power beyond ordinary nature, and suggesting that they meet in the notion of mana.

Here is scholarship gnawing its leash. Doubtless the divorce has been overdone. Warner[6] rebuts it with the Murngin of Australia. Part of this tribe has no practice of magic, but only the belief, and they save a victim of sorcery (foreign) by using rituals straight out of their regular totemic cult. The rest of the tribe fights the identical kind of sorcery with white magic. The effect is the same, and the group approves and lends its interest as strongly to the magic as to the ritual, backing up the medicine man, so that in actuality he has his "church."

We might be more concerned about the exact relations of religion and magic if primitive peoples themselves were clearer. Nevertheless the distinction is there, and the two things do indeed go their separate ways. Magic, as I have said before, exists practically everywhere, but it seldom if ever exists alone, and its status depends largely on the other beliefs of the community. For magic is typically not organized, and a church is; and when both of them are in the field of trying to do good for people, then the church wishes to arrogate to itself the things that magic does, and the priests declare war on the magicians. Magicians lose caste and become sorcerers. Because of this, any man of learning outside the Church was suspect in medieval Europe, and magic among us now is entirely disreputable. But this happens not only in the case of the Christian Church, for primitive churches also work to suppress magic. The BakXatla of South Africa once had a well-developed ancestor cult for their religion, and also the usual flourishing magical profession. Since then, the tribe has been heavily missionized; they are now Christians and the ancestor cult has gone completely. But the code of magic has persisted unchanged and in full strength, showing that it was essentially different

[6] W. Lloyd Warner, *A Black Civilization* (1937).

from and resistant to the ruling cult, whatever the latter might be.

So magic must come from a side of human nature not appealed to by any other form of religion. It is also apt to have the last word with many people; it is the final refuge of wishful thinking. In April 1942 the police of Montreal raided sixteen black-magic parlors in the city, arresting thirteen women and five men. Nine of the prisoners pleaded guilty at once, and the rest went on trial. Police seized much paraphernalia, including skulls, black cloth, crystal balls, pinwheels, and bottles said to contain the spirits of Adolf Hitler and Benito Mussolini.

5

DIVINATION: THE FUTURE IN THE PRESENT

Fortunetelling is dear to our hearts, and there is no doubt that the art of divining is the most persistent and popular of all our non-Christian religious activities. Certainly it must be the only one whose practitioners are listed in the classified telephone book. However it is done, divination means getting information about the future, or about things which are otherwise hidden (what is Uncle Ed leaving me in his will?), by some use of oracles or omens; getting word about human affairs from non-human sources.

It has always been a most important profession, and generally a respectable one. The diviner may be a magician, perhaps a specialist in this kind of work. It is easy to see the necessity of having such a man to diagnose sickness, or to discern the workings of black magic, or to identify a thief; he is as ubiquitous and necessary as the family solicitor. But divining is also something which the priests of a god practice, in order to read the will of the god, and so to pass it on to the people. Divining is too good a bet for them to miss, and thus it is, in religion generally, a bone of contention between magician and priest. The latter, if he has a monopoly on divining, gets a great deal of support from it, because it consolidates his position in the cult and elevates him above ordinary mortals. The priests of the Maya Indians were the ones who worked out the precise Maya calendar; they were able to predict phases of the evening stars, and even eclipses, which must have given them great power over the people. The calendar was used in other ways for divining, as well. Even where the diviner is not the priest, he may, like Merlin, be of importance to the king, and so a significant figure politically. People look to him for guidance, because he can find the right answer to a situation; that is why, in all the blood-and-thunder yarns and the comic books, the medicine man has become the stereotyped threat to the hero in the solar topee; he always incites the tribe to kill the intruder. On the other hand, Montezuma's diviners fell down badly: they misread Cortes as a god, and gave other bad advice, and so Montezuma in trepidation let the Spaniards come unmolested all through Mexico and into Tenochtitlan, which was no small factor in the ultimate conquest. In some cultures the chief or king may actually have developed from the diviner. Montezuma himself had duties of this kind, being expected to do a certain amount of star-gazing; and the early emperors of China had similar responsibilities.

Man's devotion to divination should hardly be surprising. I said earlier that the fuel of religion was the necessity of knowing the unknown, and if there is any general subject which can be relied on to be unknown, it is the future. Doubtless this is the reason for the bulldog tenacity of fortunetelling among us, today, after we have shuffled off most of the other typical elements of primitive religion (except for informal personal prejudices about toads and warts, or knocking wood). For with science, technology, and medicine, we have spiked the usefulness of workaday, practical magic and the fear of evil supernatural forces in our own surroundings. But the future remains fearsome, because it is unknowable. Science can take a few hacks at it, with large-scale weather forecasting, or with mathematics and the laws of probability, but we are, in actuality, helpless; I can find your life expectancy, but I cannot tell you how long you will live. There are those who are willing, for a consideration, to try. They are our fortunetellers. They may disconcert us, as a civilized nation, with their nonsense, but they make a lot of people happy.

The word "divination" comes from the same root as "divinity," implying that it has to do with the gods or is controlled by them. This is true of certain kinds of divining, done by seers and prophets, but actually the attitude of most divination is magical, and much of it is no more than a department of magic. It seems to assume the same thing as magic: that nature is a mass of invisible connections and that nothing is a matter of chance. If things which you do have effects somewhere else, as they do in magic, then someone observing those effects would be able to tell what you are doing, which is almost the same as divining. You take advantage of the fact that all nature is linked together: in magic you step in and pull the wires to operate it yourself, while in divination you merely make observations, for your own information.

William James said religion was the belief in an unseen order, and in a magical sense this means that nature is all of a piece and that nothing happens without having a meaning of some kind. You see a sign, and you know that is connected directly to something else, just as a drop in the barometer is connected with an approaching storm. You accept the usual fallacies of magic and add one more: that future events are certain rather than merely probable. When you think of the future simply as the things which have not yet happened, it is all too easy to be hazy in your logic, and to look on the future just as you look on the past, seeing the two of them stretched out from you in different directions. Convince yourself of this, as you hardly need, and the future is there to be known, if only you can find the key. This seems so obvious that not to have such a key is intolerable.

At some points magic and divination are so close that they may scarcely be told apart. It is a bad sign, you know, to light three cigarettes on a match; that is the way it is usually said. But it is not really a "sign" when you start something yourself, because you are working magic by your act.[1] Similarly, it may be that you are more likely

[1] I will entertain the argument that lighting three on a match is really a tabu, and not dangerous magic at all. If you believe that it has some known evil consequence, then it is magic.

to find a letter in the mailbox if you walk on the left-hand side of the lane than on the right, but you are doing magic if you then walk on the left in order to get a letter. In divination proper you do nothing to bring about a result, although you may go through some complicated gyrations before your work produces an answer.

The magical kind of divination, by signs and portents —it is called mantic science—proceeds either by omens, in which you simply make note of something you see, or else by some kind of mechanical "oracle," necessitating your performing an experiment in order to get an answer. The Nandi, a cattle-herding people of East Africa, use few or no devices, but they are forever watching for omens, which they have built up into a tremendous lore.[2] This seems to be their main religious preoccupation, keeping a herdsman busy when he has nothing to do. If a rat crosses your path, that is good, but if it is a snake, that is bad. If you stub your big toe, that is good, but if it is one of your other toes, it is bad. All day long a Nandi is keeping score, to see how he stands by night. In contrast to this omen taking, the nearby Azande of the Congo and the Sudan do divining by special mechanical means which they have contrived and which they use constantly; it is their great defense against witchcraft.

Omens come largely from purely natural phenomena. Astrology is the prize example of the hypertrophy of an omen system. It uses all the heavenly bodies, putting them into every possible relation, real or imaginary, significant or not, so that an infinite number of individual horoscopes may be turned out. It has been running on for centuries, unchecked by any spirit of inquiry other than books written to prove its accuracy after the event, and because of its antiquity it is all the more complicated, and can quote ancient authority and use a preposterous jargon to give itself airs. It was once deeply entrenched in more than one reli-

[2] A. C. Hollis, *The Nandi* (1909). The diviner, or orkoiyot, is also the most important political figure.

gion, of course, especially those of Central America and of Babylonia. It was respectable then; its fall from grace is recent, caused by its giving birth to a true science, astronomy. Modern astrology is the bilge which has been wrung out of astronomy proper.

Other manifestations of the heavens, like eclipses, or comets, or lightning, are used without reference to astrology, for simpler purposes of deciding whether or not to proceed with something. In Greece a sacred procession from Athens to Delphi waited upon a signal of lightning. Animals are another great source of information. This is not because they know, themselves, what is in the offing, but simply that they act as signs and as guides. It may be that their appearance alone is important; the Bushmen of South Africa rejoice to see a mantis. Or they may constitute a sign, foreordained by the gods: Cadmus had to follow a cow for a long time before she settled down to show him where to found a town, and in the very same way, the ancient Aztecs wandered until they saw an eagle sitting on a cactus and holding a serpent in its mouth, and there they founded Mexico City. These two examples are, of course, both legendary.

The art of reading a message from the flight of birds was called ornithomancy among the ancients (auspicium in Latin), and this was the main stock in trade of the augurs; if they were not suited by the way the birds flew, nothing could take place. This is by no means peculiar to the people of classical times; it is used in many parts of the primitive world. The natives of the interior of Borneo are especially bird-ridden; they will not start to build a house (a major undertaking, up to four hundred yards long) until the birds give their assent, and they will stop at once if, while they are at it, the birds change the complexion of their omens. They have found that the most practical way of getting something done is to begin the job with a rush when the birds give the sign, and thereupon to send out small boys to beat gongs and keep the birds away; then they are sure there will be no bad omens because there will not be any omens at all.

The ancients on occasion used a pit of snakes or a tankful of fish as a source of omens. Such a thing as this marks the beginning of getting the omens under your own control, i.e., to make oracles out of them, and so be able to consult them whenever you see fit. Animals are also used extensively this way. One of the classical methods was feeding grain to sacred chickens; if they ate heartily, do; if they were reluctant, don't. Recall the case of Admiral P. Clodius, OTC of a Roman force about to attack the Carthaginians in the First Punic War. Naval doctrine apparently prescribed this chicken feeding (called alectoromancy by savants) as part of the business of arriving at a sound military decision, and so he was equipped with the holy pullets, doubtless under the charge of his intelligence officer. These were duly broken out, and grain was put down on the deck for them. Alas, the chickens were stricken with mal de mer, and stood uncertainly by the rail, indifferent to food. Clodius watched this for a bit, and then lost his patience, roared, "If they won't eat, let them drink," had the chickens thrown over the side, and hoisted the order to engage. But the chickens were right: he lost the battle. Says Cicero: "This joke, when the fleet was defeated, brought many a tear to him, and mighty carnage to the Roman people."

Where the Romans used chickens the Azande use termites.[3] When a Zande has some minor question, he cuts two sticks of wood, of different kinds. He takes these to a termite mound and pokes a hole in it, to which the termites come in swarms. He speaks to them, asking them his question and telling them to eat one of the sticks if the answer is yes, and the other if the answer is no. Then he puts the sticks in the hole and fills the space around them, and leaves them overnight, coming back to see what has

[3] E. E. Evans-Pritchard, *Witchcraft, Oracles and Magic among the Azande* (1937). We call ourselves civilized, but the Azande have invented something useful for termites to do.

happened the next day. Even if neither stick (or both sticks) has been eaten, something can be made out of it.

Another principal business of the augurs was haruspication, or inspecting the entrails of animals—usually pigs—in order to read messages contained therein. It was the conformation of the lobes of the liver, in particular, which gave significant indications of the will of the gods. This again, like so many classical religious customs, is shared by primitive groups in several parts of the world.

A variation of it is making notes on the manner in which a wounded animal dies. A chicken is treated thus in Nigeria. The Nilotic Negroes along the White Nile sacrifice bulls to their high god by spearing them, but they take the opportunity to observe in which direction the dying animal staggers as it falls, and on which side it finally falls down. Still another variety of dependence on animals is the burning of bones, especially shoulder blades, which was ancient and widespread in the Far East. A shoulder blade of turtle, sheep, or deer, not yet dried out, was cast into the fire and after a while taken out again, and the cracks produced by the heating were then read much as we read the palm of the hand; this is called scapulimancy or omoplatoscopy.

From such a thing it is but a step to purely inanimate objects for divining, mechanical contrivances which call for somebody to manipulate them. Casting lots in one way or another is an old and popular fashion, the present scene of its greatest popularity probably being among the Bantu peoples of South Africa. Here there is commonly used a set of four bones, which represent an old and a young man and an old and a young woman, which are thrown on the ground to make a pattern. There may be added to these another large set of animal bones, also paired by sexes, and usually being the astragalus bone, of the ankle. These not only represent the animals who furnished them, but also other things or attributes attached to them, in a sort of zodiacal linkage: the bones of the male and female impala represent the chief and his wife; the wart hog, who roots things up, the diviner; the baboon, who is not a roaming animal, the village; and the panther, the white people; various shells also represent everyday happenings in life. When these are all thrown on the ground, a trained diviner can reap a tremendous amount of information from their various relationships as they lie. Elsewhere in Africa groups of sticks are thrown down like jackstraws, for the same purpose. In Dahomey, in West Africa, there is a much more formal system than the South African one: sixteen palm nut kernels are cast down in pairs, successively, and the results read from a rigid code of interpretation.

Our European past abounds in the same kind of thing. You need only remember that cards, dice, and even jackstones were invented for divination and not for games, and cards at least have never lost this function. Another indication is the fact that there were coined at least fifty words ending in "-mancy," each one signifying some established method of extorting an answer from the supernatural about pressing matters of personal or national fortune. People have stared at crystals, at fires, at fountains, at smoke, at the wind in the trees and the clouds in the sky and the surface of the water; they have swung rings, shears, and sieves from pieces of string; they have stuck knives into books, thrown grain in the air, dropped hot wax into water, and so on and so on and so on. And they are still at it. Perhaps the only thing we should be puzzled at is why so many methods have fallen into disuse, and why the few have succeeded. I can see the reason for the vitality of astrology, but I do not see why other methods have been largely stripped down to numerology, palmistry, and tea leaves. I suppose the last is good for tea shoppes, and the others are the most convenient: you take your name and your palm wherever you go. You can, it is true, still buy many articles for divination in the home, such as ouija boards, and gadgets which you can suspend over a letter to tell you whether the writer is male or female.

I have said that the Azande of the Belgian Congo are specialists at astral research, and I would like to describe their two main oracular methods, to show a case of a primitive nation which has come to place much of its reliance for peace of mind in this art.[4] I gave their system of consulting termites as a sample. More involved is their rubbing board. This is a miniature table, carved out of wood, which has two straight legs and a sort of curved tail, together with another piece of wood the size of the table top, which is slid around on the latter by means of an upright handle. The juice or soft meat of a certain fruit is put on the table top, and the opposite part is moistened and put down over it, and pushed back and forth. Such is the quality of the juice and the two pieces of wood that the upper piece either goes on gliding smoothly over the lower, or else it soon sticks to it quite tightly, so that it cannot be pushed back and forth and has to be pulled off.

This is all there is to it, and the worker simply asks the board a question, telling it to stick for a yes and slide for a no. It usually acts definitely, either sliding smoothly or sticking promptly, and so it gives the impression that it knows what it is saying and has no doubt in its mind. The occasions on which it misbehaves, by getting only partially stuck or not sliding readily, are easily interpreted as caused by a question being asked wrongly or stupidly, or by the board seeing complications which have escaped the questioner. It is a useful and well-liked oracle, and one that the Azande use all the time, because it can be referred to handily. They are continually demanding things of it, wanting to know if they should build a house here or plant a garden there, if a witch is after them, if they will die this year.

There is little doubt that the board is susceptible of being manipulated, just like a ouija board, and that they do tend to control its actions. The selections it makes are usually the reasonable ones, and of course it seldom tells a man who is working it that he will die soon. How far people are aware they are tampering with it, or whether they have any sense of cheating, nobody can say, but that of course is a question which is present in every kind of divination in which the performer has any chance to affect the per-

4 Evans-Pritchard, op. cit.

formance or interpret the result. This is not a complaint, because that is divination's bedside manner; it would be of no comfort to people if it dealt out harsh predictions in equal quantity with the sunny ones. I do not know of any statistics, but I should guess that reassuring trade horoscopes must outnumber disturbing ones by about a thousand to one, and I cannot imagine the most punctilious palmist giving a John Dillinger or a Baby Face Nelson even an approximation of his character and fate.

The Azande's main oracle, entirely overshadowing the others, is a poison, named benge, which they feed to chickens. Divining by poisoning fowls is widespread in Africa, but it reaches its zenith here. As they use it, benge is a red powder made from a forest creeper, mixed with water to make a paste. They have to journey to the Mangbetu country to get the plant, and it is consequently expensive. It is an alkaloid poison related to strychnine, and it has the peculiar property of killing some chickens and leaving others unaffected, within the usual limits of the doses used by the Azande.

Benge séances are held privately, away from the village, and out of sight of women, who are a bad influence on it and might spoil it just by looking at it. The man conducting the consultation mixes the poison into a paste, rolls some up in a leaf, and squeezes it into a chicken's beak, as though he were lettering a cake. He nods the bird's head to make it swallow, and at this point begins to state the question. He does this quite fully, addressing not the chicken but the benge itself, first setting out the general problem and then adding further details and expending eloquence on it when he is able. The benge is asked, as carefully as possible, to kill the bird if one answer or view of the case is the correct one or, reversing and restating matters, to spare it if the other side is right. During this time the chicken may have been given a second dose and shaken up a little. Benge serves so well as a method because it usually allows several minutes to elapse before having any effect and then either continues to produce no effect whatever or else sends the bird into spasms and kills it quickly and decisively. It is extremely seldom that there is any halfway stage, when a chicken takes sick but recovers. It is not a question of the efficacy of a given lot of poison or of the strength of the mixture, for the same batch of benge will leave the birds alive or dead in about equal numbers. Furthermore, as far as Evans-Pritchard could determine, the size and health of a bird and the number of doses given it do not have a bearing on its survival.

The Azande have a reverential attitude about benge. Though they do not personify it, they talk directly to it, and it is not looked on as an impersonal, mechanical sort of oracle. They consider it a sort of mystical force, which prevents their thinking of it as a poison, so the latter idea does not enter their heads. Evans-Pritchard pursued the point by asking them whether it would poison a man; they gave evidence of thinking this was a foolish query and said it would not, if nobody asked it a question. He also inquired what would happen if they continued to feed benge to a chicken without stopping. They lackadaisically suggested that sooner or later the bird would burst, and missed the point entirely. Apparently there is no question of their trying to manipulate this test, as they might the rubbing board, or of trying in any way to affect the result; their whole view of it would prevent such an idea, and it would be idle, because they have come to the benge for information. They guard themselves against a frightening answer by a habit of so phrasing a question that there is a loophole through which to retreat.

They rely on benge thoroughly, and its decisions have the force of law, especially when obtained by the chief or his officer. It can be asked about anything and it definitely must be referred to in certain affairs, such as where a child should be born, whether it is all right to make a journey or move to a new house, etc. A man would simply be remiss if he failed to poison a chicken before embarking on such a venture, and indeed if he had the time a Zande would ask benge about his every move, although this would run into poultry. That is why a rubbing board is such a useful supplement, because it is easier; if he can, a man takes it everywhere, and he never enters another village or leaves it without asking his rubbing board at what time and by what path he should come or go.

Zande life is obsessed by their oracles—benge, rubbing boards, termite sticks, and certain others—which sit across their psychic outlook like a pair of spectacles and fulfill some of the functions of gods in other societies; they protect the Azande against witches, their greatest dread, and they harmoniously join the present to the future, which, as far as individuals go, is one of the primary duties of any religion. Furthermore they do not seem to give rise to any practical difficulties. Evans-Pritchard, in order to gain the good will and confidence of the natives, and keep down arguments, ran his own household by what benge said, and he found it as good a way of managing affairs as any. This is certainly a touchdown for the fortunetellers.

Now there is an element about Azande oracles which makes them somewhat different from the simplest kinds of divination by animals or by mechanical means. Benge, as I said, is looked on as almost though not quite like a being, and Azande exhibit a deference to it. They also keep certain tabus in connection with its use, which would spoil its power if not observed: they cannot, before working it, eat elephant, fish, or certain vegetables, smoke hemp, or make love. The rubbing board also is looked on as something conscious and not simply inanimate, and its workers are also under obligations to eat certain medicines and to treat the board in a formal manner. Similarly, in Dahomey, West Africa, the throwing of palm nut kernels is presided over by Fa, goddess of fate, and the practice is accompanied by small amounts of prayer to her. Here we are on the border line between the idea that divination is simply taking the cover off nature, magically, and the belief that it is supplication to a conscious, knowing being for information. The magical attitude remains the ruling one, how-

ever, not so much because the trappings are magical as
because man is in control of the performance. He can employ the oracle at his whim, needing only to be correct
about it, and the oracle has no choice; it must produce an
answer, and the correct one, every time. In this light it does
not matter what the people believe to lie behind the oracle
itself, dictating its revelations, because they use it and act
toward it as a piece of magic. But there is an ambiguity
nevertheless, suggestive of the other end of the scale, where
there are kinds of divination in which the shoe is on the
other foot.

Most of these latter use a medium, rather than omens
or non-human oracles, through whom a god or a spirit
makes himself manifest, and there is much more of the
notion that this spirit talks at his own pleasure and not that
of the seekers. The tip of this end of the divinistic scale is
represented by prophets, who are singled out by a deity
as a vehicle through which to transmit a revelation to
the people. Prophets have direct-wire communication, like
Moses, through whom Jehovah issued the entire Hebraic
code of law, voluminously and explicitly. The shaman, who
is a widespread type of primitive medium, also has this
direct contact with spirits who impart messages to him.
Some prophets of history and of the savage world have
received apparitions or inspirations which were not clear
as to their meaning, i.e., signs from above rather than outright declarations, and so have had to provide an interpretation themselves. Such a prophet as this, and indeed any
prophet, is therefore in a position to lay down the law himself, or construe it to his purposes. At any rate the familiar
sects are so full of illustrations of prophecy and revelation
that there is no point in singling out a few.

Different from prophets are human oracles, or mediums
in our usual sense. They do not recount a revelation after
they have received it, but rather speak publicly with the
very voice of the god himself. The obvious example is the
Delphic sibyl, who for centuries delivered utterances while
possessed, which were enigmatic as to their meaning and

were recorded and interpreted by the priests of the oracle. This is well paralleled among the Polynesians, who had a similar subject, called a kaula in Hawaii. This person, male or female, was entered, usually at a feast, by a god who sat in his stomach. The medium shortly went into convulsions and began talking in shrill cries or a squeaking voice; this was the god's own manner of speaking, and not the subject's. As at Delphi, the communiqué was apt to be obscure as to its sense, so that the priests might have to clarify it, although on occasion the god talked quite plainly. The medium had the appetite of the god, as well as the voice, and is said to have eaten enormous amounts of food while possessed.

This is the class, I suppose, in which we should place our own minor-league spiritualists, who put out the lights and then speak for the spooks of Indian chiefs and little girls (not having quite the impious brass to represent gods). I do not see why the controls are so commonly of these two kinds—in real life they would be about the most incompetent informants you could find in a month's journey—but perhaps it is because the Indians, at least, did not get baptized, and so their shades are to be found frequenting paleface séances instead of playing a harp in the happy hunting ground.

Getting in touch with the souls of the dead is of course not a civilized monopoly at all. The business is called necromancy and it goes on everywhere, with many special diviners to do it; they commonly use an actual bone belonging to the departed in order to make the contact. Rousing the dead is also an important department of shamanism, of which more later.

There are various other patterns of personal divination, akin to those above, in which possession or control by a superior being is not implicit. Dreaming is the most general of all, and this is an endless subject in itself; however, people everywhere have about the same approach to interpreting dreams, taking them as forthright or disguised prophecies, or sometimes as meetings with the dead. It is seldom

that dreams are thought to have any particular agent behind them, sending them—notice that the Crows consider
their visions as something quite distinct—and they are usually accepted simply as a window on the supernatural. In
the Old Testament, however, the Lord used dreams to communicate with various people, and in Greece it was possible
to obtain a dream sent by a god by sleeping in that god's
temple. In the Sahara, a Tuareg woman who wants news
of an absent husband will spend the night sleeping on an
ancient tomb. A spirit of the dead, named Idebni, will come
to her, and if he likes her looks he will tell her what she
wants to know. If he doesn't like her looks he will strangle
her.

There are other diviners whose supernatural powers are
thought to be their own, and who frankly owe nothing to
the help of spirits. A Zulu seer can answer questions on
occult matters, with the help of questioners who lead him
on and warm him up; they go at it like Mr. Bones and Mr.
Interlocutor, and before getting to the real question involved, he is tested by having to find or describe some
purposely hidden object like a button to see if he is in good
working order. Some of these powers are actually based on
unconscious psychological responses. Crystal-gazers look
into the ball until they see a shape which gives them a
meaningful impression, much as we see a cloud which
makes us think of an elephant. Some, by listening intently,
believe they hear snatches of secrets from sea shells held
to their ears. And dowsers are the somewhat mysterious
people who can use divining rods to find water, or metals,
and who were once thought able to track criminals.[5]

A final and beloved branch of mystic consultation is the
ordeal. This is a trial by divination, and its special nature
lies in the fact that the accused's own person is made the
engine of the test. It runs riot through European history

[5] A delightful study of the practice of this art here at home
will be found in *Water Witching, U.S.A.* (1959), by Evon Z.
Vogt and Ray Hyman.

and goes back among the English-speaking peoples to the Anglo-Saxons (it is the same as the German word Urteil, a judgment), but it is popular everywhere, especially in Africa. It stands about in the middle of the scale of ideas sanctioning divination: in Christian Europe the belief was that an ordeal reflected the judgment of God, who would punish the guilty and save the innocent, but this was not consistent, and the common touchstone seems to be the fact of guilt or innocence itself acting in some magical way to affect the result.

An ordeal by fire could be interpreted by either belief, and at any rate an innocent person would remain unharmed. He must thrust his hand or arm into the flame, and unless he were guilty he would not be burned. Boiling water in South Africa, or burning oil elsewhere, act the same way. One cannot but feel that the percentage of convictions in these courts must have been high. In ancient Europe an accused might have to walk barefooted over red-hot plow-shares (perhaps this was first devised for third offenders, who would have no arms left). In both Europe and India people were also obliged to carry a red-hot iron in their unprotected hands for a certain number of steps, to see if it burned them, and in Arabia one touched one's tongue to a red-hot knife.

In such a trial the guilty suffered, making it appear as though this were the idea. However, that is probably wrong, because in the ordeal by swimming it was the innocent who ran the risk; the pure element of water would reject the impure, being happy to accept an innocent person into its bosom and drown him, while casting up as a foreign body a witch or criminal. This was used particularly against accused witches, and had prescriptions as careful as any other law.[6] The accused was tied up in a particular way, perhaps with hands under knees, and tossed in; he had a rope on him with a mark a certain length up, and if he sank to this point he was innocent. They pulled him out and turned him loose, if he could be resuscitated. These

[6] Kittredge, op. cit.

laws were repealed in England in 1219, but dunking witches continued for five hundred years, and seems to be the same idea.

The ordeal by poison suggests punishment without waiting, but it is not as bad as it sounds. Actually it is again more of a matter of guilt producing an effect on something you have eaten. It may be no more than water, especially holy or charmed water. Usually the guilty person will not be able to keep it down, while the innocent person will not feel it; the reverse may hold. The Bangala of the Congo have an intoxicating drug made from a certain root which they use in civil cases. The litigants have to take a prescribed dose, which blurs vision, making everything look large and causing intense dizziness. The judge keeps asking both men to step over a stick he holds out, or to catch it when he tosses it to them. By and by one of the two collapses and is adjudged the loser, even if the other keels over as well. Some other African lie detectors have a more deleterious effect than this one. The Anglo-Saxons sought divine aid in such cases by consecrating bread and cheese, which would make the guilty gag, so that he could not get it down. "I hope to choke" is believed to be a surviving remnant of the custom.

Murder may inform on itself, and dead men tell tales. Europeans and Melanesians both believed that the wounds of a corpse would start to bleed again at the approach of the killer.[7] The corpse itself may even make a move or point out the murderer. In West Africa the dead man, lying on a bier, may be carried around the village at a run, with his arms and legs flying, and he will be able to kick or strike the guilty person, or else the bier or coffin will lurch in the latter's direction. Suspects may have to file past the bier and pick up an arrow, which will prick the evil-

[7] To take two literary examples, the wounds of the dead King Henry VI "Open their congeal'd mouths and bleed afresh" at the presence of the Duke of Gloucester in Shakespeare's *King Richard III*, and in Wagner's *Götterdämmerung* Hagen gets the same greeting from Siegfried's body.

doer. All in all, the murderer will either be pointed out by his victim if he views the body, or be booked on suspicion if he stays away.

Ordeal by combat was used either to determine a criminal, whose guilt would make him vulnerable, or to settle an issue between disputants, and this was the last kind of ordeal to die out. Our forebears did not hold, as we do, that a good big man can always beat a good little man, and thought that justice would prevail regardless of fighting skill of the parties to the quarrel. This meant that you could have your case handled for you by a hired champion (who might as well be brawny anyhow), which was a convenience to many having recourse to the law, especially women and clergymen. In 1355 the Bishop of Salisbury and the Earl of Salisbury became involved in such a vicarious battle, but it was called off at the last moment; this was because it was found at the weighing in that the bishop's champion had his clothes full of written prayers and charms. This was entirely irregular, because to try to influence the outcome of an ordeal by means of sorcery or witchcraft was criminal, and also unethical.[8] The idea of champions likewise made it possible for whole groups of people to try conclusions in this way.

Divination must have wrought awful injustices through the ordeal, in thousands of cases. In its simpler forms, however, it is probably harmless and makes, as I said before, a reassuring safeguard. Doubtless it has often had a beneficial effect on a society, where the diviner comes to be a respected figure. When this is so, the position will attract intelligent and trustworthy men, who usually understand their responsibility and who, though believing generally in their oracles, will modify questions and answers to fit policies which they know to be for the general welfare. This sounds a little utopian, but it is evident that in certain cultures, like that of the South African Bantu, this does take place. Thus divining can lend its authority to good purposes.

[8] Kittredge, op. cit.

Divination certainly dies hard; it is remarkable how overwhelming a proportion of our ties with the native cults lies in this field. The reason must be that it gives people something Christianity does not, and will not. No such high philosophy as Christianity could ask its believers for patience with life and trust in God on the one hand, and on the other sanction fortunetelling, or approve of wandering spirits smuggling information across the Great Divide to a privileged few. And yet good Christians will use the Bible as a means of divining or discovering secrets, in ways for which it was never intended. And the country is full of well-dressed churchgoers who have no idea of the extent of their own heathenism in such beliefs.

6

DISEASE AND MEDICINE

I have said that religion is a barrier against fear, and I should be prepared to show it simply on the evidence of the religious approach of primitive folk to sickness. For ill-health can have no rival as man's greatest cause of earthly worry; it pains him, it dispirits him, and it raises the specter of death. And, besides, healthy individuals are preyed on by the illness of relatives. The twentieth century can be thankful for a certain abatement of this kind of fear, which has hung over most of man's ages like a pall. Modern medicine is one of the brightest facets of our civilization, and our doctors by their honesty of purpose and their compassionate efforts have set a standard for every profession; these things have made it possible for us to adopt a tolerably rational attitude, in spite of ourselves, toward sickness. Simple societies, for all the good will of their medicine men, must continue to rely uneasily on magic and pay far heavier tribute to disease. Statistics on the subject are rare, but the Navahos, for example, have been specifically studied as to what things they dread most in life.[1] First is the fear of illness, which was mentioned three times as often as any other fear for which they could find expression.

Our scientific elevation makes us stoical, as I said. We are occasionally poisoned for our insurance, by human

[1] A. H. and D. C. Leighton, "Some Types of Uneasiness and Fear in a Navaho Indian Community," *American Anthropologist*, Vol. 44 (1942).

agents, and we also talk about misfortunes being caused by an act of God, but most of our miseries we ascribe to natural causes, and write them off as plain bad luck. To the less sophisticated, however, things appear the other way around, for there is practically no such thing as a "natural" cause. A savage is aware of the existence of malice within himself and so, no matter how intelligent he may be, he is immediately apt to see in his own sufferings the hand of another man, or of some supernatural force which is consciously doing these things to him. Such an outlook, of course, makes the whole matter a social concern as well as a personal one, in which the community must band together to fight the menace in whatever form it may have.

Disease is mysterious and invisible anyhow, and this keeps people from getting a real handhold on it. When you consider how short a time it is that we have been aware of the circulation of the blood, it is not surprising that men in a simpler state should generally know little about anatomy and nothing about physiology. A broken leg is one thing, of course, because most people are familiar with the skeletons of men and animals. (The Bantu have names for the bones, but they are puzzled by the viscera and think them the seat of thoughts and emotions.) A fever or a pox, however, cannot be handled. It comes apparently out of nowhere (perhaps several weeks, as we know, after the actual contagion) and it acts unpredictably; it may be mild or severe and it may strike one person or half a tribe. Or if a tooth begins to ache and burn, deep in your jaw, it is impossible to see why it can have happened unless something has got into you by unfair means.

Because of these things, backward peoples naturally move in a more dangerous psychic world than ours. If disease is endowed with both malice and caprice, people are compelled to keep a special wariness toward it, thinking about it a little all the time. The average American can (if he chooses) lead a sensible life, get vaccinated, see his dentist and his doctor once in a while, and otherwise not trouble trouble until it troubles him. But the average citizen of New Guinea cannot be so serene, because he has seen too many random afflictions caused, as he thinks, by a broken tabu or by failure to take proper precautions against magic.

In treating disease, the first measure taken by both civilized and primitive people is the correct one: to find the cause, or to objectify it. The difference comes in whether they objectify trypanosomiasis as a piece of black magic that has been stepped on, or as a microscopic animal that is only trying to make a living. From this point the attempted cure simply follows from the supposed nature of the disease, and savages have ascribed disease to every possible kind of cause, most of them of course being what we call supernatural. We may snicker faintly at the notion of substituting an invisible devil, let us say, or a malicious charm, for the microörganism causing pinkeye, but in making a cure what help would it give a Melanesian to know about the microörganism? He can do something about the devil, but not about the bug. And when all is done, his way of attacking the complaint through the demon comes out to be nearer than you would think to our way of meeting the microbe; it starts out by being ridiculous and ends up by being fairly successful.

A very large proportion of magic consists of healing; so large a proportion that I did not include it in the chapter on magic. And the reverse is true: a great proportion of primitive healing consists of magic, because if the disease is magic, so must be the cure. The people believe they can do injury in ways I have described and others. A Zulu sorcerer can put poison on his finger and send it by pointing. A native Australian can do much the same: "pointing the bone" is to induce or "sing" an evil influence into a sharpened piece of bone, and then from a safe distance to aim the bone and use it like a bazooka; some of the deadliest of these weapons need a two-man team. As we have seen, image magic and contagious magic exist everywhere, and there are dozens of ways in which charms can be placed so that the victim will unwittingly receive their effect. Sorcerers can be much more direct than this; by proper spells they can make all sorts of mishaps, causing a man to fall out of a tree or be bitten by a snake, or if they take real professional pleasure in their work they may even be the accident themselves, turning into a snake or a crocodile for this very purpose.

Now among a people who believe in such black magic, and actually practice it to some extent, diagnosis naturally turns to causes like the ones above. The best thing to do is to frustrate evil magic before anything happens, perhaps by wearing countercharms to neutralize a dangerous one buried under your doorstep, or drinking a potion containing the ground-up head of a snake, so that another snake, which might be sent by a sorcerer, will smell this odor on you and turn away, possibly deluded into thinking you are a viper yourself. The next best thing is first aid when something happens. If the cause is image magic, you must either reply in kind or somehow get the image of yourself that is being destroyed and causing the trouble; this has happened in Polynesia. In various ways fire is used against fire: stronger magic sends the evil back against the originator, or else you threaten your attacker with the worst arts of a sorcerer, greater than he, whom you propose to hire. As soon as the source of black magic working against you is known, and brought under control, you are on the mend. It is of course the duty of a diviner to diagnose such ills.

Regardless of the cause of sickness, the bulk of medicines prescribed are magical. The pharmacopoeia based on sympathy I have already described; it depends on such things as the signatures of plants or the properties of animals: e.g., you may be given the flesh of a hawk to help your eyesight, irrespective of the cause of its deficiencies.

There is another principle behind such medicines. The rarer or more extraordinary they are the more effective they are likely to be. Rarity makes a thing expensive, and that makes it good. Nobody ever tried to cure anything with grass. In native Africa parts of a lion are always in demand, as are certain stones or uncommon baked insects.

Old European prescriptions were made up from things whose procurement ranged from difficult to almost impossible. A cure for epilepsy was the ossiculum anti-epilepticum; this was a bone occasionally found in the human skull, and was probably the bregmatic bone,[2] which grows as a separate piece at the point on top where a baby's head is soft (the fontanel) in one or two people out of a hundred, so that to get usable quantities of this bone must have entailed enormous amounts of grave robbing.

Almost any headache powder had unicorn's horn in it, which was actually the tusk of the narwhal. Prescriptions for long life called for mummy dust, which came from the Canary Islands, where the original Guanches left their mummied dead in caves; these were exported to Europe in quantity after the Spanish conquest of the Canaries. Even with narwhal tusks and Canarian mummies available, however, one can only suppose that a great many purchasers did not get what they were paying for. Chinese apothecaries still deal in similar materia medica, specializing in dragon's bones, which are in fact those of all kinds of fossil animals. A giant fossil ape (Gigantopithecus), which lived in China during the Ice Age, was for more than twenty years known to science only from three teeth rescued by the paleontologist Von Koenigswald from the stock of a druggist in Hong Kong. Chinese pharmacists, unlike those of Europe, are not forced to cheat if they are out of the right kind of dragon, because the effect may be obtained simply by writing the name of the unavailable drug down and using the document for the thing itself. This is sympathy in two removes.

Ordinary disease seems to be something which has got into you (as indeed it is). This feeling gives rise to a second important item of medical theory which is accepted by nearly all practical primitives: that the disease is a willful intrusion and usually consists of some kind of an actual

---

[2] Paracelsus thought it was the interparietal bone, another rare variation.

foreign body. It may have been introduced by magic, or witchcraft, or it may have got in by spiritual agency—at any rate, it is something to be found and removed. So general is the belief that it is sometimes taken as an example of a culture trait common to all mankind. In Australia such objects are sent by "pointing the bone," and in standard treatment the medicine man gets them out by applying suction over the sore spot with his mouth. By and by he desists, announcing that he has got it, and he plucks from his mouth the offending body, which turns out to be a piece of bone, a crystal, or a cinder. He does this of course by sleight of hand. The early English suffered from the same kind of attacks, and narratives are full of patients who vomited bones, stones, nails, hairballs, and so on. The existence of gallstones helps the belief along. The English were also in danger of being "elf-shot," or magically shot with little stone arrowheads, such as are found on the ground (they are actually arrow points of Neolithic manufacture).[3]

Disease objects are not the only kinds of intrusion, because an actual spirit may take up with you and lay you low. Sometimes this is all he is interested in. In the Marquesas Islands, such spirits were specific for a certain disease, just as our own bacteria are. The South African Bushmen are pestered by little yellow ones who have no other business in life, and do not even enter you on their own initiative, being sent by directives from other spirits higher up. If a tribe has an epidemic it is logical to explain it as a swarm of such spirits passing through, or some allied kind of mischief, like invisible worms. An Englishman who felt upset was told by a witch woman[4] that an elf had been trying to get into him, and it was a good thing it had not succeeded, or there would have been a feast of toads in his belly!

Much more important is the idea that a person has been actually possessed by a spirit. This is quite different from

[3] Kittredge, op. cit.
[4] Ibid.

an ordinary intrusion, in which you simply acquire an in-dwelling saboteur. If a devil of some kind "possesses" you, it is an independent and conscious being who is seizing your body for his own uses. Of course the effect may be the same, producing sickness of any kind. The visitor may be a demon whose profession this is, or it may be the soul of someone dead who has a reason for coming back, usu-ally because it did not get all it felt entitled to out of life the first time. The souls of stillborn infants and those who died young and unmarried are dangerous because of their desire to occupy someone and have a fling.

Possession is above all supposed to be the cause of mental illness, for which it is a spectacular and logical explanation; this is the interpretation in biblical stories, in which devils were cast out of one. There are various forms of insanity which would seem reasonable in this light, ranging from compulsions in which a generally reasonable person cannot resist performing some senseless act, through delusions about being Napoleon, to completely split personalities, in which the sufferer leads two alternating lives, neither of which has any memory of the other; this last would seem like a foreign soul periodically ousting one's own soul from control of the body and periodically allowing it to return. In some such cases the changes in personality are marked, which would give a strong impression that an entirely dif-ferent spirit was in residence. Among a people who ex-plained madness to themselves in this way, delusions would be the more apt to take this expected form, so that the symptoms of patients would in turn support the view that a devil was in possession. That is to say, just as Napoleon is part of our cultural heritage, people whose culture in-cludes the idea of possession are apt in hysterical states to cry out that they are indeed struggling with a demon, and implore him to leave them alone. They carry on, in short, like one possessed. Possession is also a good diagnosis for epilepsy or similar disabilities: a person in an epileptic sei-zure would give a tolerable imitation of two souls trying to stage a wrestling match with only one body. Possession has one benefit to offer the people who suffer from it: it is an explanation of their affliction which arouses the sympathy, rather than the contempt, of the community, and so is apt to get them more normal and humane treatment than was enjoyed by the denizens of Bedlam and of other recent English and European asylums.

The answer to possession, or to any case where the trouble is a spiritual intrusion, or a personification of the disease, is exorcism. You drive the disease out instead of battling it within. You may force it out, by means of spells, which is probably the commonest method. It is magical, of course, and is the traditional European attack. A Maori doctor detecting a subcutaneous sprite in his patient would make it easier for the sprite to leave; such evil spirits come up from the lower world through a flax stem, and the doctor, by putting his head in water, would be able to see the very stalk along which the spirit had come up. Plucking this stalk and hanging it up over the patient, he would recite a spell which made the spirit leave the body and get back into the flax.

Spells may be mixed with surgery, like bloodletting, to let the fiend forth. A doctor in France could get nowhere with one of his patients, who insisted that he was possessed by the devil and wanted to be cured of that and nothing else. The doctor put a bat in a bag and took the man into a bog; then he made a small cut in the patient and set the bat free; he pointed to it as it flew away and said, "Behold, there the devil is gone." The man was completely cured.[5] The strangely widespread custom of trepanning, or cutting a quarter-sized hole in a patient's skull, was usually for the purpose of letting out the cause of pains in the head.

Other medical recourses are dosing and a sort of bloodless surgery. A cathartic or emetic will be taken, with the same effect it has upon the civilized, but the idea is to get rid of a devil and not of some tainted fish. A sweat bath is useful, and the Navaho ceremonies in which sand paintings

[5] Ibid.

are made are built around this; other American Indians take sweat baths regularly as part of any ceremonial occasion. The most direct system is simply to manhandle the disease, treating it as though it were tangible and manipulating it out. Sucking out a definite disease object I have described. Another practice is to scrape the illness off, as though it were outside the man, and throw it away. Similarly, according to some people, it may be sponged off. Or it may be moved around by massage, until it is forced down one leg, into the foot, and out entirely.

Instead of driving it out, you may coax the spirit or the disease to leave, or persuade it forcefully. You can put out a big meal for it, so that it will vacate you with gluttonous intent; if it is simple, you may sing songs to it; or you may make a great deal of noise, perhaps because it will be curious, but usually with the Chinese idea that it will be frightened. There are endless measures in use, progressively less pleasant for the invader. The Gã of West Africa will not allow a patient to be comfortable, in the hope that the disease will get fed up with conditions and go.[6] If the patient is given a good beating, as is done by some, the sickness will form a still stronger distaste. In the Society Islands a heated stone was used to send a demon out, and in the Marquesas they built a fire over or under the ill. According to Handy,[7] the Marquesans must have had a sound knowledge of the psychology of disease spirits, from some of their other techniques. They used the ripe noni fruit a good deal, as a household remedy, of which "it may be said, that if it affected the olfactory senses of demons in a manner in any way comparable to its effect on those of a white man, it is small wonder that it was efficacious in driving out devils." Nor was this their last resource. A sick man's wife could jump over him naked, so scandalizing the demon that he would flee in speechless horror. Women, it should be

[6] Margaret J. Field, *Religion and Medicine of the Gã People* (1937). In the name "Gã" the "ã" is nasalized, so that the word sounds like the French for "glove"—"gant."

[7] Op. cit.

remembered, are in Polynesia associated with the dark and earthly aspect of nature, and to have a woman pass overhead somehow was a danger and an insult.

Rather than simply casting the illness out, some tribal practices manage to transfer it to another person or thing, thus getting a certain assurance that it will not come back to molest the original victim. This is another demonstration of how disease is objectified and considered to have will and malice of its own. An unscrupulous doctor can simply fasten it on another person by temporarily getting it into some inanimate object like a stone or box and putting this along a path somewhere, so that the disease spirit will jump into the next man who comes along and have no further interest in you. This seems to me something like getting rid of Bright's disease by giving it back to Bright. Presumably the doctor informs himself as to the ailment's next choice and, like a primitive ambulance chaser, does his best to keep up with it, rotating a series of patients through the same case of whatever he has managed to put his finger on. In some localities, however, it is thought possible to put the spirit into an animal or a tree rather than another man, so that the above rascality is uncalled for. Frazer[8] cites the case of a Scotswoman who was convicted of causing an illness simply through negligence; she had succeeded in extracting the complaint from her patient and was sending it into a tree, when she missed her aim and hit another man with it instead.[9]

Imprisonment is a further method, and one which is more considerate of the rest of the community. South African Bantu use an ant hill for a prison; a man digs a hole in the hill and puts therein a small object into which he has transferred his disease, or else he just throws up into it; the ants shortly close up the opening and seal the evil in forever.

Attacks by magic (i.e., by human enemies), and the in-

[8] *The Golden Bough.*
[9] See later in this chapter for Huck Finn's wart cure.

trusion of disease as a tangible object or intangible spirit, stand out as popular beliefs regarding illness, but they are, of course, not the only ones. Two other common explanations are that something is happening to one's soul and that a tabu has been broken. Loss of physical health may be nothing but a reflection of loss of astral health. Witches are thought, in West Africa and elsewhere, to be able to capture and eat the souls of living people at night, and as the soul dwindles so does the solid flesh melt. This, in fact, is one of the principal ways in which witches do damage in many parts of the world. In Australia, native sorcerers are able to eat the kidney fat of a man without his knowing it, and the Australians believe that this is where the soul lives. In the East Indies and among the American Indians it is widely thought that a person has fallen ill because his soul has left him, either of its own will or under evil influences, and the cure is obviously in the hands of a magician or a shaman who can find out where it has gone and fetch it back. West Africans believe that other things besides witches may injure you through your soul. It may have been captured and put to work by a deity because of a misdeed you have committed; another moral belief is that the soul itself is a naturally good and honest thing, and cannot abide jealousy and concealed anger, and gets into an upset condition at any wickedness on the part of its owner, which in turn upsets him physically.

Tabu-breaking is another cause of sickness, since such actions put a man in a bad state and lower his resistance to evil influences, and these influences generally express themselves in sickness or ill fortune. This was the Polynesian and Eskimo idea, and an Eskimo doctor had the power of seeing the bad aura caused by a broken tabu trailing after the breaker in the form of a thin black mist, invisible to all others. Personal food tabus, where they exist, will bring difficulties. One class is the common tabu on a totem, by which whole clans are prohibited from eating the flesh of the animal to which they are supernaturally related. Another class is the kind of private food tabu found among

the Eskimos, which has no apparent rational idea behind
it other than as something not to do so as not to get sick.
Such tabus may be prescribed by a diviner in a horoscope
drawn up for a newborn infant, to be observed by him
throughout life, or they may be discovered by a diviner as
a result of a man's becoming ill from breaking a tabu he
did not know he had. Natives of the Congo brew a strong
palm wine which has the sinister quality of causing headache and slight malaise on the following day. To fend this
off, a doctor may tabu it to various bibbers except when
drunk under certain conditions; one man may have to
drink through a straw, another by using a curled leaf as a
trough, and a third with a sack over his head. These things
will remind you of allergies, and while they are of course
fallacious the truth is that they are often believed in sufficiently to have as much effect as a true allergy, meaning
that a man, finding he has disobeyed a tabu, may very well
take sick over it.

Primitive philosophers are not always strict in their logic
and so may not classify causes of disease quite as neatly
as I have above, or keep them distinct from one another
throughout. Tabu and magic may become mixed, since
there are prohibitions of a sort, connected with some magic-
working, which keep a person from falling into the ma-
chinery himself. A Gã woman who exercised a strong
magic against thieves had a daughter who thoughtlessly
took a banana leaf belonging to someone else because she
happened to need it for some small purpose; the magic
did not harm the daughter but glanced back upon her
mother and paralyzed one of her fingers. A soul may be
caught or injured by magic, another mixture of ideas; the
magic does not work directly on the physique of the victim,
but imprisons his soul, with the effects of soul loss already
mentioned. Or human and divine agency may be confused;
a Gã with a grievance wades out into the water and curses
his enemy, asking the sea god to judge the case and capture
the other man. Almost every tribe and culture recognizes
a variety of these different causes for illness, rather than

one type alone, although some tend to put most of the blame on the gods and others on their fellow men.

I have not tried to be comprehensive on the subject of savage medicine.[10] However, if I have played my cards correctly, the reader should now be feeling that man has never foisted on himself such pernicious poppycock as in the name of curing. But this brings us to the psychological tenet that men and animals do not continue to exhibit behavior which does not bring a reward. Accordingly all this activity surrounding disease, false as it seems to us, must do some good. What is the good?

Some of savage practice we cannot cavil at, because it is sound, consisting of simple remedies and technical treatments. The ordinary things with which people may dose themselves without going to a doctor are partly useless and partly helpful, and many of our household drugs and narcotics (quinine, cascara, cocoa, etc.) were taken directly from peoples who knew their use; interest in such things was high, as witnessed by an extensive and detailed herb list put down for the Spanish from Aztec knowledge shortly after the conquest,[11] and the fact that most tribes were well acquainted with all the intoxicants and narcotics native to their geographical areas. It has been estimated that about five per cent of the ingredients used by a South African medicine man in his magical potions would have a drug effect of some sort (whether helpful or not), and most of his compounds contain so many things as to be likely to include such ingredients; it is doubtful, however, whether they do any good except to make the patient feel that the prescription is potent.

Better than medicines are the treatments used, like sweat baths and massage, the latter especially common in the

[10] For a fuller account see W. H. R. Rivers, *Medicine, Magic and Religion*, 1924.

[11] *The Badianus Manuscript, an Aztec Herbal of 1552*. Introduction, translation, and annotations by Emily Wolcott Emmart (1940).

Pacific. All peoples have other standard and certainly useful knowledge of this sort, like midwife practices, and some are capable of skillful operations. Trepanning—removing a piece of the skull vault—is a risky matter. This is sometimes used by primitive people in skull fractures, correctly enough, but, as I have already said, it is done more often to release disease spirits, which would rarely be of account; however, the interest lies in the fact that people of New Britain, for example, can perform such an operation with great skill, with a series of postoperational methods to help convalescence, such as washings and dressings of the wound. South Africans set a broken arm by burying the hand and wrist in the ground and then steadily raising the man's body. I am not sure I would not rather undergo this than take my chances with a Boy Scout.

Nevertheless all this is beside the point, for two reasons. Such useful knowledge occurs only at random amidst all the flummery and, more important, the fact of its being scientifically sound is meaningless. It is not religious in this aspect, and it is the religious side which counts here; the significant thing is the huge, scientifically inaccurate side of curing, which is nonetheless effective because it is believed in. Faith may not actually move mountains, but its power over the body is greater than even sophisticated people allow for.

This is a fact which has great bearing on the belief in, and certain real effects of, primitive cures as well as tabu, magic, and witchcraft. I will cite some evidence, but I will eschew that of modern faith healing or religious cures, because of the argument as to the miraculous element which rages around them, and instead use that which seems to apply best to the very kind of primitive belief I have described. Deaths because of tabu, black magic, or witchcraft have been recorded from Polynesia, Australia, West Africa, and South America especially, and these are well-founded cases in which there is no reason to suspect poison or any factor other than fear. Imagine first of all the utter dread possessing a man who has become hopelessly tabu from a chief's food, and who can expect no help or perhaps even sympathy from his relatives and friends. Given that, Dr. Walter Cannon has described the actual process which might cause his death.[12] He can be killed by his own sympathetic nervous system which, when stimulated by fright, prepares the body for an emergency by supplying higher amounts of sugar and adrenalin and causing certain blood vessels to contract. If the bodily action for which these changes are intended does not take place, and if the emergency does not subside, continued activity of the sympathetic system is harmful, bringing about the effects of shock: blood pressure falls, the heart deteriorates, and contraction of the arterioles near the skin reduces oxygen in the blood here and allows the plasma in the blood to leak into the tissues, leaving the red corpuscles stranded. Lack of food and water would accentuate this vicious circle, and continuing fear, producing only normal amounts of adrenalin, would prolong the condition until the man died.

A large variety of actual ills can be induced among ourselves by hysteria or suggestion.[13] These are real organic complaints and not delusions. The skin is particularly susceptible, and people readily develop hives as an embarrassing response to various psychological situations. There is the case of a married woman who was having a lobster luncheon in a restaurant with another man for whom she entertained affection; her husband showed up and she was so disturbed that she developed a case of hives spontaneously, and always did the same whenever she ate lobster thereafter. Similarly, natives of Dutch Guiana who had personal food tabus got hives when they were put in the army and forced to eat some of their forbidden foods. People may suffer from a real allergy and yet have the same asthma from various purely psychic causes; sufferers may get it from the sight of a paper flower or a dust storm in

[12] Walter B. Cannon, "'Voodoo' death," *American Anthropologist*, Vol. 44 (1942). See also Warner, op. cit.

[13] See H. Flanders Dunbar, *Emotions and Bodily Changes* (2d ed.; 1938).

a movie. One woman who never had asthma laughed once at an acquaintance who was sneezing his head off, and in remorse began to fear that God would punish her for laughing, and thereafter developed asthma herself. A Berliner, for a reason undiscovered, was taken with asthma whenever he was in the Alexanderplatz, and for no other cause.

Hair actually goes white from fright, it is believed, but verified cases make it seem much rarer than is popularly thought. Other such changes because of fright or hysteria —loss of hair altogether or in patches, loss of hair color in spots, temporarily or permanently—are well attested. Suggestion or autosuggestion has shown various other susceptibilities. A woman who had an obsessive fear of being beaten by her husband, although he was paralyzed, was being treated by a psychoanalyst, who discovered this. He touched her on the arm and told her she would have a mark there as though her husband had beaten her, and next day her arm was swollen and discolored. By hypnosis, experimenters have been able to suppress the effect of a mustard plaster on a patient's skin, or else to produce the effect of one by using nothing more than a postage stamp. Frequency statistics indicate that many doctors develop angina pectoris simply from fear of it, because they know its symptoms and worry over its approach. Similarly, worry has been known to produce all the symptoms of gastric ulcer, sufficient to call for an operation, which reveals no ulcer but is very apt to cure the patient by reassuring him.

Now if these are all things which can be cured by psychiatry, they are also things which might be cured by a medicine man. (Notice how many of them sound like the effects of witchcraft or black magic anyhow.) We can no longer afford a simple, standard belief in magic in our society, and so we must turn such cases over to the more conscientious and personal probings of a psychiatrist. Plainly, fear of magic or of the displeasure of a supernatural being could bring on these physical ills and others in the same way as more civilized worries; and plainly a primitive doctor is doing his patient a real service if the latter is a natural neurotic and worrier, and the doctor can discover a believable, acceptable cause (however fantastic to us) for his worries. In either case, if the doctor can win the patient's confidence by convincing him that he has control over the trouble, the patient is as good as cured. Huck Finn (in *Tom Sawyer*) had three recipes for getting rid of warts, preferring this one: take a dead cat to a graveyard where somebody who was wicked has been buried, and at midnight when a devil comes to fetch him, heave the cat after them with the right spell; your warts will follow. Is this folderol? No, it is a perfectly good cure for warts. Warts have been cured easily by suggestion; directly in the case of some types of patients, and indirectly (i.e., by fooling them with harmless injections, fake electric machines) with others. Dr. Bruno Bloch[14] went after this systematically, and found that he and his colleagues could cure from a quarter to a half of wart sufferers in these ways, with some men being able to do it better than others, according to their ability to win the confidence of patients.

The kind of evidence I have been quoting I introduced in order to show how strong is the connection between physical and mental states generally. (One present school of thought insists that medicine should be based squarely on the view that they cannot be separated.) I mentioned certain kinds of cure which arise directly from this fact, but these are of course availing only when the ailment has some basis in neurosis or hysteria, and are no good for the mumps. In all this the more important and more general point is the value of what can only be called the bedside manner. It is a great asset to the civilized doctor, and it is far and away the greatest asset of the savage one. This sounds rather obvious, but its significance in primitive life is worth a little repetition.

To begin with, primitive medicine is perfectly rational and consistent, for a magical and supernatural world. It is not a hodgepodge of conflicting gibberish, but a logical sys-

[14] See Dunbar, op. cit.

tem of diagnosis according to the tribe's belief, by a competent diviner, followed by a course of treatment dictated by the supposed nature of the disease. This means that a highly intelligent savage and his doctor can get together on an explanation and a cure for his disease which will appeal to their reason. It is probably wrong, but remember that very few civilized patients, no matter how intelligent, really understand anything their doctors say, or grasp the complex biology of the situation. The important thing is that the sick man is convinced that the proper thing is being done. Think of the reassurance a Pueblo Indian will feel when he is given a healing ceremony by a special curing society made up of people who have already recovered, in the same way, from the same disease that he has.

This is half the battle, when the psychic factor has been enlisted. Among ourselves, the spectacular side of medicine has long been surgery, not curing. Recent strides, in immunizing, in antibiotics, and in highly specific compounds, have changed the face of medicine, but we cannot cure colds, measles, or mumps, let alone many more serious afflictions. Much of our treatment is still to give nature all the help we can, by disinfecting the patient, making him rest, and keeping him in a good frame of mind. Unless he has strong personal reasons for staying sick, or has a really dangerous disease, he will get well, in an overwhelming percentage of cases. And this is so even under primitive conditions of life, because man is an animal with tremendous tenacity of life. A tribal doctor, therefore, has all the ordinary power of nature on his side when he takes on a case, and his contribution is faith, surrounding his patient with a helpful psychic climate. Faith is the essential ingredient; it comes from his past successes and his personal attitude, and from a system of ideas which seem to provide the people with the hold they need upon disease. So armed, the doctor is able to give to the sick man a strong interest in his own case, and to the well the assurance that he can be rescued when he in turn falls sick.

Not only do people defy disease by making it plausible.

It is probable that they go further, and actually take much advantage of it—since they suffer from it anyhow—to point morals and strengthen parts of their philosophy. They may believe in love or hunting magic just because it seems useful. But illness is a real physical scourge, like hunger. So people put a special earnestness of faith in the methods by which they meet it, whether these are medicine men or religious rituals. Thus it helps to discipline them into general submission to certain important group beliefs; it is, so to speak, the teeth in the law. Now we have seen, for example, how the system of tabu appears to act as a social directive, organizing group attitudes in a useful way. Ostensibly tabu is a method of avoiding misfortune and disease, but actually disease, which is the real element in the situation, is the reason for observing tabus, and believing strongly in them, and so it helps give them the force they exert in society.

7

WITCHCRAFT: EVIL IN HUMAN FORM

So far I have been describing strange forces which primitive people see in nature and which they try to grasp and use. But there are also men and women who are strange in their own right, having special powers which are in themselves. On every continent there are those who possess an unnatural ability to do evil. Such a person is a witch.[1] Every one of you must have felt, at least once in your life, that nothing would be finer than being able to get even with people who had offended you, and to make them sorry just by wishing, unless it were being able to fly through the air. Witches can do both.

This does not mean that witches may not be guilty of black magic, or of raising evil spirits, or of every kind of abomination, and so they are, among such people as the Navahos as well as in Europe. However, our own witches were particularly loaded down with such fearful crimes for a special reason: the assault of Christianity. As the Christian faith spread across the simple culture of western Europe, it found the religious landscape dotted with a variety

[1] The sense I am giving this is one often used in anthropology: it is an idea quite different from a worker in magic, as will appear, and "witchcraft" here means simply the possession and exercise of the power of a witch. This is etymologically bad, but we have no proper English word and the distinction in ideas is a necessary one, so that the above convention has been commonly used. See the quotation from Evans-Pritchard on p. 114.

of objects: wise women (those of our fairy tales), diviners and magicians, good and bad, and everywhere local gods and spirits, together with a widespread cult around a god who appeared as a human being or an animal at the meetings of the worshipers.[2]

Now we know that during the Dark Ages one king and court after another became converted, and that today the "Witch Cult" is dead, surviving only in some of our holidays, like Halloween and May Eve. But it is hardly likely that whole populations did any immediate flipflop, and in fact Christianity fought the old cult tooth and nail for centuries before it won the battle. It did this partly by a propaganda war in which the old god was identified with the devil, and the worshipers were regarded as demons, as consorters with demons, and as evildoers of every kind, especially witches who rode to the meetings on broomsticks. Many people remained pagan, however, and plenty of them died for their faith, as did the early Christians for theirs.

While the established Church was conducting this campaign, it did not at first try to destroy the wise woman, who ranged from a respectable seeress to an old crone who knew magic and could be asked for help, but who was apt to be crabbed and was best left alone. Instead the Church competed with her and her ilk, by allowing a certain amount of Christian magic to be used and sanctioned: holy relics, exorcism, and so on. But the Church could not tolerate this opposition indefinitely, and finally felt compelled to take sole charge of the dispensing of all supernatural benefits, and so it sent the wise woman out beyond the pale along with sorcerers and demon worshipers. True witches, those with supernaturally evil attributes, had been there all the time, and so these several personages, banished into the darkness by Christianity, became rolled into one. (The recruiting of the wise woman may be the reason we now always depict witches as old hags.) So it could be that

[2] For a description and history of this, see Margaret Murray, *The Witch Cult in Western Europe* (1931), and *The God of the Witches* (1937).

when Dame Alice Kyteler of Kilkenny was tried as a witch in 1324 she was accused of denying Christ, of consorting with demons, of sacrificing roosters and compounding their entrails with herbs, spiders and black worms, with the brains of an unbaptized infant, and with the hair and nails of corpses, all boiled together in the skull of a beheaded robber, and finally of working spells to catch and kill husbands. (This was apparently the real charge; it was her fourth husband who accused her, alleging fear for his own skin.) The only odd thing is that she had not been seen flying through the air by hysterical children.

But Kittredge, who cites this famous case, puts his finger on an important point.[3] This is that in the last period of English witch trials (the seventeenth century) it was not black magic or broomstick riding that was considered a hanging matter, but only the power and the ill will of the witch. It seems clear, and it is interesting, that in these late cases the people believing in witchcraft had fastened once more on its basic, formidable nature, paying little attention to other things that had come to be associated with it. One party to a grudge would make some silly threat—a crotchety old woman would burst out at a tormentor or at someone she envied—and some piece of bad luck would befall the person threatened. It would then be believed that the threatener had brought this about because she was a witch and had the power to do it, and it was for that that she was denounced and tried. If at the trial witnesses then came forward and said they had seen the accused flying by night, consorting with devils, eating dead children, and making hoptoad stew, this was almost invariably embroidery on the fabric of the indictment, and not the cause of arrest at all.

Kittredge illustrates this with the case of the Trevisard family of Devonshire: Michael, Alice, and their son Peter, who were tried in 1601. All three had long been suspected

[3] Kittredge, op. cit. Anyone who has not read this marvelous book has been doing himself an injustice.

of witchcraft. That is to say, while nobody claimed to have seen them at the black arts, all had repeatedly given evidence of their power as witches, and at the trial eleven people or groups of people bore testimony as to their sufferings from the Trevisards over a long time. Actually it is obvious that the family was sharp-tongued and always at sword's points with the neighbors; that they foolishly indulged themselves in spiteful remarks and shallow threats; and that in this way the Trevisards managed to get themselves held responsible locally for most of the ordinary hazards of Elizabethan life. A few of the accusations quoted by Kittredge follow.

A sailor, William Thompson, used abusive language to Alice Trevisard in the street and then, as he left her, fell down and nearly broke his neck. Alice laughed merrily, as she might, and William rose and hit her with a musket rod. Sobered, Alice said, "Thou shalt be better thou hadst never met with me." When William next sailed, three weeks later, his ship burned and sank; he was picked up by a Portuguese vessel and held prisoner in Spain for a year. When he returned and Alice heard of it, she told his wife that he would be imprisoned again. He was: on his next voyage he was captured and held once more, this time for two years.

Alice Butler wished aloud that her child, who was ailing, might be able to run and play like other children. Michael Trevisard heard her and said, doubtless from native cussedness, "It never shall, until you have another." The child died not long after. Later, young Peter Trevisard tried to borrow a hatchet from Alice Butler's maid and was refused, whereat he said sarcastically, "I will do you a good turn within a year." Within a year, the maid died, as well as Alice's husband and another of her children.

Joan Baddaford complained that Alice Trevisard had quarreled with her husband and had said to him, in effect, "Why don't you gather up your wits?" This was not too direct a threat, but the husband made a trip three weeks afterward and came back out of his head. Alice told Joan herself that she would not be worth a penny, and Joan lost her house. Joan once dunned Alice for a penny she owed for washing; Alice paid it but said as she did so, "The penny will do you little good." It is dangerous to take money from a witch and Joan should have been warned by this time, but she recklessly spent the whole penny on drink and found she couldn't get it down and fell sick instead. Still Alice was not done with Joan; after she had been accused by her neighbors of witchcraft, she met several of them in the street, among them Joan, to whom she said, "Thou or thine will be burned." Now on her guard, Joan made no fires in her house for several days, and when at last she did, the ruff on her child's neck caught fire and killed him.

Nobody said anything about compacts with the devil, or cat familiars, in accusing the Trevisards. One boy said he had seen Peter Trevisard shove his skiff off from a dock, telling it to go to a certain place on the other side of the cove, which it did. But apart from this there was nothing laid to the members of the family except the power of their ill will. It seemed clear that the Trevisards were deliberately causing suffering and were a terrible danger to the town. Alice Butler and Joan Baddaford had proper complaints: Alice had lost most of her family, and Joan had lost her house and her husband's mind, and in each case the Trevisards had told them in advance what would happen, or had seemed to. So the townspeople at last felt compelled to appeal to the authorities for protection. That is why a witch suffers; it is not because people like to see witches die, but because they are forced to seek protection from them. Nor is it a case of zeal on the part of the law in attempting to root out witchcraft. It appears from the records that English judges who had cases of witchcraft before them usually tried, being men of more intelligence and education than the accusers, to prevent convictions and neutralize evidence, and often allowed convictions only because they could not do otherwise, and gradually in this way brought the trials to an end.[4]

It is not easy to see the slightest excuse for the existence of this wretched business, especially since, though our forebears held to it, we have now shaken it off. In the relations of individuals it appears superficially as an agent of discord pure and simple. But institutions like the belief in witchcraft do not exist for so long and in so many places unless they confer some reward commensurate with the penalty of trouble they exact, and hints of such benefits can be seen by studying the people among whom witchcraft still flourishes. Its actual outward effects on popular behavior differ in different cultures, according to the aspects of it which people choose to emphasize and the official attitudes they take toward it. Some peoples talk about it constantly and absorbedly, while in West Africa and among the Navahos the subject is considered indecent and furtive, in spite of the awe in which it is held. Some, like the Azande, control reactions to witchcraft by a careful protocol, while others, like the Navahos, have no such prepared channels for it, and its outbreaks commonly lead to murder. But it seems to be a fact that witchcraft works in several ways as a safety valve through which may escape the accumulations of anxiety, irritation, envy, and neurotic tensions that arise in all human groups, and which are particularly painful in a

By Dahl

SALEM IS THE PLACE WHERE NO WITCHES WERE BURNED. THEY WERE HANGED.

AWK!

PLEASE REMEMBER THAT.

[4] For the Salem eruption of 1691–1692, which cost twenty people their lives, see Kittredge. In the light of English and Scotch history of the seventeenth century, this was only one of a series, and not even especially severe, although late. There is some evidence that such aberrations may be associated with times of stress, as in the case of the Navahos, who had a great period of witch hunting after their national catastrophe of being rounded up and temporarily imprisoned at Fort Sumner in 1864. Famous catch question: How many witches were burned in Salem? Answer at left, by the kindness of Mr. Francis Dahl, Curator of Witches for the Boston *Herald*.

small, closed, primitive society from which there is no escape. This we shall see.

One more thing to notice is the astonishing number of parallels in witch beliefs on different continents. Witches are almost always thought able to fly, or at least to travel very rapidly. They are thought to gather in a witches' sabbath, to plot evil, and to eat or otherwise make use of the corpses of victims which have been killed by the members. And they are generally associated with animal familiars. Cats have got a particularly bad name in this regard. In a similar way witches may be werewolves, being able to assume the shape of wolves, cats, or other beasts to carry out their missions. Above all, however, witchcraft is always looked on as utterly bad, an unredeemed evil which cannot be sanctioned, while even the blackest of sorcerers is theoretically capable of good magic.

Among the Gã, a representative tribe of the Guinea coast of West Africa,[5] women are the worst offenders. The cause of witchcraft is possession by a demon, who lives in one permanently. Usually he is born in you, being passed on from mother to daughter, or he may be sent later on in life by a dead mother or some other relative. (Certain villainous people are said to buy them.) It is possible to have more than one at the same time, and if they get to breeding in you, you may be harboring a hundred; so they have no particular market value. The demon is not necessarily bad, and may even be used for curing, or knocking down trees, but if he once is put to evil he is like a shark that has tasted blood, and he will force the witch he lives in to kill neighbors against his or her will, and with no ordinary motive, and may actually kill the witch. In this way even people with good dispositions and intentions may become witches. In fact, one is usually possessed against her will, and makes a struggle against it. The victim pines away, goes through mental anguish, and may develop a real psychosis. The demon usually triumphs, of course, and the newly fledged

[5] Field, op. cit.

witch then resigns herself to the fact, and feels much relieved and more settled in her mind.

Gã witches' crimes are the usual injuries, commonly mortal, of innocent people. They steal a soul, it is said, ordinarily that of a child of one of them, and eat it in company, and drink blood. As the soul is slowly consumed, so does its rightful owner sicken and die, while the witches flourish and get strong. Witches also can steal a person's luck, which is something not dissimilar to his soul. Or they may cause a woman to be sterile, by stealing her womb without her knowing it. In a puckish mood they may do the reverse, sending children to be born where they will give the most embarrassment. These misdeeds the witches do in company. As in Europe they have a court, presided over by a king, and they travel to the meetings at night, following along invisible threads to guide them, riding through the air on the backs of leopards and antelopes. And how is all this known about witches? Because they confess it!

Individuals really believe, that is to say, that they have become witches, and they own up with gusto and pleasure to all sorts of things they could not possibly have done.[6] Although there is no sign of its actually taking place, they report that they have been to witches' sabbaths, where they have partaken of the astral menu, and they may name various other individuals who were there, all of whom are of course also innocent. The witch is picked out in the first place by a doctor or medicine man, who may be able to see tiny spurs on the witch's heels. To prove the case, he may test her with a certain kind of drink which will cause her to vomit serpents if she is guilty, or with some other ordeal. He can make a cure, furthermore, which begins with a hysterical confession, followed by various rites, including a cleansing bath and a renunciation of witchcraft. There may not even be a punishment, unless there has been a complaint about witchcraft traced to this witch, in which case there will be an appropriate fine. The attitude seems

[6] This has happened in Europe as well.

to be that the witch is not held completely responsible, and the doctor has managed to defeat the witchcraft and save the onetime witch.

It is obvious that confessed Gã witches are people of neurotic tendencies, and that the "cure" is actually pretty good psychotherapy. The witch has heard murmurs about witchcraft from babyhood, of course, and knows all about it. If later on a real neurosis makes itself felt, the pattern is all ready. Someone who is struggling against anxiety, morbidity, a feeling of social inferiority, or some other such cause of tension will under this stress begin to wonder if she is becoming a witch (some even develop temporary blindness or deafness, doubtless hysterical) and, absorbed by the notion, will finally accept it, in spite of a feeling of guilt, as the unavoidable cause of her personal unhappiness; this is apt to bring a relaxation of tension, especially as it makes an exciting fantasy to compensate for the lack of ability to deal with her troubles in the actual world. But the cure is even more satisfactory than the supposed disease. The doctor, who is believed to tell witches by their spurs, does no such thing; he knows who is a likely "witch" and takes such a one in hand by common-sense methods, although the ritual is treated with complete seriousness. The witch confesses and receives a gratifying tribute of awe, interest, and even sympathy from her fellow villagers, such as she never had before, which gives her a satisfactory counterbalance for her previous unnoticed maladjustment. This, therefore, is one useful aspect of witchcraft. Everybody has had a pleasant and rewarding experience: the "witch" has achieved a degree of psychological compensation for her feeling of inferiority, the doctor has made a coup, and the people have had some rather scandalous excitement.

There is another reward, reaped by the people bewitched rather than the witch, and it is more usual than the one described above. There are many people, less neurotic perhaps than those who actually believe they are witches themselves, who suffer from tiny delusions, unnamed worries, the fear that they are disliked, accumulated frustration, and so on, who have no direct way of draining these irritants off other than by a violent emotional explosion, such as no society can tolerate. Since there is nothing very real on which they can expend their suspicion and venom, it is better to have them expend it against something imaginary before they reach the flash point.

Witchcraft seems to have been invented simply to fill this need for an imaginary something, and it falls short of being ideal only because real people, when accused of being witches, fall into its toils and vitiate its work as a remover of discord. But those people who seem to be sitting on a psychological tack can project their psychological difficulties onto witches. Instead of being unable to give vent to their fear or anger, they can claim that their troubles are due to witchcraft; they can talk about their troubles in an interesting way, and other people, having nothing to lose, will agree and sympathize with them. They will have made their complaints public in an acceptable form, however fantastic. And because it is fantastic, and thoroughly evil, society can without argument present a solid front against witchcraft, as it can against the man-eating shark, and the individual finds surcease from his worries in public support, as well as in the catharsis of getting the whole thing off his chest. Public concurrence in the fantasy is necessary, of course. If little black people are doing square dances on your counterpane, the doctor cannot help you if he cannot see them too, but if everyone sees them, perhaps they can be shooed away. In sum, it is easier for most people, primitive or civilized, to believe in witches, which are imaginary, than in the facts of psychiatry, which are real.

Contrasting somewhat with the Gã-speaking people, the Azande of the Nile-Congo watershed emphasize this second aspect of witchcraft; instead of a somewhat disapproved subject of conversation, actively manifesting itself mainly in rare exhibitionist eruptions by slightly unbalanced individuals, they make it into a down-to-earth forum for the expression of indignation against ill fortune. Among them it is socially important, but it also has a pronounced and unfortunate effect on the public disposition.

The Azande believe that a person is a witch by virtue of a mysterious organ in the body, called mangu, which some people possess by inheritance. They are only one of a number of African nations who consider witchcraft to be an internal substance. Says Evans-Pritchard: "A witch performs no rite, utters no spell, and possesses no medicines. An act of witchcraft is a psychic act. They believe also that sorcerers may do them ill by performing magic rites with bad medicines. Azande distinguish clearly between witches and sorcerers. Against both they employ diviners, oracles and medicines."[7]

They are not positive as to just where the mangu is, but it is roughly underneath the bottom of the breastbone; it is described as an oval blackish swelling, or a reddish one with pumpkin seeds in it, or a round hairy ball in the belly, very dreadful to look at. The gall bladder is something like it, but it does not do the harm of witchcraft, only making its owner spiteful if it is large. Mangu is inherited, and all sons of a male witch get it, and all daughters of a female witch, but not vice versa. Approaching it scientifically, they may determine by autopsy whether witchcraft was present in a man, by examining his intestines, where experts can detect its presence. This is done mainly to clear a man's name after his death, and that of his living brothers and sons. That is, a man who has had to pay a fine for witchcraft may get it back if a relative dies thereafter and he can get an autopsy proving that the relative, and therefore he himself, is no witch. On the other hand, it would seem as though the fastening of witchcraft on a man would put all his male relatives in jeopardy, but they escape this by saying he is obviously illegitimate, because others of the family were found not to be witches when they were opened up.

Witches cause many kinds of accident and illness. To attack a man directly, a witch sends his mangu soul to capture the soul of some vital organ (different organs have different souls) of his victim. The mangu soul sails through the air like a fireball, and must be directed by the owner, since it cannot find the target alone and must have him pointed out. This means that witchcraft cannot travel far, and so the witch is usually somebody within the village; and a man who is fearful that he is under attack can go into temporary hiding at a little distance.

The mangu brings back the captured soul, or a part of it, and the witch eats it a little at a time; if he gets a bigger portion on one excursion than he wants, he hides the uneaten part in the roof of the house for later attention. As the soul of one of his necessary parts diminishes, the victim sickens, dying only when it has been eaten entirely. (Sudden sicknesses are caused by sorcery rather than by witchcraft.)

As elsewhere in the world, witches are believed to get together for feasts, and may there decide on attacking a certain person; in the main, however, witchcraft is thought to be simply the working of one man's spite against another. Although, as Evans-Pritchard says, witchcraft is purely psychic, witches have a few other common accouterments at least partly magical. They have an ointment to make themselves invisible. And they may injure at times by shooting small things into people in the way I have described.

Zande witches are also associated with cats in a loose way. Some female witches may have cat daughters or cat familiars, and may kill people simply by showing the cats to them. However, it seems that the cats are feared in their own right, because people will fall deathly ill at the mere sight of a certain species of bush cat, and on hearing a cat cry they will rush to blow their anti-cat whistles, and sit near their anti-cat plants, which grow in every homestead. Even people of royal blood, who are immune to witchcraft, die of cats, and sudden deaths among them are believed to be from this cause. It is interesting that witches and cats are here feared for the same reason without being bound together as firmly as in the lore of Europe.

Witches are detected by benge.[8] (The autopsy method does not enter into most cases, since few people would be in such a fret to clear themselves as to submit to an immediate post-mortem.) A man may do some preliminary exploration with the help of his relatives, but to give an accusation the proper sanction it should be based on the chief's oracle, which is infallible; consequently people who have decided on the identity of the witch who is troubling them will go to the chief and petition for a judgment. He consults his oracles in private and informs them of the result.

Sometimes vengeance is attempted by magic, once the chief's oracles have assented. This is done entirely in secret, and the only signal that it has been successful is that the relatives of the witch's victim stop wearing mourning. If the witch succumbs, his family is forbidden by the chief to practice magic again, although it is all right for them to fake the procedure of doing so, to hide the fact that their dead relative was a witch. But all this magic is apart from the usual resort, which is direct confrontation of the supposed witch through the proper forms. To begin with, unless the suspected witchcraft has caused somebody's death or very serious illness, or extreme damage such as the failure of a whole crop, action by the aggrieved Zande is not usually taken, because even if the witch is discovered he cannot redress the damage or call back the witchcraft, and because indiscriminate accusations of witchcraft are dangerous. In minor matters, therefore, the witchcraft is simply accepted as the bad luck in life, and nothing is done. When, however, a man is dangerously ill and feels that a witch is working against him, steps are taken to find out who is responsible, through various oracles. Then, instead of exposing and denouncing the witch and crying for public vengeance, relatives of the sick man approach the witch

[8] See p. 75.

tactfully and suggest that he desist. If they have asked the chief for a judgment from his oracle they may bring a wing of the chicken killed by the benge to show that they have the goods on him. It should be remembered that after all it is not his fault he is a witch, and since he is a neighbor, the victim will have to go on living with him in the same village. The accused witch will protest that he meant no harm and will blow water on the chicken's wing, telling his witchcraft to cool off. He is not insulted by the accusation, but rather takes this diplomatic visit as a favor, since he may be involved in a witchcraft trial and vengeance magic if the sufferer dies.

Now of course this accused man is not conscious of having caused witchcraft (witches are a conversational commonplace among the Azande, and there is no pattern of occasional semihysterical confessions or hallucinations). But accused people do not shout to heaven that they are innocent, a kind of reply which might end the whole institution. For they are not sure they have not caused witchcraft, or if they are, each feels that he must be the exceptional guiltless person wrongly accused; and so instead of making a scene he establishes his good will by accepting the imputation, and the chicken's wing, and declaring his good intentions. There the matter will normally end. Sooner or later everyone is taxed with being a witch, and it is understood that one or two flings at witchcraft should not be held against an otherwise respectable member of the community. However, a malicious, quarrelsome, or spiteful person would be the object of the greatest number of accusations or suspicions, and might come to be regarded as an intentional, dangerous witch.

The Azande have made of witchcraft an important social mechanism. They do not fear or despise it as do most other cultures, because they know how to deal with it, and it is an almost normal thing, a matter of everyday gossip. It has a certain ethical value, because socially disruptive activities —quarreling and so on—are apt to give rise to witchcraft and are accordingly inhibited. It gives them a universal explanation for bad luck and sickness and an immediate course of action against them. It does, of course, place the guilt on an innocent person, and a fellow villager, but it provides a formula for bringing the whole thing to a head and resolving it, and relieving the victim with a protestation of good will by the accused, and when you consider how often among ourselves cranky people wrongly blame neighbors for their troubles, it seems possible that the Zande system may nip more incipient feuds than it causes. To a Zande, witchcraft is the explanation for every mishap that cannot be better explained. If a man is killed hunting, that is witchcraft *unless* his wife has been unfaithful in his absence, which is breaking a tabu. If a beginner at making pottery cannot keep his pots from breaking while they are being fired, that is lack of skill (and he should heed his teachers more carefully), but if the pots of a skilled potter break, that is witchcraft. If a granary collapses, injuring a lot of people, that is witchcraft. The granary fell, they know, because termites had eaten the supports, but it was witchcraft that caused the people to be in it at the time. All in all, witchcraft gives the people something socially legitimate to wax indignant over, some outlet for anger and annoyance when affairs go wrong, and it steers the anger along a careful channel until as a rule it dries up.

It has its unfortunate aspects, however. It gives rise to a lot of minor resentment, causing people to store up the memory of every mean remark, to be used later as an indication of witchcraft. The idea of the casual roving malice of witches sets the tone for everyday Zande life, and the expression of envy in gossip is given full rein. The natives are quick to accept any small action as a slight and an injury; they delight in seeing misfortune befall others, and they look for witchcraft on every hand. Witches are to us pure fantasy. Witches are pure fantasy in Zande territory, too, of course, but the Azande have given themselves over to the complex wholeheartedly, and anybody can see from Evans-Pritchard's account of it how much very real behavior is determined by it. If this constant sense of danger and hair-trigger suspicion sounds like something hardly bearable, however, you may recall that two hundred years ago civilized gentlemen went armed, and never knew for certain but that in a meaningless quarrel they might suddenly lose their lives from sword cuts.

Differing from the Azande, our own Navahos view witchcraft, and also black magic, with a good deal of terror and consider its practice a heinous offense; and instead of being handled by a well-modulated etiquette, it is a dark subject and a suspected witch is exposed to murder by his victim in aggravated cases. Nevertheless Kluckhohn, who knew the Navahos intimately and did a careful and enlightening interpretation of their witchcraft,[9] believed "that the euphoric effects of the witchcraft pattern assemblage are considerable, perhaps even outweighing the dysphoric effects at the present moment"; i.e., it does more good than harm.

Although the results are the same, in Navaho ideas witchcraft is less clearly defined, having a distinct name but being associated with other supernatural evildoing. We meet kindred beliefs already familiar: black magic of the usual sort, the practice of shooting objects into victims to cause illness, and image magic or harming through contagion, using hair, nails, dirt, clothing, etc. All of these things are detested, but it appears from Navaho stories about them that witches are abhorred above all. Witches constitute a group, and to be initiated one must kill a near relative, preferably brother or sister; witches revel in death and incest, and they meet in a sabbath, presided over by a chief witch, where they plan action against victims, eat human flesh, and do other fouler things. In accordance with Navaho ceremonial patterns witches have an evil ritual corresponding in type to the usual ones, with chants and sand paintings. Those sorcerers who work spells through conta-

[9] Clyde Kluckhohn, "Navaho Witchcraft," *Papers of the Peabody Museum*, Vol. XXII (1944).

gion or images are also thought to go to the witch meetings, but the other types of malefactor do not.

Although it would appear that once a witch always a witch, the special quality of being a witch is not too explicit. When on business, Navaho witches go as werewolves, although not in the sense that they turn outright into the animals involved (wolf and coyote, and sometimes bear, fox, and owl). Rather they go in the skin of the animal, otherwise naked but painted and wearing jewelry, so that they remain detectably human and can be identified if seen closely. However, they can move with preternatural speed. "They can travel as far as Gallup in a minute." "They would go from Zuñi to Laguna and back in one night."[10] And they leave tracks like those of the animal cloaking them, but larger.

In a hogan the witches, as werewolves, eat the meat of corpses to strengthen them, and make a poison from dried and ground human flesh, especially that of children, and of twins if possible. A witch takes the poison powder and goes to the hogan of the victim, where he drops it down through the smoke hole while everyone is sleeping, or else puts it into the nose or mouth of the doomed. It may even be blown into a person's face in a crowd, generally at a ceremony, so witching is not necessarily done at night or in fancy dress. The poison at once causes something like fainting, lockjaw, or a swollen tongue, and thereafter the victim wastes steadily away, unhelped by any ordinary curing rituals. There are certain specific anti-witchcraft ceremonials, but the best cure is to force, or even torture, a confession out of the witch himself, which will reverse the witchcraft, allowing the bewitched to get well while the witch suffers and perishes from the very illness he has caused. Best of all is to forestall witchcraft with gall medicine, which acts as an antidote, and is made from the gall of eagle, bear, mountain lion or skunk, or certain other animals. Careful Navahos never go into a crowd without taking it along. Kluckhohn made a check of thirty-two households in the Ramah area

[10] Navaho informants quoted by Kluckhohn.

of the Navaho country, and with his own eyes he saw gall medicine in thirty of them. This would indicate, as he says, that the Navahos take witchcraft seriously and not as an amiable diversion like the Oz books. To the same point, Navahos are still being killed over witchcraft, and the Navahos are no more casual in matters of homicide than anybody else.

This is not all that witches do. One will make a partnership with a doctor, and the witch will strike a man ill for the doctor to cure, the two of them splitting the fee. Witches also rob graves by night, for the jewelry of the dead, a hideous crime to the Navahos, who are usually too much afraid of ghosts and dead men to commit it anyway. In these and other ways witches may get rich, which is a second major motive, besides spite or vengeance, for indulging in witchcraft.

In the belief in witches the Navahos have created a pageant of all that is most fearful, horrible, and shameful—most anti-social—to them, and Kluckhohn has shown why, given their particular kind of culture, they embrace it with such fascination, and why it is actually a force for social good. Some of the reasons are obvious; they are "manifest functions" which belong to witchcraft and magic generally. Witchcraft furnishes the credulous with exciting though vulgar drama, with plausible if unsound medical information, and with constant support for time-honored ceremonial formulas (by explaining, if they misfire, that witchcraft caused it). But this is only superficial, corresponding with what we derive from, let us say, television. It is the covert functions, operating at one remove from the visible ones, with definite psychiatric value, which are of significance for the social balance, and which, though unadmitted and unrealized, may do more to explain the fidelity of the Navahos, as well as other peoples, to the witch belief. One such function we have seen before: that of giving soul-satisfying public attention to thwarted individuals of no personal force or social account. Among the Gã of West Africa, such people sometimes confess to being unwilling witches themselves, while among the Navahos they may draw attention by claiming to be the victims of witches. Victims in general are from every social stratum and both sexes. Some may have a standing illness diagnosed as witching by a doctor, while others may be suddenly seized with one of the known, violent symptoms of witchcraft sickness. Kluckhohn analyzed the cases of seventeen persons who, fainting at large gatherings, claimed they were bewitched —i.e., came down with witch sickness in the most public way possible—and found that of the seventeen, thirteen "were persons known to receive a minimum of prestige responses in the normal run of things," eleven of these being women.

Larger than this accommodation of a few frustrated individuals looms the relief provided from the twin disturbers of society, anxiety and aggression. Navaho life is harsh: sheepherding on poor land is precarious, children are easy victims of disease, privations are constant, and the Americans add to the woe by insisting on new kinds of behavior which are not welcome. The pressure of this difficult existence makes the Navaho a prey to anxiety which he is unable to fend off. This is bad for the whole group, lowering the effectiveness and morale of one member and thereby acting as an irritant to all. Witchcraft, however, lets him talk about his moroseness in a way which is acceptable to the others, and through which they can close ranks and lend him their moral support; it therefore has a unifying influence on the oppressed.

Anxiety is both a cause and an effect of aggression and hostile impulses, with which all human beings bulge. Every single one of us has something of the crank in him, fostered by the fact that society and family must curb his freedom of action, and then must curb the resentment he feels thereat. As Kluckhohn says, "Always and everywhere human beings have hostile impulses toward other human beings. But every society restricts and channels the expression of hostility . . . unless there are some forms of hating which are socially approved and justified, everyone will remain in an intolerable conflict situation, and neuroticism will be endemic in the population." As far as the Navahos go, this can be severe because of the closeness of family life and certain features of it, as well as the anxieties already described. Personal bitterness is common, but family and clan responsibility represses it. And there is little to relieve the tension. War is no longer allowed for the Navahos, and drink or the possibility of leaving the tribe are insufficient refuges; furthermore, honest composing of ill-understood differences between men is no more likely than among ourselves. Witchcraft will act as a safety valve for all this accumulated antagonism, releasing it where it will at least do less harm than within the group where it was generated.

Most simply, Navahos fire off an emotional charge against a witch believed to live a long distance away, so that the pent-up feelings of aggression are displaced to an object in which nobody near by has any interest. Instead, therefore, of feeling any resentment, even if only at the display of rage, the plaintiff's circle approves his tantrum. This is the commonest pattern. However, some of this release by accusation of witchcraft takes place within the group; here it allows a satisfactory indirect attack against an object of hostility, but is kept simply as gossip. A young wife living in the confining atmosphere of her husband's family has a difficult time, with no means of outlet, and she may soothe her raveled feelings by telling her own family, when she visits them, that she—shh!—rather thinks her father-in-law is a witch. This is highly scandalous, so it is a real blow on her part, yet it can be approved because of the general uncertainty and attitude regarding witchcraft. Finally, witchcraft also causes an occasional killing, e.g., where a man has been goaded to the breaking point, perhaps by the death of a child, and so it allows and approves a release of fierceness in which many people can wallow and dump great loads of stored-up hate. That this is a just appraisal is indicated, says Kluckhohn, by the fact that such murders are particularly bloody and sadistic, and have much in common, I should say, with our lynchings.

Kluckhohn recounts still other features and relationships of Navaho witchcraft. I have not followed every line in his analysis, because I am writing about witchcraft in general and I would like to stick to its clearest aspects. Other cultures have witchcraft, or something standing in its place, without being so much obsessed by it. The Bakongo of the Congo Basin believe certain people are ndoki, and can turn into spiders to suck out a victim's heart's blood at night; here, as in the Navaho country, a relative must be turned over for eating as the price of initiation. In Hawaii, evil sorcerers could create evil spirits, unihipili, from otherwise innocent spirits of the dead, and these were sent by the sorcerer on errands of murder. Werewolves in general, and such things as the evil eye, are related to witchcraft in spirit if not explicitly.

And even where there is no such institution, many cultures if not most have a chosen whipping boy to absorb the exasperation and frustration which torment them, so that it is now commonplace that the treatment of national minorities may be ascribed largely to the same thing. I think it is sober judgment to say that witchcraft is a much more humane solution, because it is a more socially useful prescription. Under it as a heading, a tribe can gather and impute to witches a number of recognized evil desires and emotions, and so make the witches serve as a horrible example; witches are easy to believe in, and witchcraft can be hated communally, so that it makes a bond; and for these reasons and because it is beyond the pale it makes a safe shooting gallery in which to expend the floating hatred present in a group, which cannot be shot off in the group's own circle. It is true that individuals have come to grief at times, at the hands of the Navahos and of our own tenth-generation grandfathers. But witchcraft is less dangerous a fantasy than the one in which the Nazis placed the Jews.

8

THE SHAMAN, A SIBERIAN
SPIRITUALIST

Witches are all evil, and hide themselves from common men; they are "secret, black and midnight hags"; fell creatures, they hypocritically put on the mien of ordinary folk, the better to stalk and strike their prey unknown. But there are other men and women with extraordinary powers of their own, who have no need to skulk, because their purposes are good, and who are given public recognition and respect. The type specimen of such people is known under the Tungus word shaman, and the shaman is a figure of importance among the aboriginal people of Siberia and the Eskimos, among most of the American Indians, and to a lesser extent among various other primitive tribes elsewhere in the world. He has been sometimes called a witch doctor, especially with reference to Africa.

A shaman is a medium and a diviner, but his powers do not stop there. He differs from men in general, and resembles a witch, because he can shift gears and move in the plane of the supernatural. He can go at will to the other world, and he can see and treat with souls or spirits, meeting them on their own ground. And that is his business. He differs from a witch, who exists solely in the heads of the victimized, in that he is an actual person, who not only conducts his profession publicly, making the people think that he goes on brave errands among ghosts and goblins, but in many if not most cases really believes he has the powers he claims. This, of course, would be something difficult to get the truth of. Nonetheless he acts as though he can and does do the things which are traditionally his to do, and the public believes and acclaims him. That is the important thing.

His duties are to ride herd on the souls of the departed and to discover the general disposition of other important spirits, according as it is swayed by the behavior of human beings. He may do only a little of this; among some people there is a shaman in every family, who simply makes contact with the spirits from time to time to flatter them and assure himself of their serene humor, as we look at a barometer. Elsewhere he may do it as his trade: general divining, diagnosis of sickness, and ghost chasing. And he may be the most important person of the village, as well as the center of religion; this position he has in easternmost Siberia and among the Eskimos. With such people communities are small and religion is otherwise crude, and the people look to the shaman to take care of their relations with the supernatural both public and private. While he thus acts for them much as does a medicine man or a diviner, he is no magician. He does not endeavor to find the formula to the supernatural, working it as though it were made up of wires and joints, while remaining on the outside; instead, he boldly enters it himself and meets its inhabitants man to man. Nor is he a priest, who leads the people in supplication and represents them before their gods. He may work in their behalf, but he does not represent them; he is acting on his own hook, and through skill and power, not through supplication.

The stronghold of the shaman is among the reindeer herders and fishers of northeast Asia: the Yakuts and the Tungus, two widespread groups of tribes, and others living around the western shore of the Bering Sea: the Chuckchis, the Koryaks, the Gilyaks, and the Kamchadals of Kamchatka. Some of these live nomadically in felt tents and others in wooden villages, and in the long arctic nights of their bleak environment the comfort and entertainment that the shaman gives them is very well received. Typically it is believed that there are three realms of nature: an upper one, of light and of good spirits; a middle one, which is the world of men and of the spirits of the earth; and a lower one, for darkness and evil spirits. Men of the usual sort can move about the middle realm, and have some dealings with its spirits, but only a shaman can go above or below. A shaman also has the power of summoning spirits to come to him. Thus he can speak directly to spirits and ask what they want, which is his form of divining. Not only this, but a shaman deals with sickness in various ways through these same powers. If you have a disease spirit inside you, he can detect it and he knows how to send it off, perhaps by having a personal contest with it. Or you may have lost your soul—this explanation of illness turns up almost everywhere in the world—and the shaman gets it back. It has probably been enticed against its will by a stronger demon, and taken to the lower regions, and only the shaman can go after it, see it, identify it, and return it.

Both in Asia and America shamans, like witches, are generally believed to have familiar spirits, or animal souls, which are the things that give them their peculiar qualities and powers. A Yakut shaman has two or three.[1] One, called emekhet, is the shaman's own guardian angel, which is not only a sort of impersonal power like mana but also a definite spirit, usually that of a shaman already dead. This spirit hovers around its protégé, guiding and protecting him all the time, and comes at once when he calls for it, and gives him the advice he needs. Another spirit, the yekyua, has more character but is less accommodating. This one is an external soul, which belongs both to the shaman and to a living wild animal, which may be a stallion, a wolf, a dog, an eagle, a hairy bull, or some mythical creature, like a dragon. The yekyua is unruly and malevolent; it is dangerous and enables the shaman to do harm, rather like a witch, so that the people are in awe of him, but at the same

[1] M. A. Czaplicka, *Aboriginal Siberia. A Study in Social Anthropology* (1914). I. M. Casanowicz, "Shamanism of the Natives of Siberia," *Smithsonian Institution Annual Report* (1924).

time it has no consideration for the shaman himself and gives him continual trouble and anxiety, because his own fortunes are bound up with it. It is independent and lives far away, rather than upon the immediate tribal scene, and only another shaman can see it anyway.

"Once a year, when the snow melts and the earth is black, the yekyua arise from their hiding places and begin to wander."[2] When two of them meet, and fight, the human shamans to whom they are linked undergo the evil effects and feel badly. If such an animal dies or is killed, its shaman dies as well, so that a shaman whose yekyua is a bear or a bull can congratulate himself that his life expectancy is good. Of this phantasmal zoo the least desirable soul partners to have are carnivorous animals, especially dogs, because the shaman must keep them appeased, and if they go hungry they are not above taking advantage of their connection with the poor shaman to gnaw at his vitals to stay their appetites. When a person takes to shamanizing, the other shamans round about can tell whether a new yekyua has made its appearance far away, which will cause them to recognize the new shaman and accept him into the profession.

Siberian shamans all dress the part, as do so many shamans and medicine men of North America. The northeastern Asiatics wear clothing which is made of skin and tailored. A shaman has a cap and a mask, but it is his coat which distinguishes him like a collar turned around. It is a tunic made of hide—goat, elk, etc.—and usually comes down to his knees in front and to the ground behind, and is decorated to the point of being a textbook of shamanistic lore. On the front may be sewed metal plates which protect him from the blows of hostile spirits which he is always encountering. One of these plates represents his emekhet, and usually two others suggest a feminine appearance, since shamans have a hermaphroditic character, as we shall see. All over the tunic are embroidered or appliquéd the figures

[2] Czaplicka, op. cit.

of real and mythical animals, to represent those he must face on his travels in spirit realms, and from the back there hang numerous strips of skin falling clear to the ground, with small stuffed animals attached to some of them, all this alleged to be for attracting to the shaman any spiritual waifs of the vicinity, who might like to join his retinue. The whole getup would remind you of the unusual headdresses and paraphernalia in which medicine men are turned out among Indians of the Plains and Canada.

Siberian shamans have a tambourine drum whenever they are working, and this is true of Eskimo shamans as well. It is a round or oval drum, covered like a tambourine on one side only, and decorated with the same kind of symbolism as the coat. It is held by a crosspiece or strips of hide in the frame, and is beaten to accompany all the invocations of spirits.

When a shaman goes into action the result is not a rite but a séance, which is full of drama and which the people enjoy immensely. A typical performance is a summoning of spirits, and is carried out in the dark (for the same reasons as among ourselves—i.e., to hide the shenanigans), in a house, a tent, or an Eskimo igloo. The people all gather, and the shaman says what he is going to do, after which he puts out the lamps and the fire, being sure that there is little or no light. Then he begins to sing. There may be a wait, and he beats his tambourine drum first of all, an immediate dramatic effect. The song starts softly. The sense of the song is of no consequence as far as the listeners are concerned; it is often incomprehensible, and may have no words at all. Jochelson[3] knew a Tungus shaman who sang his songs in Koryak. He explained that his spirits were Koryak and said that he could not understand Koryak himself. Jochelson found this last suspicious statement to be quite true; the shaman had memorized the songs subconsciously when he had first heard them.

[3] W. Jochelson, "The Koryak," *Memoirs of the American Museum of Natural History*, Vol. 10 (1908).

As the singing goes on, other sounds begin to make themselves heard, supposedly made by animal spirits and said to be remarkably good imitations. The shaman may announce to the audience that the spirits are approaching, but he is apt to be too absorbed or entranced himself to bother. Soon voices of all kinds are heard in the house, in the corners and up near the roof. The house now seems to have a number of independent spirits in it, all moving around, speaking in different voices, and all the time the drum is sounding, changing its tempo and its volume; the people are excited, and some of them who are old hands help the shaman out by making responses and shouting encouragement, and the shaman himself is usually possessed by a spirit or spirits, who are singing and beating the drum for him. The confusion of noises goes on increasing in intensity, with animal sounds and foreign tongues as well as understandable communications (among the Chuckchis, the wolf, the fox, and the raven can speak human language), until it finally dies down; the spirits give some message of farewell, the drumming ceases, and the lights are lit. Often the shaman will be seen lying exhausted or in a faint, and on coming to he will assert that he cannot say what has been happening.

This is all a combination of expert showmanship and management and of autohypnosis, so that while the shaman knows perfectly well he is faking much of the performance he may at the same time work himself into a trance in which he does things he believes are beyond his merely human powers. He warns his audience strictly to keep their places and not try to touch the spirits, who would be angered and assault the offender, and perhaps even kill the shaman. When the show starts, the shaman produces his voices by moving around in the dark and by expert ventriloquism, getting the audience on his side and rapidly changing the nature and the force of the spirit sounds he is making. He may allow the impression that some of the visiting spirits are possessing him and speaking through his mouth and beating on his drum, but he may hide the fact that he is using his own mouth at all.

A shaman need not perform only in the dark. He carries out some of his business in full view, especially when it is a matter of his going to the spirit world himself, rather than summoning the spirits to this world. The idea seems to be that he is in two places at once; i.e., his soul is traveling in spiritdom while he himself is going through the same actions before his watchers. He does a furious dramatic dance, rushing about, advancing and retreating, approaching the spirits, fighting them or wheedling them, all in a seeming trance. He may foam at the mouth and be so wild that he must be held for safety in leather thongs by some of the onlookers. After vivid adventures in the other realms, portrayed in his dance, he will accomplish his purpose, which may be to capture a wandering soul or to get some needed information from his spectral hosts. Then he becomes his normal self again and gives an account of what he has done.

After a death it is a regular thing for a Mongolian shaman to be called in to "purify" the yurt (felt hut) of the deceased's family, by getting rid of the soul of the dead, which of course cannot be allowed to hang around indefinitely. The mourners assemble late in the day, and at dusk the shaman himself comes, already drumming in the distance. He enters the yurt, still drumming, lowering the sound until it is only a murmur. Then he begins to converse with the soul of the newly departed, which pitifully implores to be allowed to stay in the yurt, because it cannot bear to leave the children or the scenes of its mortal days. The shaman, faithful to his trust, steels himself and pays no attention to this heartrending appeal. He goes for the soul and corners it by means of the power in his drum, until he can catch it between the drum itself and the drum stick. Then he starts off with it to the underworld, all in play acting. Here at the entrance he meets the souls of other dead members of the same family, to whom he announces the arrival of the new soul. They answer that they do not want it and refuse it admission. To multiply the difficulties, the homesick soul, which is slippery, generally makes its escape from the shaman as the two of them are on the way down, and comes rushing back to the yurt, with the shaman after it; he catches it all over again. It is lucky the people have a shaman! Back at the gate of the lower world he makes himself affable to the older souls and gives them vodka to drink, and in one way or another he manages to smuggle the new one in.

Europeans who have seen Siberian shamans perform say that it is tremendous and exciting melodrama for them, and it must therefore have still more of an impact on the natives, whose belief and interest are greater. Aside from ventriloquism and histrionics, shamans use other tricks to heighten their effects, and even give small magic shows to maintain the awe of the populace. They are masters of prestidigitation, especially considering that they must work with little apparatus—no trap doors or piano wire. In their séances they can make it appear that there are spirits in several parts of the yurt at once, mischievously throwing things around. Many stick knives into themselves and draw them out again, making the wound heal immediately (all faked, of course). Or they will have themselves trussed up, like Houdini, and call on their spirits, who will set them free. Bogoras saw a Chuckchi woman shaman take a rock between her hands and, without changing it in any way, produce a pile of smaller stones from it, and to defy the skeptics she wore nothing above her waist. She repeated the trick at Bogoras's request, but he could not find out what she did.[4]

The shamans know, of course, that their tricks are impositions, but at the same time everyone who has studied them agrees that they really believe in their power to deal with spirits. Here is a point, about the end justifying the means, which is germane to this and to all conscious aug-

[4] W. Bogoras, "The Chuckchee," *Memoirs of the American Museum of Natural History*, Vol. 11 (1904–09).

menting of religious illusion.[5] The shaman's main purpose
is an honest one and he believes in it, and does not consider
it incongruous if his powers give him the right to hoodwink
his followers in minor technical matters. If shamanism were
a conspiracy or a purposeful fraud, it would attract only
the clever and the unscrupulous, interested in their own ag-
grandizement, and the public would shortly see the snare,
being no bigger fools than we are. But shamanism is an
institution, and the things that keep the public from reject-
ing it are religious characteristics: shamanism does something to help them, and the shamans themselves are inside
the system and believe in it too. A sick shaman will call
in a superior shaman to cure him. Actually, shamans are
among the most intelligent and earnest people of the community, and their position is one of leadership.

Evans-Pritchard has the same thing to say about Zande
witch doctors,[6] who do shamanizing of a less distinct type.
They divine for the people, usually dancing in a group. A
question will be asked one of them, and he will "dance" to

[5] Shaw has the following to say about it, through two characters in *Saint Joan:*

THE ARCHBISHOP: A miracle, my friend, is an event which
creates faith. That is the purpose and nature of miracles. They
may seem very wonderful to the people who witness them, and
very simple to those who perform them. That does not matter;
if they confirm or create faith they are true miracles.

LA TRÉMOUILLE: Even when they are frauds, do you mean?

THE ARCHBISHOP: Frauds deceive. An event which creates
faith does not deceive; therefore it is not a fraud, but a miracle.

Elsewhere the archbishop says: "Miracles are not frauds because they are often—I do not say always—very simple and innocent contrivances by which the priest fortifies the faith of his
flock. When this girl picks out the Dauphin from among his
courtiers, it will not be a miracle for me, because I shall know
how it has been done, and my faith will not be increased. But
as for the others, if they feel the thrill of the supernatural, and
forget their sinful clay in a sudden sense of the glory of God,
it will be a miracle and a blessed one. And you will find that
the girl herself will be more affected than anyone else. She will
forget how she really picked him out. . . ."

[6] Op. cit.

it, very vigorously, working himself into a transport or half frenzy, throwing himself on the ground and perhaps gashing himself. In this state he begins to make an answer to the question, at first tentatively and in a faraway voice, but then more certainly and finally in loud and arrogant tones, although the terms of the answer remain a little obscure, with no names mentioned, and probably phrased in such a way that only the questioner can gather up the meaning. They do not claim to be guided by spirits, and they could be accused of making any answer they chose. It is unlikely, however, that they do such a thing consciously; actually they possess a knowledge of the village and its people, and of the background of any question asked them, so that they have a good basis for judgment, and they juggle all these elements loosely in their heads until, under the stimulation of their abandoned physical activity, they feel struck by an inspiration, an effect which they would not experience without the dancing. These witch doctors also cure by sucking intrusive magical objects out of their patients, if that is the cause of illness, and at their shindigs the doctors who are not busy dancing to a question will stage contests of shooting the same kind of thing—bones or beetles—into one another, or into the spectators, if they are unruly, and then removing them again. This is generally known by the Azande to be nothing but sleight of hand, good as it is, and the doctors will admit it, saying that their success is really due to their medicines; the people are also often skeptical of them to the point of laughing outright at them, because a doctor may fail completely when tested by so simple a question as what is hidden in a pot. Nonetheless Evans-Pritchard feels that these doctors, who do not occupy as responsible a position as the Asiatic shamans, are basically honest; and also that they are usually above the average mentally. In spite of their higher intelligence, and their awareness of their own trickery, they believe in their magic and their powers as much as anyone else, and the people, laugh as they may, always go to them when taken sick.

In Asia and North America some tribes think that shaman spirits run in the family, and that a boy or young man will sooner or later be seized by such a legacy. This is the usual thing on the Northwest Coast of America, so that normally only the descendants of shamans became shamans. However, a man with none of them in the family tree may nevertheless become one by going to the bier of a newly dead shaman, which in the northern region was set out in a hut on a point of land, and there he will sit and bite the dead man's little finger all night long. This will offend the departed soul, who will react by sending a small spirit to torment the offender, and the latter, if he is courageous and has his wits about him, may capture the spirit for his own ends, and so become a shaman.

The most general belief as to recruitment is simply that a spirit appears, to anyone at all, and insists on the person's becoming a shaman, which is tantamount to accepting the spirit as an internal boarder, whether it is wanted or not. Being a shaman is considered dangerous and burdensome, because you are committed to it and have to observe certain tabus, and so people generally try to avoid it. If you play on a drum, or show yourself in any way receptive, you are laying yourself open, and anyone not wishing to become a shaman will be careful to do no such thing. Usually the spirits pick out young men. In Siberia there are as many woman shamans as men, and they are by no means subservient to their male colleagues. In this area also, there is something of an assimilation of male and female shamans; the former, as I said, wear some marks suggestive of femininity, and may braid their hair, and vice versa, female shamans acting somewhat like men. They may go so far as to marry someone of their own sex, a woman getting a wife to keep house for her. This is considered strange, as you might think, and it is not approved of by right-thinking people, but right-thinking people do not like to antagonize shamans and so they keep their mouths shut. Actually, shamans are not thought of as bisexual so much as sexless.

This is one significant thing about the temperamental

nature of individuals who become shamans. Another is the reason often given as to why they do so deliberately. A Siberian will say that he became ill, and that in desperation over being melancholy, or on the verge of dying, he began to solicit a spirit and prepare for a shaman's career, whereupon he got well; he now has a bull by the tail, however, and must continue to shamanize or fall ill again. He has to undergo a long training, under the tutelage of an older shaman, and during this period he is subject to mental suffering and sickness; but once he is a practicing shaman he regains his balance, and no shamans suffer from insanity. Europeans report that they can distinguish a shaman by his expression, which is nervous and bright compared to that of ordinary people. Furthermore, the Buriats allege that a future shaman can be told while he is still a child, by certain signs: he is meditative and likes to be alone, and he has mysterious dreams, and sometimes fits, in which he faints.

It is clear from these clues that shamanism is a calling for a certain psychological type: those who are less stable and more excitable than the average, but who have at the same time intelligence, ability, and what is vulgarly called "drive." They are familiar to us, perhaps most so in what we think of as the artistic temperament; they fail of the balance and solidity and self-confidence, not to say aggressiveness, that are necessary in a business executive, or a politician, but their mental powers and their quickness demand expression, goaded by their dissatisfaction at being somewhat maladjusted socially. We are given to calling them introverted, and think them somewhat difficult. They find the expression they need mainly in the arts. Now of course I do not mean that every artist must have bats in his belfry, but only that there is some relation between one variety of human temperament and the insistence of artistic expression. There are plenty of placid and well-adjusted artists; nevertheless, we often say that artists are temperamental people, actually meaning that it is temperamental people who become artists. So it is with shamans, who have in their profession a socially useful exhibitionist release, and a device by which they can discipline their own nervous tendencies by orienting them according to a defined pattern. We have a somewhat stereotyped parallel in people who soothe their nerves by playing the piano; and Conan Doyle made Sherlock Holmes (who was such a bad case that he was addicted to the needle) play the violin.

Some of the native diviners of South Africa, of either sex, are much the same as shamans, being recognized as people of a special type.[7] They enter into this life because of an illness, or hallucinations, or spirit possession; and since the novitiate involves months of solitude, training, and medical treatment by an older diviner, few go into it voluntarily, and most will try to resist it as long as possible. When they come out of this phase they are believed to have second sight and spirit connections, and have developed a peculiar faraway look. As elsewhere, the profession automatically picks out people of a high-strung temperament and appears to give them social satisfaction and psychiatric help.

Shamanism is the more adapted to Siberian and North American native cultures because hysterical tendencies seem to be common among the peoples of the Arctic, giving rise to the term "Arctic hysteria."[8] Hysterical seizures, cramps, and trances are the simpler expressions of it. Eskimos will suddenly run wild, tearing off their clothes and rushing out, plunging into a snowbank and sometimes freezing before they can be caught. In Siberia, victims fall into a state, generally on being startled, in which they lose command of themselves and cannot help repeating the words and actions of others. Jokers used to tease known sufferers by tricking them in this way into throwing their belongings into the water, and a Russian colonel was once faced with

[7] Winifred Hoernlé, in *The Bantu-speaking Peoples of South Africa* (1937), edited by I. Schapera.

[8] For this and the following, see Czaplicka, op. cit., and W. Jochelson, "The Yukaghir and the Yukaghirized Tungus," *Memoirs of the American Museum of Natural History*, Vol. 13 (1926).

a troop of natives who had gone hysterical in a body, and were helplessly roaring his orders back at him, and his curses too. A native boy, who knew two older men were both subject to this failing, managed to get them each repeating the other, which they kept up until they both collapsed. I do not know what the basis for this is—i.e., whether it is culturally suggested, like running amok among the Malays—but it is not as merry for the people concerned as it sounds, and is a disturber of the normal social welfare of a group. The contribution of shamanism is not only that it exhausts the special tensions of the shaman himself, and makes him a figure of consequence rather than a slightly psychopathic social liability, but also that it drains off the potential hysteria of the whole community, through the excitement and the drama of the shaman's performances.

Shamans seem to flourish, as might be expected, mainly among people whose religion is not highly organized and whose social structure is also simple and loosely knit. Something that can be called shamanizing often exists in other cultures and cults, but when it does, it is apt to be subservient to some higher political or religious authority. A true shaman is a lone wolf, following his own dictates, and so a well-developed cult, with important gods in it, cannot tolerate any such freebooting approach to the supernatural, and is bound to restrict this kind of activity, and to deprecate the importance of shamans, mediums, and their like. Two generally similar examples will show this. I have already described the kaula of the Polynesians, the prophet who was temporarily occupied by a god, and who then spoke with the voice of the god, often going into violent frenzies while possessed. These prophets also held séances of an entirely shamanistic kind, conducted in a dark house, with ventriloquism, sleight of hand, and all the other appurtenances of shamans as I have described them. Handy[9] refers to a well-known story about a Maori priest whom a missionary was assiduously trying to convert: he stopped

[9] Op. cit.

the missionary in his tracks by holding up a sprig of dry brown leaves and causing it to turn green before the good man's eyes. The report does not say whether the missionary saw the light and became a Maori. At any rate, the public business of the Polynesian prophets was limited to divining —the primary overt, if not actual, office of all shamans—and in their public appearances at Tahitian feasts they were kept under the thumb of the priests proper, who received the word of the gods in the indistinct mutterings and shouts of the kaula, and then interpreted it themselves and divulged it to the people.

A good parallel to this exists in female functionaries, called woyei (singular woyo) by the Gä of West Africa,[10] and common to many tribes of the same region. It is an area of polytheistic cults, in which worshipers are free to choose their favorite god, with each god having his own temple, manned by a priest. Such a god enters and possesses certain women, who will therefore be officially appointed to his temple; and their duty is to dance and become possessed at any ceremony, and while possessed to speak for the god. They show various typical signs of possession, and dance in a semiabandoned manner. If a practicing woyo becomes possessed while no ceremony is going on, a dance is organized at once in order to maintain the possession and get the message which the god is transmitting. Such a woman generally has her first seizure at a dance, having an apparently genuine fit, and acting bewildered and abstracted, talking incoherently. This is a sign that the god has chosen her, and she must leave home and go into training. Eventually she becomes able to deliver the words of her god with more coherence. Sometimes one has been found to talk in languages of other tribes, which she once knew but can no longer speak in her ordinary conscious state. On completing her training she resumes her normal life, and may be appointed to a temple, serving un-

[10] Field, op. cit.

der the priest at ceremonies, and becoming possessed; or else she may practice free lance, as she sees fit.

I have not seen any comments of the same sort on Polynesian kaulas, but Miss Field states that Gã women who become woyei are, like shamans, individuals of a more nervous and less stable temperament than the average, and that the satisfactions of office, together with the license to throw a periodic fit of prophylactic hysterics, actually result in their living more serene, well-balanced, and happier everyday lives than perfectly "normal" women.

If you follow native philosophy, shamanism can be made to look something like witchcraft, as I said earlier. And it also resembles witchcraft, as we have seen, in the psychological benefits it bestows. Both of them relieve certain kinds of tensions in individuals, such as can be harmful to the social climate, and both of them do it dramatically, which means artistically, which in turn means in a manner calculated to give emotional satisfaction. Shamanism should be the more successful, because witchcraft is more of a fantasy and brings its own difficulties, while shamanism is a real emotional exercise, with practically no drawbacks. It allows some of the people to let off steam by indulging in uninhibited antics, while it allows the others to enjoy these antics and at the same time to make use of some of the shaman's real gifts.

9

ANOTHER WORLD

I have been describing a series of religious odds and ends all relating to unnatural science or unnatural people. Fantastic as they may be to us, the happy civilized, they are not only real but very immediate to those who believe in them. They are, in fact, the closest parts of the supernatural, through which people can best manage the ordinary things of the present world. In a general way, tabu, divination, magic, witch beliefs, and shamanism are all a kind of lore by which affairs can be made to turn out right in the end, or kept from going wrong in the first place; people with this knowledge can calculate their behavior sensibly to accord with it, and the whole seems only just over the boundary of the invisible.

There is another world, however, where there live other beings, different from men, and where men themselves may go, but only as souls. Of the religious phenomena up to this point, only the shaman takes any pronounced interest in spirits, and he does not defer to them. This other world is never seen, but it stands large in the beliefs and attitudes of men, overshadowing the attention they give to the ideas with which I have already dealt. It is the real core of the majority of tribal religions, because around it is formed the public cult which explains the universe and the tribe, and the relation between them. Up to now what I have been describing were attempts to get across to the supernatural on a mechanical basis, and not a personal one (again with reservations as to shamans). No attitude has been seen to which the word "pious" might apply. But in what follows there is a different disposition, in which people think in co-operation and actually try to project their own world in toto into another one, in which it is recreated, perfected, and fulfilled. By means of the realm of spirits and gods, men have a chance to adjust their whole lives as units, and not merely certain gobbets of behavior, to this more complete model; and this applies to the lives both of individuals and of the group. Usually, but not always, the prevailing atti-tude is submissive and conciliatory, differing from what one would adopt toward anything so impersonal as magic or mana.

There is thus a certain broad distinction between the cults of supernatural beings, to which I shall now proceed, and the less organized practices of the last few chapters. As an emotional influence, gods are more positive and less negative: they serve less as first aid for anger, individual neuroses, or the dread of illness, and more as stimulants of ordinary confidence and a sense of adjustment to nature and the community. And as a focus of interest they are more collective and less personal, more public and less private, and so they are better able to reflect the concerns of the whole group, and to act as a dramatic medium in which the group can formulate its own particular philosophy of living.

At any rate it is this side of religion which has bur-geoned and become the prop of advanced cultures and complex societies. You will notice that tabu, magic, and witchcraft can all be classed together under what we now call superstitions, and all of them tend to decline among advancing civilizations, because they turn out to be blind alleys. In *The Golden Bough*, in fact, one of Frazer's prin-cipal assumptions was that the worship of gods—true reli-gion, as he defined it—grew out of the failure of magic; that there had been a stage in human development when magic prevailed as the proper approach to the supernatu-ral, and that a "tardy recognition of the inherent falsehood

A Zande of the Belgian Congo feeding benge to a chicken.

She loves me—she loves me not.

A Zande consulting his rubbing board.

A Cheyenne Indian with thongs in his back, in preparation for the Sun Dance.

Shaman's coat, Gold tribe, Siberia.

A Yakut shaman in his robes of office.

A Koryak woman shaman performing.

6

Arunta tribesmen making up
for corroboree, or rain dance.
*American Museum
of Natural History*

Onandaga (Iroquois) False Face Society dancers exorcising disease spirits. From models in American Museum of Natural History exhibition "Masks and Men."

American Museum of Natural History

and barrenness of magic set the more thoughtful part of mankind to cast about for a truer theory of nature." People realized slowly that magic to control death or the seasons was a waste of time, and that there must somewhere be beings of vast power in charge of the universe, who were conscious and personal, and that it behooved man to throw himself upon their mercy.

This is far too simplified and detached a reconstruction, its main fault being the implication that man shaped his religion consciously. Nevertheless there is a germ of truth in it. Magic and its fellow ideas have their functions in primitive cultures, and their appeal to unsophisticated minds in any nation. But there is no future in them. To peoples who have reached a higher social and political organization they have nothing to offer except a drag, and a surcease from thinking for the stupid. This is not so of the conception of a godly society superior to this one, a conception which can be expanded like a Gladstone bag so as always to be able to act as a pattern to the imperfect community here below.

10

SOULS, GHOSTS, AND DEATH

What is a soul? It is not known to science. No surgeon, using his scalpel on an appendix, has ever made a soul bleed or caused it to expostulate. Neurologists, physiologists, and biologists have always arrived at other names and explanations for the myriad oddities of life. Physicists, whose objects of study run from the vast to the infinitesimal, have revealed the presence of nuclear energy by measuring the one per cent difference between the weight of an atom's whole nucleus and that of its separate component parts. But physicists have not yet detected any aberration which could be laid to the influence of an indwelling spirit. Never mind; it is none the less a religious reality, and people understand and believe in a soul who never heard of atoms, and who could not understand them if they did, and who would not be interested if they could.

Is the soul a creature of poetical allusion? We talk about it enough, making it stand for our better selves, or our inner selves, or our artistic selves, and so on. I find that in the newest Bartlett's *Familiar Quotations* "Soul" is referred to two thirds as often as "God" and one third as often as "Man," but nearly twice as commonly as "Mind." (It is not quite up to "Heart" and "Love," but it easily beats those old throat-catchers, "Home" and "Mother.") Such preoccupation must be deserved. Actually, of course, neither poetry nor science could make the belief in souls so compelling.

There are better reasons, both for ourselves and for primitive people.

The latter have essentially the same conception that we have, and there is, I think, no tribe where the conception cannot be found. Christian theology has refined our own ideas, especially through the moral notion of the effects on the soul of sin and its final consequences, but otherwise our idle imaginings portray a soul in a simple way, as the supernatural part of man, that part whose chosen uniform is the robe of an early Christian and whose greatest joy is music, especially harp music. A soul has the personality of its owner, but it can be separated from the body, and it is indestructible, so that it survives when the body dies, and lives forever. We are by no means orthodox in our beliefs; properly, we suppose that souls, on their separation from earthly service, head at once for heaven or, as the case may be, hell, or purgatory, but we also hug our half belief in ghosts, which linger on the earth, and with which we adore to frighten ourselves. The incongruity between ghosts, some of them in doublet and hose and centuries old, and souls which bustle off immediately for the better world does not seem to disturb us at all.

Untutored tribes have many good intellectual reasons as to why living people have souls which can leave the body and which possess supernatural powers. First of all is sleep, and dreams. A man, who without a second's interruption all day long has seen and heard everything around him, and has had something going through his mind continuously, lies down at night; in a short while he is different; he is only an inert breathing body which does not see or hear, and cannot stand up; he lies peacefully where he is, uninterested in things about him and doing nothing beyond twisting on his couch occasionally. Something has changed: his soul has left him, as it may, and is off on business of its own. He knows this himself, because his soul—which sees and hears—has adventures which he can recall when he wakes up. It does extraordinary things, like flying or gliding, or traveling immense distances to scenes far from the body;

and it also meets other souls, some of distant friends, some
of strangers, and some even of people who have died. And
all the time his body has not moved; he can get witnesses
to this. Some tribes even think it is bad to be wakened too
suddenly, in case the soul cannot get back at once, which
would leave the body all discombobulated. A native of
Fiji, who feels that he has wakened abruptly, might shout
to guide his soul back. We, when trying to shake off the
fingers of slumber, may ask, "Where am I?" but not he—he
cries, "Here I am!"

This is a matter of every night, but souls may act irregularly. One lacking in a strong sense of duty may suddenly
desert its owner by day, and leave him in a faint. Or hallucinations may be explained in a similar way; a man's soul
has made a quick round trip somewhere, gathering impres-
sions which were not seen by other people around the man's
body, which has stayed at home. More striking still are
those cases of split personality which I mentioned before,
where the patient is now himself and now someone else.
To some primitive thinkers, this is a case where his own
soul has been ousted and replaced by the other man's, who
possesses the body while he wants it and then retires.

Here we have grist for pseudo science and absorbing de-
bate among the unsophisticated, though we, with our superior knowledge of these little oddities of life, can easily
detect the fallacies. But there is always one thing which
nobody knows about, and which turns everyone to reverence and dread: death. And so death gives us heavy reasons
for the belief in souls, which are psychological and not intellectual alone. If sleep is thought by savages to be the
temporary withdrawal of the soul, death is thought to be its
permanent withdrawal, by savage and civilized alike.

Human beings live a long time, and each one has a personality, a constant combination of the qualities of character and mind, which impresses itself upon the sympathies
of all who know the man, and profoundly upon those who
know him best or are his relatives. This essential nature is
remarkable for its constancy, so that his intimates may be

adapting themselves to its familiar form—loving or hating it—for over half a century. It is also remarkable, and particularly human, in its vividness, flashing in his face and words, enlivening his body and his mind and stimulating those around him. And when he dies, especially in his vigor, the effect on his circle is far more than mere sorrow at his dying; it is a real psychological amputation. The personalities of a family, or a whole group, have all been fitted together like carpentry, and when one suddenly vanishes, it is as though a side of the house had fallen out. Something is missing, and with it has gone a sense of security. Gradually the gap is closed, but in the meantime, while the feelings of bereavement last, the bereaved are strongly preoccupied with the one who has disappeared, so much so that they are apt to imagine they feel his disembodied presence, and even, by suggestion, half see it. But still more universal, I should say, is the astonishment we feel at the disappearance itself. The body, no matter how beautifully it might be mummified, is no real comfort; what we have lost is the person himself. It is practically beyond belief that anything so alive as his personality, so highly organized, so valuable to us, perhaps so learned or so gifted, has in a moment disintegrated. Somehow it must still exist, as it was. We abhor to think otherwise.

We all agree about that, because we have other personal reasons. We have our occasional big shocks, when a friend or a relative dies, and we wish with our whole wills that he may yet live somewhere, if not here. But it is for ourselves as well that we detest death, or rather this catastrophe of disintegration, and we never escape the fear of it. We cannot; we know we must die in the end, and that is everyone's personal hell on earth. This little rankling fright is a bigger goad than the death of relatives and it is purely psychological; somebody else's death may suggest the existence of souls, and almost make us see one, but the prospect of our own ends would force us to invent souls anyhow. Much as we would like to live here forever, we can be willing to relinquish the body if our real inner selves can remain imperishable. The idea of an immortal soul fulfills our wishes, and there is no society, anywhere, that dares to disbelieve it.

Primitive people are usually not so shamefaced as we are about trying to picture to themselves what a soul looks like, and they have, in one place or another, probably exhausted the logical possibilities of what or where it is. It is often thought, naturally enough, to be a replica of the living person, a shade which cannot be seen or touched except possibly by a shaman. This would mostly be the same size as the body, but some say otherwise; many of the American Indians think it is a manikin and Malays believe it to be no bigger than your thumb. Have you ever thought where it may live? Savages have.[1] Many tribes say it is in the blood, which is reasonable, since, if you lose enough blood, what happens to you? Some natives of the Congo would rather have a ferocious beating than the least scratch in their skins, because they fear to lose a single drop of soul. Others think it is in the heart, for similar reasons, and also because the heart pounds when you are excited, and stops when you die. Still others conceive it to live in one or the other of the internal organs, commonly one for which they have figured out no better use. The liver is a favorite choice. The head is not selected as often as you might think, considering that it is the seat of the senses, although the eye is more popular; Tylor quotes the Macusi Indian description of a soul as "the man in our eyes."

Of course, not every people has imagined some definite form for a soul, or some definite anatomical enthronement of it; it may permeate the system like a drink of whisky. In this case especially, or when the soul is believed to be an

[1] For a large number of ethnographic citations as to the nature and residence of souls, see J. G. Frazer, op. cit.; C. H. Toy, *Introduction to the History of Religions* (1913); and E. B. Tylor, op. cit. Tylor must be credited with having discussed the question in so thorough a fashion that one can only follow to a great extent in his footsteps.

invisible replica, it is frequently thought to manifest itself
in various ways. Some hold it is in your shadow as well as
yourself, and you should therefore be careful where your
shadow falls; South African Bavenda may have it seized
by a crocodile, should it lie on the water. It may be in your
reflection in a mirror, and Frazer cites the European custom of turning mirrors to the wall when one is sick and
one's soul should not be exposed unnecessarily. Zombies,
you may recall, have neither shadow nor reflection, because
they are only walking corpses. The custom has existed of
burying the dead at night, when there is no shadow and the
ghost is therefore not about; the ghost will lose track of his
body and will glide off to other haunts. Many people think
the soul is in the breath, because like the heart it stops at
the end of life. You may have noticed that we ourselves
have the same word root in "spirit" and "respiration," and
the eldest son of a dying ancient Roman took this seriously,
making an effort to breathe in his father's last outgoing
breath, and so catch his soul. Similarly, we go in for such
expressions as "the breath left him," thus identifying breath
with the vital spark. Many other languages make breath
and soul synonymous. Polynesians used to try to save an
expiring man by stopping up his nose and mouth, to keep
his soul from escaping. This is of doubtful use, but it shows
that their minds were running like ours when we shout
"Gesundheit!" to a sneezer; in origin, we do it from fear
that his soul might get blown out by the internal pressure
of the sneeze, and not because we think he has a cold. It is
not even safe to yawn, say some, and I would not be too
sure that, in the beginning, we did not delicately hold our
hands before our gaping mouths more to keep our souls
from taking French leave than to hide the tableau of golden
grinders.

Still another class of things in which the soul may be
present are portraits or photographs, which are akin to re-
flections. This reminds us that black magic works through
such things, and on images or parts of the body like hair,

and in fact it is often based on the idea that a person is being attacked through a captured particle of soul.

It is by no means everywhere thought that a man has one soul alone, and actually beliefs in multiple souls are common, the numbers being two, three, or four, usually, though thirty or forty are envisaged by some tribes. The reasons are good, being based on conceptions of souls for different parts of the body, or for different aspects or functions of a person. In general, there is apt to be a distinction between a ghost and a soul, so that in some tribes you may have both, or else between a soul representing your consciousness and one representing the vital principle which keeps you alive. A typical, and excellent, example of such beliefs is that of our oft-cited Gã people of West Africa,[2] who hold that a man is composed of three elements: his body, his susuma, and his kla.

His susuma is his conscious personality and everything that enters into it; it is what leaves his body in dreams, and it is the susuma which may be late getting back to work when the body wakes up. It is also a wonderful alibi. Its owner is controlled by it, rather than the other way around, and they say it may know more than he does. In other words, the Gã realize vaguely there is such a thing as the subconscious, and they ascribe it to the susuma together with the conscious mind. Furthermore, they say that the susuma of one man may seize that of another, an elliptical way of recognizing the greater personal force of certain people. The kla, on the other hand, is simply the principle of life. It has no individuality like the susuma; it is as uniform as water and is present, and must be present, in everything living, even an egg. Your susuma can go roaming while you sleep—that is why you dream—but if your kla leaves you, you are done for. The two are not related to each other. Somebody very ill may say that his susuma and his kla had a fight in the night and that his susuma won, luckily. Witchcraft (see p. 109) is carried on through these

2 Field, op. cit.

souls: the susumas of the witches gather (while the bodies of the witches are of course at home in bed), and eat the klas of their victims, nibbling away as though at ginger-bread men, to the detriment or death of those the klas belong to; this nourishes the klas of the witches themselves, and therefore people who live to be very old are suspected of doing so by witchcraft. When a man dies, his kla simply returns (in the form of a shooting star) to join the heavenly supply of kla from which every newborn living thing is outfitted.

Belief in the possession of two souls like the susuma and kla is common throughout Negro Africa, and this belief may add a third component which is practically the same as a soul: one's name. This is a vital part, and your true name is apt to be kept secret, so that you may not be injured through it. (This association of ideas crops up all over the world, e.g., in Oceania, and it may be considered insult and injury to speak a person's true name aloud, if you know it.) The Gã add still another personification to a man's consciousness and his life: his luck. They call this gbeshi; it is not quite the same as a soul, since it is not essential, but is more like tonsils. It should walk behind a person, but it may turn unruly and get in front, and lead him into trouble. It is generally possible to tell when somebody is being led astray by his gbeshi, which is flouting his good intentions, and allowances are made for him; if the gbeshi gets completely out of hand, it may be forcibly shut up in a bottle and tied to a stake in the town dump.

Given practical ideas of all the kinds that I have been describing, primitive cultures advocate everyday, logical precautions to keep one from coming to harm through his soul. Some I have mentioned: proper secrecy about a person's name, or being careful about yawning. A lot of curing depends on catching souls which have been lost. There are many other notions. The soul of a newborn infant is silly, because it is so young and so new to this world, and may not like it; so it may be necessary to keep the windows and doors shut until it is used to things. But such notions and measures are as nothing to the attitudes and practices connected with death.

Universally, religions promise their adherents life after death. This does not signify that the soul never perishes; it may be destroyed in mishaps on its journey to the other world, it may die out if its living descendants become extinct and do not feed it, or it may finally fade away as a matter of course. But it is always believed to survive the death of its earthly mansion for a time (i.e., while the living are still deeply concerned with it), and death is usually looked on as a mere transition, with the deceased still living in another state to which he must become acclimated. The myths of many tribes, in fact, pretend that death is unnatural and accidental, being caused by a blunder on the part of the creating deity, or the first man, so that human beings can no longer cross the Great Divide in both directions.

Taking the beliefs about it by and large, the soul generally has a future. It may be born again, perhaps instantly, like the soul of the Dalai Lama of Tibet, or perhaps in a descendant born some time later, as in East and West Africa. In some groups here, and in New Zealand, an infant may indicate its identity by sneezing while a list of its ancestors is being recited to it, and parents who favor a given name may pop some pepper up the child's nose at the right point, to give that ancestor a better than even chance. It is also a common enough belief that men's souls appear again in animals, either for no reason or because of their behavior in this life.

The usual destiny of souls, however, is the other world, which of course has been conceived of in hundreds of different ways. It is sometimes in the sky, and sometimes in the earth, and sometimes on the earth itself, perhaps in an inaccessible place like a mountain where nobody has ever been and consequently never goes. It is apt to be in a westerly direction, because that is where the sun travels at night. As a usual thing the soul has a hazardous journey to make, full of terrors which may keep it from its goal or perhaps do away with it entirely; the pattern is very common, with icy mountains, fiery roads, and monsters; it may be that the dead man needs to take certain things along, or can be helped by them, like the little red-haired dog of the Aztecs, which was killed and buried with his master, so that it could carry him across a Stygian stream.

A fairly typical primitive odyssey is that of the life soul of a Menomini Indian[3] (his other, the intellect soul, lives in his head, and this becomes a local ghost, which whistles at people after dark). This soul has to travel four days, westward to the home of the creator over the Milky Way. It must not eat or drink on the trip, though it will pass a huge strawberry and a beautiful fountain. Just before the village of the dead there runs a swift river, with only a slippery log for a bridge, and a great dog guarding the log. The dog decides who has lived a good enough life to enter the spirit world, and he washes out at once those who have been mean to dogs. (Fijian souls have to get by a giant who hates bachelors, and every man therefore takes along a lock of his wife's hair as passport.) On passing the dog, the ex-Menomini still has to cross the log, and he may fall into the water and be carried off for good, but once over he is joyfully greeted by all the old people of the tribe, who are radiantly clad, with their faces painted vermilion, and the happy company nevermore does anything but eat and play lacrosse.

How the soul fares may be related to some extent to the way in which the body is disposed of; in any case these practical obsequies are usually a matter of care and importance, and are almost infinitely various in type. The corpse may be meticulously prepared and dressed: Bangala of the Congo have professional corpse painters, something like sidewalk artists, who attire the departed beautifully and paint him every color of the rainbow, and who get their

[3] Alanson Skinner, "Social Life and Ceremonial Bundles of the Menomini Indians," *Anthropological Papers of the American Museum of Natural History*, Vol. 13 (1913).

fees by charging admission to art lovers who want to see the work. The position in which the body is buried may be important. Perhaps it should face the future world, so that the soul may get a proper start: Todas of India are burned, on a funeral pyre, face down because the place of souls is below ground.

It is hard to generalize from other burial customs, except to say that they serve the purpose of getting rid of the body; people simply do what they think best. Probably most tribes bury, and usually away from their villages, but not always; ancestors of the Pueblo Indians simply dug a hole in the hard floor of their houses. Berbers of the Rif make every grave one size even if they have to shoehorn its occupant into it, because they conceive that making the grave larger would harm the soul. Some flex the body instead of extending it, saying that this is the position in which it entered the world, and so is the best one for leaving it; some probably do the same thing merely for convenience, as in our Pueblos above. Variations on ordinary interments are burials in caves or in shafts; or else in special monuments like pyramids, or the beehive tombs of the Mediterranean, or the large mounds of the Ohio Valley.

Cremation is today not common outside of southern Asia, but as a custom it swept over Europe during the latter part of the Bronze Age, for a reason not known. It is sometimes due to a wish to send the soul off, because when the body has been burned the soul cannot delude itself that it is any longer human. This idea is apparent among such people as Congo tribes which smoke the body without burning it: the soul is in the blood, they think, and when the blood is gone, then and then only has the soul finally left the body.

Here and there people use the simple measure of exposure. The Eskimos do this mainly from necessity, being quite unable to dig in frozen ground. The East African Masai think it is proper and essential for the deceased to have the same fate as dead animals, and simply leave the body in a small enclosure for the attention of carnivores. The Parsees have philosophical notions on the subject; they do not wish to pollute the earth with the corruption of corpses, and so they leave the dead out for the vultures in their Towers of Silence. Bodies were put in a box or rolled up in a mat, and tied high in a tree, both in North America and in central Africa, and in the former place some of the dead (especially shamans) were also exposed on a platform.

At the other extreme of concern for the corporeal remnant are the customs of secondary burial and of mummification. The former is a final interment, or enshrinement, of the bones after the flesh has left them, with the first burial being only preliminary and temporary. It was very widespread, occurring in many parts of America, in Polynesia, Asia, and Stone and Bronze Age Europe. The collected bones are found wrapped in a skin, buried in a pot, or otherwise concentrated, and may have red ochre on them; this last is well known in Indian remains along the coast of Maine, and Wisconsin abounds in bundle burials. Some recent tribes bury the dead and later dig the clean bones up, while others encourage the dissolution of the flesh in other ways; in Tibet they simply strip it off. It is not necessary to suppose that all of this is due to a single idea or source. Some Polynesians thought that the soul could not settle down in the other world while any flesh remained, but other cultures may feel that attention to the bones is the best they can do in the way of respectful preservation or final deposit of the body.

Mummifying the dead may be in part simply a more successful attempt along the same line, and is not necessarily done to save the body for a day of resurrection; it does not appear to spring everywhere from one idea alone. A few peoples have been successful at it, like the Egyptians or the Canary Islanders,[4] but some of the other practitioners cannot quite manage it. In Polynesia the natives often

[4] Here we cannot include chance mummification, like that of Peruvian Indian burials, or the Basket Makers of our Southwest, or some Eskimos, all of which are due to favorable climate; or fortuitous cases where a cellarful of cadavers has accidentally got tanned, as in the crypt of St. Michan's in Dublin, or the Tour St.-Michel in Bordeaux.

tried to oil the corpse, or salt it, but could keep it in condition only for a time; and in Melanesia, in the New Hebrides, they made a combined attempt, by saving and stuffing the skin and surmounting it with the skull, though burying the whole after a while. (The Maoris of New Zealand successfully smoked the beautifully tattooed heads of slain enemies, the best collection of which is probably in the American Museum of Natural History.) The reason for this complex in the Pacific—halfhearted mummification and secondary burial—is obscure.

But let us not be too entranced with such "reasons." They are in any case only rationalizations, whether supplied by primitive undertakers or by Ph.D.s. Burial is simply a part of funeral rites, which have deeper-lying compulsions.

So much, then, for the man who has died, and for his assurance of more life. Now, what about the people he has left behind, whose serenity is bleeding out of their severed ties with him as blood comes from a severed vein? What faces them, before they can once more take up their usual affairs? They feel compelled to go through some ostentatious affirmative behavior, allegedly because the ghost-soul expects or needs it, but actually of course for its effect upon themselves, giving them comfort and safety. These acts are connected with the funeral, which is the proper ceremonial farewell, and with the rites of mourning, which follow along during what can be called the convalescence—the period when they and the ghost are accustoming themselves to the separation.

People think, of course, that a soul remains conscious, and aware of what they are doing, and that it feels strongly about human affairs and has new powers, like any supernatural being or force. Further, many cults see no guarantee that the soul's attitude is exactly the same as before it died; it is something new and may be positively dangerous. Projecting their own feelings onto the soul, such societies imagine that the freshly dead cannot reconcile itself to its new condition, and that it goes through a sort of purgatorial stage, or at least a period before it is content to leave the world and relax its interest therein. When it does, then it becomes a perfectly benevolent spirit, perhaps highly so, if it is ever thought of again.

All this simply reflects the turmoil in the living and leads to a strangely two-sided attitude toward souls. People brought up in the Christian tradition can meet all such tribulations by faith in God and heaven, and so are not troubled by having their supernatural concerns scattered about piecemeal; they feel only heightened affection for the memory of the dead. But primitive folk who must deal with souls directly are apt to regard them suspiciously and fearfully, as something not to be trusted. Love or good will for a soul is present, of course, and is exhibited in real grief, and in such simple actions as leaving out food for it or, as the Eskimos do, trying to keep it from coming to harm through foolishness, by not leaving knives lying about on which it might cut itself; and the burying of weapons or pots with the body, or even whole households and riches, as in Egypt and Sumer, shows a concern for the soul's welfare.

But the dominant attitude in most simple cultures is fear, and distaste for any contact, the more so as the poor ghost has little to do except watch the living and wish he were one of them again. Luckily ghosts and souls are not hard to fool, being poor of eyesight and slow to perceive what is going on, and they can be fobbed off with any old kind of a sham. You can show them an empty plate, and they will think there is no food in the house. You can sacrifice a goat and call it a bull, and they will never know the difference. So there are means of protection.

Usually the most difficult ghosts are those who feel cheated, because they died childless or before their time. In Sumatra a medicine man may recognize a disturbance as due to a lingering, discontented shade and will inform the family involved, offering to handle the case (for a fee). He makes a large puppet of the dead man, and on a given day all the latter's former possessions are laid out before his house; the medicine man, encased in the puppet, comes thus magically as the ghost; the puppet looks sadly over his goods, does a doleful farewell dance with a woman of the family, and takes one last long look inside the house, making gestures of renunciation and weeping. Then the medicine man gets out of the effigy, sits it down, and puts out its eyes so that it can see no more, and while everyone sets off firecrackers to confuse it, it is rushed down to the river.[5] Such a ghost is mild; that of a Gã who has died too young is much more malevolent, and jealous of the living: if it meets a man at night who has been to a party enjoying himself, it will be infuriated, and will chase him until his heart gives out. His only chance is to throw the ghost a white cloth, which is like a red cape to a bull; it will worry the cloth while he escapes.

Formal funerals of different tribes vary in plan and detail, but the same feelings as those above are usually present. Exhibitions of grief are a constant feature, but so is a tendency ritually to separate the dead from the living. This may lie in the treatment of the body, as I have said (e.g., by smoking it), but the people may also go to some trouble to foil the soul. Very commonly the house where the man died must be burned or torn down, which is such an inconvenience that people in extremis will be carted off into the bush so that they can die in a small hut made for the purpose, which will be no loss to destroy. The Bushmen of South Africa will stay away from a camp where a man died for two years. Other tribes will go so far as to leave the house of the deceased standing but pull down the rest of the village, leaving it all to his ghost; this looks like a kindness and an honor, but it is also a desire to leave him to himself.

Others keep the house, but fool the ghost by taking the corpse out through a window (Menomini), or a hole in the wall (Navaho, Hottentot), so that the soul on retracing its path will be stumped in trying to find the entrance. At fu-

[5] S. Dillon Ripley, "Laying a Ghost in Sumatra," *Natural History*, Vol. 45 (1940).

nerals of still other tribes they try to keep the ghost from finding its way back from the graveyard at all; it is something like trying to lose a dog. Among the Menomini Indians the nearest relative—the one most likely to attract the attention of the soul—will leave the cemetery before the rest of the party and sneak home through the woods, while the soul is still absorbed in its own funeral. Chinese will set off firecrackers on the way home, to frighten it. Congo ghosts will not cross water, and the returning mourners dig a ditch across the path and put water into it, as a convenient river over which they can jump.

So we have, superficially, a spectacle of the dead being separated from the living. Actually it is more the reverse, being a matter of the living renouncing their attachment for the dead. Psychologically, this is absolutely necessary; the living cannot go on and on sorrowing, and failing to disentangle themselves from the non-living, or the society would become morbid. And yet this cannot be done too cheerfully and quickly. Small societies depend heavily on their individual members and cannot tolerate any irresponsibility of attitudes as to what the individual stands for; as Radcliffe-Brown and Durkheim say, funeral ceremonies act as a reaffirmation of group solidarity. Thus they are not entirely unlike our periodic oaths of allegiance to the flag. Mourning customs are a means of handling the whole transition through which the living are passing; they definitely signalize the gradual release of the living from the psychological tentacles of the dead, but also, because these customs are always unusual behavior, they act to emphasize the acknowledgment by the group and its members that they have lost something significant and are in an unsettled state, trying to re-form their ranks. And these customs do it with propriety, and adjust the degree of mourning for different mourners according to their nearness to the departed, although involving all of the immediate group.

It may seem paradoxical and ambivalent that people appear to be ravaged with grief at the very time they are

taking steps to forget, but as far as the community is concerned it is really all one process of adjustment, like the
physiological reaction to a wound. Let us look at some of
the typical aspects of mourning.

To begin with, a widow (or to a less extent a widower)
is of course greatly exposed to the approach of the dead
spouse, who for a time is naturally supposed to remember
his human appetites and habits.[6] Accordingly mourning by
the widow is deeper than by others, and in many places
the presence of the ghost puts her in a tabu state, making
her dangerous to other people, and a Menomini widower
must handle objects with twigs, to avoid infecting them. In
parts of New Guinea widows wear sacks over their heads,
and in the southeast of that island they must even crawl
along completely hidden by a mat when they go out, so
that the eyes of others will not fall on them; in such cases
what looks like deep mourning may be for the protection
of the public. The dead are commonly thought capable of
having sexual connections with their living spouses, which
is dangerous if not deadly for the latter; this is a particular
reason for some of the careful seclusion or ritual purification of widows. The same interest of the dead can make
it dangerous, if she remarries, for a widow and her new
husband, and this is often dealt with, in Africa, by having
the widow feign intimacy, or actually indulge in it, with
her dead husband's brother, or clan relative, because these
are the persons she should most suitably marry next, and the
ghost, noting her action, will be satisfied and pay no more
attention.

This all illustrates a keen desire to avoid any contact with
the ghost via the surviving spouse, its most natural avenue
of return, but with a respectful appearance of lament at the
same time. More general mourning rites, for the whole
group, are too varied to describe, but they are apt to include two elements. The first, practically universal, is to
wear mourning dress, or to change one's personal appear-

[6] See Edwin Sidney Hartland, *Ritual and Belief* (1914).

ance radically away from that of every day. It may mean taking off ornaments, but it may mean putting them on. It may mean cutting one's hair, or not cutting it, or arranging it a different way, or not arranging it at all, but wearing it at any rate in a manner foreign to the fashion. In dress, the color may be changed, often to white, or the whole shape may be altered; people may leave their clothes off, or wear them inside out or even upside down. Tribes who dress very little anyhow will paint instead, perhaps only a little face paint, but perhaps a complete suit, of black, white, or red. Native Australian widows go about daubed in pipe clay for as much as two years.

Both savages and anthropologists have made suggestions as to the fundamental reason for mourning garb. One is that the ghost will be pleased by this attention, especially if the mourners debase and uglify themselves and look as though they, too, might be better off dead—this will soothe the soul's jealousy. Another is that people may escape the attention of the ghost in this way, because mourning is a disguise, and the ghost will not recognize them. But few tribes say this, and I doubt that either ghosts or people are so simple as all that in general. It may be that several reasons underlie the customs, but it is also likely that primitive people do not altogether understand their motives. Wearing mourning is a rite, by which the bereaved express their grief and their general perturbation, and which serves as a rallying point and a reinforcement of such feelings, which are a group concern.

A second element of mourning seems to suggest the same things more emphatically. This is the common custom of mourners deliberately injuring themselves. They will beat or scratch themselves, or have whipping bouts, or put dirt or filth on themselves, or cut off a finger joint; the last has been found in widely separated parts of the world. All this, it has been claimed, is either to show extreme sorrow or to appease the envy of the dead. But there may be more to it; it may be a drastic manner of concentrating the bereaved people's emotions on their psychological wound, so that they can discharge their feelings of unsettlement and find a community of sentiment through which to recover. In the general ideas of Durkheim and Radcliffe-Brown, a group unconsciously feels a moral obligation to go further in behavior than their natural grief would take them, but for their own sakes, and not for the ghost's. In the face of an extreme situation they take extreme action and find a solidarity therein which they need in their loss of equilibrium; and this common experience gives them a basis for rebuilding the mutual adjustments of the parts of the group.

I must repeat that this of course applies above all to the simplest of peoples, who live in small bands with few established resources, whose life is precarious at all times, and who feel with shattering force the blow of the death of a member, unless he is quite young or very old. Such a people are the native hunters of Australia, some of whose behavior in mourning has been cited by Durkheim as illustrating his contention. Their small camps need the full co-operation of all individuals, and the life of each person is intimately intertwined with that of every other. There you have people to feel the shock of death. They need their solidarity like the crew of a submarine, and they maintain it partly by a careful discipline of the emotions clustering around group behavior, which is something on the order of patriotism. Lloyd Warner[7] describes a custom of the Murngin of North Australia. Here a man must use highly correct behavior toward his sister, never even speaking directly to her, although their relationship is important. And he cannot stand hearing curses or obscenity addressed to her, even by her husband—it acts as an insult to him and calls for a show of resentment. But group unity prevents outright quarreling over a really minor matter between the two men, who must go on working and hunting together all their lives in this tiny group. So the brother gets his spears, and throws them, in real anger, *at his sister,* and at his other sisters as well, however innocent they all are. He

[7] Op. cit.

knows this is absurd: "It is silly, but when I hear those words at my sister I must do something. I throw spears at her." Thus he replies publicly to the insult in these not uncertain terms. I repeat this story to show how such a group may demand certain emotional behavior, but cause it to be expressed obliquely. This may be a true factor in mourning.

Spencer and Gillen were present when a man of the Warramunga of central Australia died,[8] and witnessed an orgy of self-mutilation among the other members of the band. Before the dying man had actually breathed his last, groups of men and women had begun throwing themselves down on top of him, in a scene like a goal-line stand; following this, the women cut into their scalps with their digging sticks until blood poured down their faces, while near male relatives gashed themselves deeply across their thighs with stone knives until they could not stand. When in a few hours the cause of it all actually succumbed, this business was repeated and intensified, with the women pairing off and battering one another over the head with war clubs. Next morning a number of men were lying about with gashed thighs but the women were still lacerating their scalps, and the deceased's widows were searing their own wounds with burning sticks. Now the natives say that this Donnybrook Fair placates the ghost of the dead man, but it is obvious that the angriest ghost in Australia could not harm them as much as they harm themselves, and also that, were this statement the true reason, ghosts would be the most important thing in Australian religion, which they are not. So we are led back to the idea of a psychologically explained benefit to the living rather than an intellectually explained benefit to the dead: the society unconsciously seeks this violence as a way out of despair and to assert its

[8] Baldwin Spencer and F. J. Gillen, *The Northern Tribes of Central Australia* (1904). See also *The Native Tribes of Central Australia* (1899); Sir Baldwin Spencer, *Wanderings in Wild Australia* (1928).

cohesiveness. Of course such ferocity is unusual[9]; and furthermore, the above reason may not be the universal one behind mourning; as an allied element, the bereaved family is gratified to have outsiders mourn, and in some places mourning is a good way to avoid the charge of witchcraft.

So it is that the doctrine of souls, and the hereafter, with the things that grow out of it, is a technique by which men defeat death and parry its blows. It does not rise out of the instinct of self-preservation alone. For feelings of security, all individuals depend also on the society in which they live and must assure themselves of its continuity in spite of death. Death is like a cliff over which society is always being pushed, but society, by turning it into a mere transition for the dying and for those remaining, can make it seem not like the edge of an abyss but like an infinite vista. This is not all the belief in souls can do, as we shall see.

[9] The Australians have a cultural tradition of self-mutilation anyway, subjecting themselves at various stages of growth to having a tooth knocked out, circumcision, having large welted scar stripes made by cutting, and removing finger joints.

11

ANCESTOR WORSHIP

As a witch is more powerful than other people, so is any
supernatural being, by its nature, more powerful than an
ordinary mortal man. Every kind of spirit, large or small,
enjoys at least the suspicious respect of human beings. And
therefore any soul, released from life, at once comes into
special powers and a certain degree of divinity. That should
be clear from the descriptions in the last chapter of how
carefully mourners deal with the soul of one just dead:
this shade may be myopic, or downright stupid, and it may
be well disposed toward the living, but it has powers nonetheless which they have not. Men with a grudge have been
known to kill themselves with the purpose of promoting
themselves to ghosts, and so of being able to take advantage
of their enemies.

It is therefore natural that in one culture or another the
dead have furnished deities of a great many sorts, and indeed the sociologist Herbert Spencer theorized that the idea
of gods in general had arisen from the ghosts of men. Some
human beings have become public gods, especially when
they had been living people of importance, like great warriors or kings. (Examples of the latter are common enough
but they may, like the Caesars and the Incas, be deified for
purposes of propaganda, and so be highly artificial.) But
when people revere their forebears simply because of being
descended from them, they have a true ancestor cult.

The Polynesians had something of the sort: the gods

were the ancestors of men, and most directly of the chiefly line, and so the chiefs and priests worshiped the gods on behalf of the people as a whole. But they were gods of a pretty high order of development and had important special attributes, and the fact that some of them were ancestral to the islanders was a secondary matter. In the kind of ancestor cult I shall describe, the spirits are not extraordinary in their nature; they are simply those of the dead members of the tribe, older and more important, perhaps, than the living; their community is the other half of the mortal one, recreated in another world.

By such a cult, tribes have organized the idea of souls into something far more useful than the simple belief in life after death. The latter is present, intensified; there is the same glad assurance of meeting again that speaks out from the slate tombstones of New England—"Not dead, but gone before." Not only do those who have died live again; they live together, as they did here, and so the whole community is guaranteed survival in death, as are the individuals who make it up. Much more than this, however: ancestor worship puts before the people the importance of their community life; interesting them in their ancestors, it makes them feel that their ancestors are interested in them, and in what they are each doing to maintain the village; it presents them with a means of feeling the dignity of the community and of the individuals within it, of feeling the importance of the responsibility and the good will of each man for the common weal.

The people I have in mind when I say this are the Bakongo, a group of Bantu-speaking tribes just to the south and east of the Congo River near its mouth on the west coast of Africa, in the region of Leopoldville. The religion of these tribes has been superbly described, and from a thoroughly anthropological point of view, by Father J. van Wing, S.J.[1] Ancestor worship is found in China, and in a simpler form in southeast Asia and in the Indies and the Philippines. But it is especially characteristic of Negro

[1] Op. cit.

Africa, from the Slave Coast through the Congo Basin down to the territory of the Zulus.

The daily life and culture native to the Congo forest are much the same in all parts of that area. The people are, to begin with, primitive farmers. But they are not primitive men; that is something I should like to repeat here from the beginning of the book. It is always so easy for us to lose a sense of perspective and put into one "savage" and "primitive" class all the peoples not deriving from the high civilizations of Europe and Asia, who do not have writing or coined money. (As a matter of fact, I allowed this simple distinction to stand largely unqualified in Chapter 1.) But such living "primitive" people are not "early" men; they have no more to do with really ancient man than we have. More important, they are not all at the same level of culture, which is the difficult thing for us to see. It is true that we are civilized, and that the natives of the Congo (or of most of Asia, Oceania, and the Americas) lack our technical and political advantages, but nevertheless the natives I have named live a fairly advanced way of life which has existed for only ten thousand years or less, a very minor period in the whole history of man. They support themselves by raising their own food and animals instead of depending on hunting, and the achievement of this domestication of food is doubtless the most significant single discovery ever made by man. It allowed him to settle down and develop all his other industries and higher institutions. Its early stages can be referred to as the Neolithic phase of human progress, and the living tribes who belong in it stand culturally far ahead of those few other peoples who have remained nomadic hunters into our own day, even though we are given to calling them all "primitive" indiscriminately. The hunters have almost no industrial arts, but only skills, and they have no leeway for cultural advancement; the farmers have many arts (though rudimentary ones), their feet are all potentially on the path to civilization, and their lives have a security which those of hunters lack. By all of this digression I want only to inspire a more sensitive perception of the relations of uncivilized peoples to nature, to each other, and to us.

The Congolese, then, are agriculturalists. For meat they are forced to depend to a considerable extent on game of the forest, since where the rainfall is heavy the tsetse fly prevents their keeping cattle; however, they have goats, pigs, and chickens. Principally they are gardeners, and able ones; their original crops are millet, yams, bananas, and sugar cane, and since the discovery of America they have grown corn and manioc as well. So they seldom go hungry; they are also good cooks and have various delicacies, and for stimulants they smoke tobacco, chew the kola nut, and drink palm wine. Their villages are varyingly substantial, with well-built thatched houses, whose sides may be clay walls or matting, in different regions. After a number of years, however, the villages move, because the soil used for gardens roundabout becomes exhausted; but when this happens the rights to the old village are by no means abandoned, and groves of palm trees which are still vigorous are particularly considered to be private property in good standing.

Their arts may be familiar to you: they are indifferent potters, fairly good weavers, especially at baskets, and are workers in wood and iron of a high order. These things are all made by professionals, and reach the consumer through village markets which are held periodically. By a simpler trade the Negroes even get special forest products and game from the Pygmies, whose life is all hunting, and who therefore exemplify those really primitive hunting cultures I mentioned above. Among themselves the Negroes use "money" to some extent, in the form of cowrie shells and other standard objects, but they pay the Pygmies off in iron arrows and spear points and vegetables. Socially the Congo peoples are grouped into clans, which are dominant in importance over the family in our ordinary sense of it; clans are a common feature of people living a tribal life and constitute a sort of corporation, which owns property, governs much of the social life of its members, and generally acts as a unit in religious affairs. While a large part of native Negro Africa is governed by petty kings, politics are simpler in Kongo territory and authority rests with the hereditary head of the clan, which is the same as the village. The clan is therefore so much the more important. Van Wing says, in a statement which applies to clans generally: "To the clan of his mother he [a Mukongo] feels himself bound in a manner which cannot be expressed in our European concepts; it is a profound feeling of dependence, of solidarity and of reciprocity which we, in our individualism, cannot grasp."[2] (A repetition of Lesson Number 1 in cultural anthropology: that a people can be understood only in the light of its own outlook on life.)

A Mukongo marries a woman of another clan, or village, and brings her to live with his own. The children, however, belong to her clan and not to his, since descent is in the female line. Although their bonds with their father and his clan are strong, they are most closely bound to the members of their true clan, their mother's, and especially to their maternal uncle, their mother's brother; when they are about ten years old they leave their parental house and village and go to live with their uncle, and this is the clan into which they build their lives. Naturally this village has ties in all directions, through its married daughters whose children come back to rejoin it, but it is knit into a single body with great firmness by its common maternal descent, which outweighs all other relationships. And here is the point of religious importance: its members are knit almost as strongly, in their feelings, to the dead ancestors of the clan as they are to one another. It is all one clan, which marches through time like a parade, and the dead are simply those who have passed a point which the living are still approaching.

The ancestors are not the only important religious feature of the Bakongo. They are great dependers on magic, through fetishes, as we have seen (page 58). In common

[2] Ibid., p. 117.

with the rest of central Africa, they have a hearty belief in witches. They have an important secret society into which large numbers are initiated, with long and complicated rites, about once a generation. Without being monotheistic, they believe in a supreme god, Nzambi Mpungu, the maker of everything, who cannot be described; he intervenes in daily life for his own reasons, but he is a moral god and punishes crime, oath-breaking, adultery, and the like. Thus they ascribe absolute wisdom, power, and righteousness to Nzambi, and they hold him in reverence and ask him to witness oaths, but they do not otherwise worship him. (They leave this to the missionaries, who are obviously priests of Nzambi.) Bakongo know other spirits, including a major demon and a powerful spirit in the form of a serpent.

Apart from these, beings are souls of the dead, of different kinds. The Bankita are those who died violently, in war, by murder, or by suicide; they are spirits of great power and are normally white-bodied, but they appear sometimes as bats or hummingbirds, at sight of which people spit on the ground on general principles. The Matebo are the souls of sorcerers and worthless people who are spurned by the community of ancestors; these creatures are small in size and have long red hair; they are very ugly and smell intolerably. They are wholly foul: they come from their huts in the woods at nightfall to steal the goods of the people, and if they can capture a lone man they will take him home and eat him, because they love human flesh, as the finest pork, and call men "pigs." Of the dead Bakongo, only the good can join the true clan ancestral spirits, the Bakulu; only those who have led blameless lives, keeping free of debauchery, troublemaking, and sorcery.

Thus purged of undesirables, the Bakulu, who get a new white body on dying but otherwise remain much like the living, are reunited serenely in a village which is the counterpart of that of the living clan, and is located underground somewhere—it is unknown just where—in the neighborhood, perhaps under the river; at any rate it is a richer and better place than the land of the living. Furthermore, they are the real owners of the country, the animals, and everything good. Nzambi made these things but the ancestors dispose of them, and every benefit the Bakongo desire —children, health, and long life; fortune in hunting, crops, and trade—they ask of the Bakulu. The Bakulu can give, freely or not, as they like, and so the Bakongo interest themselves in these, their ancestors, and leave Nzambi, who metes out only punishments, to his own devices. The Bakulu sometimes bestow on a favorite a particular piece of luck, recognized by a particular name, mbambu, which might best be translated as "jackpot." A hen which is an extraordinary layer is a mbambu, and the eggs must not be eaten, but hatched; similarly a specially fine crop, or a windfall of money from success in trade, must not be dissipated but must be conserved and multiplied, otherwise the good luck will not come again. Here is a fine example of a religious belief rationalizing a moral principle and sharpening the edge of husbandry.

Accordingly the Bakulu are asked for their aid and generosity, especially in the hunting of big game. When a large hoofed or clawed animal is killed in a group hunt, it must be butchered, cooked, and distributed in special ways, out of respect for the ancestors; and if a lone man bags such a prize he should send parts of it to all the members of his clan, including women in other villages, because it was in the forest of the Bakulu of the clan. However, although the ancestors send game and mbambus to the living, the relationship of the two is more than simply begging, or giving and receiving. For, in Kongo eyes, it is really all one affair, the welfare of the clan, and the village above ground and the village below ground are both concerned in it, and have their reciprocal interests in it. Without the help of the Bakulu the clan must perish, and this would leave the Bakulu isolated from the world, to fade away, with no one to tend the graveyard or the land. Thus, while the ancestors demand industry and moral strength in the living as their

contribution to the continued life of the clan, so the living
are within their rights in expecting the ancestors to protect
them in health and to send them children and food. (Look
carefully and you will see that the living assume responsibility for the things which call only for the proper will, and
ask the ancestors for what they can control less surely.)
The more formal relations with the Bakulu take place
through the head of the clan, or its elders, acting as priests,
and it is here that the Bakulu appear as the organized religion, the cult proper, of the Bakongo.

The place where the ancestors are approached is, naturally enough, the cemetery where the older people of the
clan lie buried, which is apt to be apart from the present
village, due to the occasional moving of the latter over the
years. In it there is a shrine to the Bakulu, a small hut
where there is a constant fire watched by a boy, and in
which is kept the basket of the ancestors, containing relics
—hair, nails, and a finger joint—of all former clan heads,
and of all albinos as well, since their whiteness signifies
that they are great ancestors reincarnated. To this shrine
the priest, or village head, comes every fourth day to hold
a small service for the ancestors. He sprinkles palm wine
on the basket and then, kneeling, makes a little mud on
the ground with wine, and touches the mud to his chest.

This is ordinary homage to the ancestors when the village is in equilibrium, but if there is bad feeling or sickness
abroad, he holds a larger ceremony: "pacifying the village." All the clan members come to the cemetery and
anoint themselves with wine mud, as above, after which
the priest delivers himself of a recitation which is like a ser-
mon, reminding the people that anger is wicked and quarreling forbidden and exhorting them to tranquillity and re-
spectability, telling them to expend their ardor on the game
and not on one another; this ends with a series of set questions to which the people respond in unison. The priest
speaks on behalf of the ancestors, sounding almost as
though he were one of them himself, and the whole mono-
logue, which is formal in nature, contains a strong con-

sciousness of the value of social integrity to the life of the people.

In addition to these usual attentions, and offerings made for the good of the hunting, the clan from time to time holds a major series of ceremonies, the Feast of the Dead. This is done when the Bakulu are demanding more fulsome attention from the living, which a diviner will recognize as being the cause of one or several people falling sick. The priest of the clan begins the rites by going to the cemetery with his people, taking palm wine, to announce to the Bakulu that the feast will be held; assuming a tone of outraged reasonableness, he tells them of the sorry state of affairs: how he, as the clan head, is having a hard enough time making ends meet, and now the Bakulu are asking for services—they who should be supporting the clan and making it flourish in health like other clans. This is how his dissertation goes, a well-organized prose poem of considerable sonorousness and beauty[3]:

"You, now, you old ones, who have gone, leaving us in the
    clan,
Listen to the reason which brings us here.
When you were alive you said to me,
'You, you must stay with the clan, and the clan will be
    your help,
Take good care of these riches in human beings.'
But see how now, in our domain,
The earth is not well, the sky is not well.
The diviner tells us: 'Use the fetishes!' and we use them.
And we are told again: 'Still more fetishes!'
We go to the diviner, to find the trouble,
And he tells us: 'Go, honor the old ones.'
That is the reason we have come.
I, the old one who remains with the clan,
With me you have left all the human treasure,

[3] Ibid., p. 65. This is my translation from the French of Father van Wing's translation from the Bantu.

The women and the men;
Some of them women you gave in marriage yourselves,
You yourselves have held in your hands the bride-price!
Now then, in the clan here on earth,
Death was sleeping; see, he is sleeping no more.
The children of the village are leaving,
The women have children and the children die.
Why should there be such a fate?
Clans which were weak when you left us become strong;
Their Bakulu send them fecundity.
But you, you come back into the savannas,
And you take away our young people.
Can it be that you do this of your own wish?
Or are witches making you do it?
We are told that you want funeral honors,
But I tell you this: before you look for honors,
Leave our young people in peace,
Give us back our fecundity and plenty.
Today all our work is in vain.
I have not yet paid the government my taxes.
If I have one franc they tell me: 'Such a woman needs
*   care.'*
If I have half a franc they tell me: 'Such a one's child
*   is dead';*
'The brother of this or that relative is dead'!
How then am I going to pay for your honors?'"

(He offers the Bakulu wine and mushrooms—a love potion
—and beseeches them to have consideration for the birth
rate. He goes on:)

"*You gave us this proverb:*
The drawer of wine shall be fed by his trade,
And the hunter by his hunting.
But I, as soon as I earn a little money,
See! It has disappeared.
I raise some chickens,
The ferret gets them!
If I let a goat out to pasture,

The leopard is waiting in ambush.
And you, you are asking for honors in the cemetery!
How can I cover the cost of them?
If that is what you want, then open your treasure of good.
Then I will come again to your graves,
When the youths go out to the forest,
When everyone who sets a trap catches big game,
And everyone who climbs a palm tree
Comes down with two gourds full of sap.
These offerings you see are the last that there are.
Do not look for any more plates,
Any more palm wine, or any more camwood powder.
Unless perhaps you would like to have me steal some?
But then people would say: 'A certain person is a thief;
Have his ancestors left him nothing, that he must steal?'
Make things fertile, so that all of us, your servants, may
   remain alive and flourish.
And if any one of us has been going about at night,
To our women in other villages, to eat their children by
   sorcery,
If you see such a one, catch him and take him away.
We here want only to be free of every evil desire.
And you also, where you are, be like the hairs of a dog,
Rest all smoothed out together.
Then we will know the meaning of joy.
If the hidden treasures are opened for us,
Then your tomb will be beautiful.
But otherwise do not look any more for honors,
But simply come here where we are
And take us away; it does not matter to us.
When the last of us is dead and gone,
Then we shall see who comes to honor your graves!
And who then will eat the fruits of our palm trees and
   sagos?
It will be strangers, taking over your village.
Now that I have spoken so, I have finished."

On this somber note the elder leads his people back to

the village to await the effects of his harangue; it is the ancestors' move and nothing more is done unless the sickness which they have sent is recalled. Then the actual feast is decided upon, goats, pigs, and chickens are collected, and taken by the clan members and all their outlying relatives to the cemetery; here the clan head draws the attention of the Bakulu to the animals and tells them of the coming feast, in compliance with their wishes, and acknowledges the return of prosperity. After spilling wine on the graves, and leaving kola nuts as well, the people go back to the village, where a small reception is held for the visitors. This the elder addresses, setting a date nine "weeks" (of four days) away for the beginning of the feast proper, and saying that he hopes all members, relatives, and children of the clan will be present and in good temper.

For the real ceremony, visitors arrive during several days, and dances begin with the firstcomers, lasting twelve days; the visitors bring presents and are given food in return. Finally, after an all-night celebration with drumming and volleys of gunfire, everyone repairs in the morning to the cemetery, where generous offerings are made to the Bakulu. Now the elder makes the ancestors a final address, like that of his first visit, but out of the other side of his mouth, and more humble; he reports that everything is well, and thanks them, asking only that things go on like this and wishing the ancestors such contentment as the living clan now enjoys.

Ceremonies like this, of course, make for a renewal of confidence and a release of happiness, as well as for solidarity and good will within and without the clan. But this is only an addition to the whole philosophical attitude which the ancestor cult acts to instill in the Bakongo. Father van Wing's own words cannot be improved on[4]; this attitude, set forth in their addresses, comprises "Feelings of dependence and of humble supplication, familiar and confident avowals, with here and there a few subtle injunctions

4 Van Wing, op. cit., p. 75.

and even climaxes which pose threats, what though conditional ones, of abandoning the whole cult if the ancestors fail to grant the favors asked for. Compare these prayers with the spells used for fetishes, and you will see the difference between the ancestor cult and fetishism.

"Nothing could give a clearer and more objective idea of the 'morale' of the Bakongo, or of its wide and healthy base. In it man is beheld as the continuator, and not only as the inheritor, of the work of the ancestors. Right and duty never appear as separate. A Mukongo is not an odd creature who for a time eats, drinks, and gesticulates in the sunshine and then disappears. He is rather a man who has received the gift of life, who values this gift above every other, and feels the obligation to pass it on to as many others as possible. In this purpose difficulty does not daunt him, because he has the sense of being an individual in the service of the group which includes him, a group living the same life as that of the ancestors. You will sometimes find in him an appalling egotism, but never the egotism of those for whom personal pleasure is the end and the measure of everything. What he asks of the ancestors is simply life, and the honest and natural means of keeping it and of handing it on again."

So the worship of their ancestors makes the Bakongo feel that life is well worth living, that their individual and communal efforts are worth making, and that the world about them is in safe and friendly hands. And it gives the clan head, charged with their welfare, a highly dramatic way of bringing their attention to the qualities of forbearance and mutual help, and of condemning the forces of disunion.

12

TOTEMISM, A PRIMITIVE PHILOSOPHY

Recognizing souls within themselves, men have been wont to see souls also in other aspects of nature—in animals, plants, rocks, stars, and rivers. When Homo looks on Felis in this way, what he is really doing is making the latter like himself, and therefore understandable, for if a cat, or perhaps a rock, has thoughts and feelings, what should these be but the thoughts and feelings he has himself? At any rate simple societies tend strongly to identify man with nature and nature with man, through the device of souls, or something very like it.

Tylor termed this "animism," and it has been a basic and favorite notion in the study of religion for nearly eighty years. There has been some disposition to talk of animism as a belief, or a doctrine, which suggests that men worked out such an idea by a process of thought, and then by further thought developed further ideas from it. Now doubtless there would be an element of thought in it, but it may be safer to think of animism more as an attitude than as a belief—as a willingness to accept things in nature as having human reactions, thinking up an explanation afterward rather than beforehand. If you take this view it seems more natural that animism should be so characteristic of human groups, and it does not call for any extended theorizing about an evolution of religious thought.

Be that as it may, the files of anthropology will yield

innumerable examples of the endowment of things, animal, vegetable, or mineral, with souls or spirits, and the logical consequences of this. Borneans who hook their enemy, the crocodile, drag him out on the bank and truss him up to starve; they will not kill him outright and so have the guilt on their heads, for fear the other crocodiles would be roused to vengeance. There is no worship here, only diplomacy, but nevertheless they humanize the crocodiles. The Eastern Crees hunting the bear take care not to insult him, and apologize humbly for killing him, explaining that they must eat; and they treat his bones with respect, returning his skull to the forest. This is propitiation; apart from the soul of every individual bear, the whole bear species has a major spirit which must be humored if bears are to be taken. The Ainus of Japan raise bears from cubs and then kill them with lamentations, in a definite ritual. Here is something which is almost a cult, or worship. These cases make up only a part of the scale: there are animal gods, and gods with animal attributes, and so on. As a matter of fact animal deities and animal worship are not particularly important in the whole range of primitive cults, nor are such things as sun worship; animals in particular are more important in myth than as cult figures. Nevertheless one could write a fat book on souls in this and that; I will not even write a chapter, however, because it has been done many a time and would result only in a crowded catalogue of the sort of thing I have given in example above.

But allied to all this there is a special and altogether extraordinary phenomenon—totemism—which is of great interest and significance. No wonder it has always bedazzled anthropologists: not only is it most striking in its nature, but it has been claimed to exist somehow in every continent, especially America, Africa, and Australia.

Totemism is an idea, not of worship of animals (or other objects), but of affiliation with them. Basically, it is an association of human groups with animal groups, in both a social and a religious way. It is not sensible, or even possible, to define it much more closely than this,[1] but it has several similar features in different places, and that is what is extraordinary about it. Socially, it goes with clans. The human community is divided into clans, and each of these has non-human relatives of a particular kind—let us say lions, or kangaroos—and goes under the name of this totem. Also, as a general thing, the clans are exogamous—i.e., the members must marry someone of another clan and totem. (A tremendous amount has been made of this connection —note the title of Frazer's book in the last footnote—but clans and exogamy occur independent of totemism.) Furthermore the clans are generally explicit about their relationship, through common ancestry, with the totem, saying that they are descended directly from such animals, or else that a woman or female creature gave birth both to the totem animals and to the first people of the clan, or else that the kangaroos and the people of the kangaroo clan have souls of a similar nature; in parts of Australia, a kangaroo-human soul would enter a woman, causing her to conceive.

More definitely "religious" are the attitudes people hold toward their totems. Typically, they may neither kill nor eat their totem animal (or plant), though they usually do not take it amiss if members of other clans do so. Indeed, in the famous "increase ceremonies" of Australia the clans go forth to encourage the plenteousness of their own totem animals for the benefit of others: the Witchetty Grub men paint themselves with the totem emblem and, with the aid of a large chrysalis made of boughs, re-enact the hatching of the grubs. Later, when the season for collecting the edi-

[1] Sir James Frazer's definitions: "A totem is a class of material objects which a savage regards with superstitious respect, believing that there exists between him and every member of the class an intimate and altogether special relation" (from *Totemism* [1887]); ". . . totemism is an intimate relation which is supposed to exist between a group of kindred people on the one side and a species of natural or artificial objects on the other side, which objects are called the totems of the human group . . ." (from *Totemism and Exogamy* [1910]).

ble grubs comes around, they go out with the other clans and must be the first to eat a little of the bag. This is of course in contravention of the normal prohibition, and is a highly ritual affair, like a mass, and is not an ordinary, profane meal. Otherwise the prohibition on the totem animal, to the totem membership, has the nature of a tabu. So far as eating goes, this conflicts with the supply of food for most people, but not fatally, though it can be a nuisance: in semicivilized Dahomey, guests invited to a dinner party must come in the middle of the afternoon to let the cook know what they cannot eat, so that the menu can be abridged accordingly.

This tabu attitude to totems may express itself in other ways than not eating or marrying. Some tribes will not even look on their totems or speak their names. Others may have secondary tabus, specific but seemingly meaningless (resembling those of the Eskimos—see p. 41). The Nandi of East Africa represent these. Here a Lion man may not eat meat killed by a lion, or wear a lion-skin headdress; he may fight only on the right flank in battle and may strike no person in the head; and he may bleed his oxen for blood pudding only in the morning. His neighbor, a Bush Pig man, may in hunting not kill an animal wounded by a member of a different clan, and may not touch a donkey; he may marry only a girl who has previously conceived a child, a thing expressly forbidden to most clans.

Instead of an extension of tabu there is, in some places, a feeling of brotherliness, good will, or dependence between the men and their totem. Among the tall Dinka of the White Nile a Crocodile man will swim fearlessly among his reptilian relatives (although even a crocodile *can* make an occasional mistake) and a Lion man will sleep in the open when away from his village, while any other man would fear lions and make a barricade of thorn. The Lion man also from time to time leaves meat out for Brer Lion, especially at his wedding feast. Once a Lion man killed a lion, following which another lion destroyed twenty head of the tribe's cattle; the tribe looked into the matter and decided the lion had every reason to be outraged, so they did not hunt the lion but fined the man instead.

So, in many parts of the primitive world, people are found grouped into totemic clans with tabus on the totems. The occurrences of this have been searched out and described with enormous enthusiasm; Sir James Frazer, who was only one of totemism's apostles, turned out five fat volumes full of evidence. In the course of this, totemism has also been stretched to cover some things which do not fit cleanly into the description I have given. For example, in Australia men may have individual totems, as well as clan totems; that is all right and there is small doubt that it should be called totemism, as we shall see, but in North America totemism has also been generally applied to individual totems which are more in the nature of adopted guardian spirits, often acquired in adult life in a dream and grading into the sort of vague patron who sends visions to the Crow Indians. Should that be called totemism? "Totem poles" of the Pacific and Alaskan coasts are also not well named, because they stand for special spirits, or for family crests which share more the character of European heraldry than of the trappings of totemic groupings. These, and particularly guardian spirits, may simply be something which had different beginnings but came to look much like totemism found elsewhere. This is not an important point for us, who are trying only for an appreciation of totemism as religion, but it does bring up one of the great difficulties in interpreting such a thing as totems, and religion in general. It is this: as soon as you have given some social or religious phenomenon a name and a definition you begin to see it everywhere, and in other forms. Everything becomes totemism, and a primitive group would no more fail to show some signs of totemism than I would go out without my fingernails; built of pieces from here and scraps from there, totemism turns into a monster that obsesses its creators.

This is not an exaggeration. It is what happened just before and after the turn of the century. I must say that since that time anthropologists have not been given to treating totemism as an uprooted Frazerian spectacle. I do not mean to condemn this practice harshly; I only mean that, aside from the sin of tearing totemism loose from its tribal setting, such a treatment makes it more definite than it has a right to be, and may mislead you into easy but false beliefs as to how it came into being and what it means.

Certainly this seems to be a factor in some of the theories of totemism's origin. These theories have been many, and a few of them seem childish enough now. Clan totems have been ascribed to a confusion growing up after several generations because of an ancestor's nickname: supposedly a grandfather called Old Goat finally was believed to have *been* a goat and his foolish descendants thought of themselves as half goats for this reason. Transmigration is another suggestion: the clan imagined the souls of their dead becoming animals, establishing totemic relationships so. Or the idea was founded by neighbors, who called a given group after the kind of food they ate. These notions and others like them ignore or contradict the visible facts—of course, they are old hypotheses.

Frazer made three different suggestions, sensibly opining that all three might be applicable in different places. One derived group totemism from the belief in individual "external souls," human souls which might reside in animals, like those of the shamans of Siberia. Some of the older American anthropologists had a similar idea, that group totems came down from individual guardian spirits which were inherited, and so passed on to a widening circle of related descendants. Frazer's two other suggestions were based on increase ceremonies and on conception totemism respectively. Increase ceremonies (Australia) gave a form of totemism growing out of ordinary propitiation of animal spirits; a given clan took up the business of simple magic to increase the supply of a given animal, and denied themselves the eating of that animal in order to fool the animal spirits into thinking their hands were clean. Totemism based on the belief of conception occurring by an animal spirit entering a woman (also Australia) grew from sheer ignorance of the actual biology of conception, combined with notions of prenatal influence (one of our own strongest superstitions).

Some later theories were more complicated, more sophisticated, and involved the hypothesis that totemism was a necessary stage of development in religion and society. Reinach thought totemism and its attendant tabus organized primitive society and provided for the step from hunting to domestication: the tabus conserved the game (while the religious aspects lent the tabus their force) and led gradually to the taming and breeding of the animals, following which the animals became so common that they lost their sacredness, and the cult of totemism collapsed. So Reinach believed that all animal veneration, sacrifices, or food prohibitions are vestiges of totemism, and was able to affirm that even the absence of totemism (in an advanced culture) is proof of its former presence!

Freud has had his say on the subject, managing to keep totemism, tabu, and exogamy in the air all at once, without dropping any of them, by using the Oedipus complex and a whiskery old conception, the "primeval horde," this being the imaginary first social stage of man, or man-apes, having no more refined organization—e.g., marriage, family—other than its existence as a group. This group was dominated by one powerful old man (or pithecanthropus), who kept all the women to himself and brutally pummeled any of his growing sons who attempted to take a practical interest in the females; the young men finally staged a revolt, assassinated the old beast, and *ate* him; then their former submissiveness to the patriarch reasserted itself, they adopted a father substitute in some animal form, and in the anguish of a sense of guilt not only would not harm that animal but renounced the women they had won, and looked elsewhere for their own mates. This may be good Freud but it is wretched anthropology—there is no shred of evidence for this reconstruction, and reason to doubt that the earliest human pattern resembled a primeval horde.

Durkheim, who made totemism the earliest type of religion, explained it in a more subtle and plausible way,
using the natives of Australia. He started with a religious
feeling caused, so to speak, by the mana of society: individuals feel a certain force or power of the clan or group
in which they live, which affects them without their being
able to see it or put their fingers on it; it is all the things
that fellowship, group spirit, and public opinion mean to
us, and is greatly intensified on those occasions when many
groups or clans have come together for social and ceremonial purposes, when men feel enlivened and strengthened
by their contacts.

So, for Durkheim, the force of religion is in society itself, because the society is able to make its members feel
that they are dominated by something outside themselves,
restraining them at some times and exciting them at others.
They cannot understand what it is, however, because it is
too abstract, but they need some kind of symbol on which
they can hang these emotional attitudes, which will crystal-
lize their feelings and reawaken them more readily both
from day to day and at the times of their meetings and rites;
they need an emblem, as we need a flag. It is something
which can communicate these religious feelings to all the
group, bring them forth and sustain them. The emblem
they choose comes from the most obvious objects in nature
around them, their common animals; in fact, as Durkheim
correctly pointed out, the emblem is the important thing,
being based on some natural species but used in the form
of paintings and drawings, so that the actual living totem
animals, though respected by tabus, are secondary.

Durkheim's penetrating ideas are certainly sounder than
most of their forerunners, which generally called for primitive people to be either very thoughtful or very naïve and,
while trying to serve as an explanation of totemism, did
not give a reason for its continued existence—i.e., what
kept it up? Why should a confusion about the nature of
one's ancestors, or a pother about killing a horde leader, be
maintained as a cult? At least Durkheim's moral force of

society can serve both as an explanation and as a reason for religious behavior, and Durkheim also followed the actual facts as they had been reported from Australia.

Totemism remains inadequately explained, especially its wide distribution. In many places, of course, its accent is social, having to do with clan names and practices, and it does not serve as the cult. Nevertheless it is a religious affair, not because the living totem animals are raised up or venerated—they are not—but because the connection between them and men is mystical and spiritual. In Australia it is most certainly a religion, and gives a picture of how fully religion, knowledge, and philosophy can be merged.

Any discussion of totemism finally comes to rest here, in aboriginal Australia, the anthropologist's paradise. The natives are the largest surviving body of really primitive hunting people, and their culture has been lovingly studied by many talented men, notably Spencer and Gillen and, recently, Lloyd Warner and A. P. Elkin,[2] whose under-

---

[2] Warner, op. cit. Elkin, *The Australian Aborigines, How to Understand Them* (1938). Here are two quotations from the latter: "I do not regard the Aborigines as interesting survivals of man's early ancestors, nor their customs as cultural curiosities —noble, barbarous or amusing. I am concerned with their culture as a means of life worked out during the past centuries—a culture which is being strained to breaking point by contact with ourselves. . . . We are apt to make the mistake of thinking that because a people is primitive and poor in material possessions, it has a very elementary form of social order and religious life. Some folk carry the metaphor of child-race too far. A child-race is so called because it has not attained to the stature of our civilization; its grown men and women, however, are adults; they do not think as children but as social personalities who are responsible for the development and maintenance of the social, economic and religious life of their community. Therefore, we should not expect the understanding of that life to be a matter for the kindergarten; it is a subject worthy of our best efforts." Also: "There are many white folk who are said to be great authorities on the Aborigines. I have frequently been told to consult them, but ever and anon I came out by the same door by which I went in. They had some idea of the sub-

standing analyses of their totemism and its meaning are most illuminating.

Now Australia is a paradise only for anthropologists, and not for the blackfellows who long ago brought into the continent an economy which is that of the Old Stone Age. Australia has a moderately varied wild life but it is not rich in vegetable food and is poor in water, and the natives, in their own culture, know no means of extorting from their environment what is not already there; they are dependent absolutely on the natural supply of things. What there is they are amazingly skillful at collecting. They are superb trackers; they can tell whether an opossum is still up in a tree, or has come down, from claw marks in the bark, and can follow other game through brush and desert for long distances. Warner says that, among the Murngin, an eight-year-old girl can identify even a stale footprint of anyone she knows, among a hundred or more. Australians have many ways of taking fish and also of birding—here is a sample, on which the State rests: duck hunters wade downstream to raise a flock of swimming ducks; the ducks fly down past other hunters who shout to speed them up, until they come to men who imitate the cry of a duck hawk and throw pieces of bark over the ducks to simulate the hawk himself; to escape, the distracted ducks bend on all sail, skimming the surface of the water, and crash into a sort of tennis net which has been stretched across the stream against their arrival.

Australians also collect honey, grubs, moths, lizards, and

---

sections or sections, of the mother-in-law taboo and a few obvious customs such as circumcision, but they had no real knowledge of the inner life of the natives. It may seem surprising to be told that a settler, missionary, policeman or settlement manager can spend years and years amongst such an apparently primitive type of people as the Aborigines, and yet know very little of importance about them, but it is a fact, and no one knows it better than the Aborigines themselves. But such is their loyalty to their secrets, that they never drop a hint to the white 'authority' of the great world of thought, ritual and sanction of which he is unaware."

so on, and the women make an important contribution by going out with their dilly bags to dig wild vegetables. But the natives were originally, of course, absolutely innocent of domestication—of any way to increase the natural food by sowing or breeding—and, when all is said and done, their subsistence was like that of other animals in one way: they could not even save or store their food for any length of time, and so have something on which they could depend between hunts. Only, in some parts, a few wild seeds were kept, to be ground into meal if needed. Think how crippling is such a life to all further advance: food is not only limited, but uncertain as well, and the people must move camp every so often before the game and the plants give out, and must live (except for occasional get-togethers) only in small bands so as not to exhaust the food more rapidly than they themselves can move.

The things that such a people can make and carry with them amount to what you would expect: almost nothing. If they house themselves at all, it is typically in rough, impermanent shelters. With minor exceptions, clothes do not exist, but only decorations. A woman has her net bag, and perhaps a wooden bowl, and a man has his boomerang, his spears and his spear thrower, or launching stick. (They lack the bow and arrow.) But with this pathetic stock of goods, and their nomadism, they are nevertheless not mere drifters, in either purpose or abode. The life of these meanest of savages, these fag-enders of man's Pleistocene days, has order, richness, and glamor.

Though they wander, they wander in their own land, to which they are deeply attached. There were once about three to five hundred "tribes" (about a third of a million people or less) in all, this being the probable number of different languages. But tribes are not too distinct; while their members tend to recognize closer kinship than with other people, and have a tribal name and ceremonials, there are cross-tribal contacts, and the true unit of living is a small horde of about thirty-five people. This is made up of a group of related men, having the nature of a clan, and their wives, who are drawn from other hordes. The group is exogamic, and not as a matter of ordinary clan exogamy: a man thinks of his father's brothers as his own "fathers," so that his uncles' children are "brothers" and "sisters," rather than cousins; and he cannot marry his sister. Thus quite distant relatives may be "sisters"—he knows they are distant as well as we do, but he cannot marry them, because they rate the treatment of sisters. On the other hand other relatives are arranged differently, particularly his cross-cousins, e.g., his *mother's* brother's daughter and son. To us these are first cousins, like the "brother" and "sister" above, but to certain Australian tribes this girl cousin is not only a possible wife but the preferred wife, and the kinship name for her means both "wife" and "mother's brother's daughter," and the word for "father-in-law" also means "uncle (mother's brother)." (Some Australian systems follow more generations out, providing for marriage with a second cousin, and reaching a complexity that makes college students gnash their teeth.)

These principles, in much of the continent, result in dividing whole tribes up into two, four, or eight groups, or sections, which specify whom you cannot marry, whom you must marry, and whom your children must marry, and these sections have names of their own. Now both these sections and the kinship names for relatives are bound up with etiquette and behavior aside from marriage; an Australian must not speak to some relatives, may be familiar with others, and must be especially deferential and helpful to still others. So, knowing his kinship to another, he knows his duties toward him, and thus neighbors in other hordes, distant acquaintances, and perfect strangers, can by using the formula all be brought into the right relationship when necessary, and these relationships might theoretically be carried as far as a man could ever travel. There is a tendency to weave all people, and all social relationships, into a single skein. The same feeling imbues their totemism.

Now a man's totem spirit, amounting to his soul, comes

from a totem home in the band's territory, entering the womb of his mother and causing her to feel that she is pregnant. The spot where this happens may tell her what totem it is, or she or her husband may know its nature from a dream. It may not be the same as that of the father (whose true biological contribution to his existence is not recognized—"father," in Australia, simply means "mother's husband"), but this is desirable, and is usually the case anyhow, since the horde is most apt to be in the vicinity of its principal totem home, which is that of the husband. This totem is of deep importance to a man, being the cardinal religious fact of his life. (Women also have spirit totems, but it is of no consequence since women are excluded from ritual.)

But it is not his only totem; he also has a social one which is called his "flesh." This one recognizes that he is flesh and blood with his own mother, since he gets this totem from her and is joined by it to a clan tracing descent in the female line. This totem is more social than religious in nature, but a person will not kill or eat its animal, nor will he marry another member of it, no matter what the kinship relations of the two may be.

Totems do not stop here. Each sex may have its own totem, and each marriage group or section may have its totem; and these will also be respected, and not eaten, by the totemites. Individuals may even have totems special to them, particularly magicians, whose totem animals are their familiar spirits and give them help.

Thus most of a native's recognized affiliations are reflected and expressed in totemism. Nor is this yet all, because the Australians welcome the rest of nature into their system as well, putting other animals, lightning, stars, and clouds into the totemic clans or marriage groups, and according them both respect and brotherliness in this way. So, as Elkin says, totemism is a way by which the Australian "makes nature at home within his own social organization," a way through which he looks at nature as a whole and classifies it in a manner which to him is logical and complete, so that when his rites are directed toward the key totems he is dealing with the true system of the universe.

Thus Australian totemism is many and one. While it is all religious in background, it takes definite form as a religion in the cult of the local totems of the horde and its land. These are the spirit totems responsible for a man's very existence, and the beliefs and rituals concerning them are the doorway to the secret life, the mystical but true one. The women know nothing of it, nor do the boys. When the latter are of an age to be initiated (old enough to take the serious responsibility of cult knowledge), the elders escort them out of the camp, to the accompaniment of weeping and feigned protest by the women, to a special corroboree ground where other tribal members are also gathering. Each boy now goes through a long and harsh series of rites which seem to suggest death and rebirth. During the course of these at least one mutilation is performed on him; most generally he is circumcised or has a tooth or so knocked out and usually, according to local custom, undergoes both, as well as being gashed on the torso to raise a pattern of large welted scars. Little by little, he is now admitted to some of the lore of the cult. After the operation (to "kill" him?) he lives for months in the bush, being taught and disciplined by the older men, and seeing from time to time things and places sacred to the cult. The elders also ceremonially shed their own blood on him, to give him strength, and make him one with them. Finally, after a ceremony of being tossed onto a smoking fire, and a washing, the full-fledged initiate is taken jubilantly back to the camp of the horde. During all this time the young man has suffered pain and been cruelly frightened, but the older men have also helped him, and even shared his pain; what they have done is to kill, not him, but his childish brashness and individualism, substituting a new sense of being a man in the social sense, of being an integral, important part of the group's life, and an inheritor of its cult. He feels, too, that by his ordeal he has won something beautiful and valuable in the secrets he has been taught. And this is what he has learned.

He sees his native land with new eyes. He has learned of the altjira, the dream time, when there were totem-ancestor heroes, who were either men or animals or both. For the first time he is shown the churingas (decorated slabs of wood or stone, kept in a hidden and holy place) which represent and commemorate the heroes. In the dream time the heroes made things the way they are now, or-dering the life of man and leaving reminders of their pas-sage: they gave patterns of behavior, but they also made lakes or springs, and above all in certain places—totem cen-ters—they left spirits, to be born later, some as animals, some as men. The cult members know where these totem centers are, and they know the paths along which the heroes walked, and where, here and there, a deposit of red ochre, or a certain stone, shows that one of them shed his blood, or left part of himself, or died.

This is the haze of sanctity on the country that the newly initiated man now perceives, and the cult member lives in. The land is crossed with the paths and dotted with the relics of the ancestors. For the men of the cult, this is their own land, from which their spirits, left by the ancestors, were born into their mothers; they know it and feel a part of it, and are not comfortable when in a country they know only partially or not at all. As the owners, the incarnated spirits of the land, it is their business also to know the myths that tell of the doings here of the heroes, and to know the paths they used. But the heroes wandered beyond their own bor-ders, and so the myths and the paths dovetail with those of other bands, and a pious elder may learn from allied cults a whole cycle of myths about the same hero, and actually follow his path for hundreds of miles. So, as society is linked throughout by kinship, and nature by totemism, the country also, so sacred to the aboriginals, is in a way knit together by the travels of the ancestor-heroes.

But why is this religion? Why is it more than fairy tale? Because the myths are like mana; they not only explain nature but are a necessary part of nature, and so also are the heroes. The heroes lived and hunted and made totem spirit places and died, but they are not gone; the dream time was a miraculous age, and that is past, but ineffably it still exists,[3] and the natives can enter it through their cult and their myths and, individually, by "dreaming," or fixing their minds on it in a concentration that is almost a trance. The heroes still act, and their past actions are still effective. By their secrets, and their possession of the churingas, the Australians link their lives with the dream time; they recreate the past in the present, or rather join the present to the past. In ceremony they re-enact and recite the myth—this is their worship and their prayer—and make the myth live again to revivify nature. They go to the totem centers and clean the exits for the totem spirits and ritually coax them out to be born, as human beings, or emus, or fish; they cut themselves and shed their own blood at totem spots or hero monuments, to lend their own life to the totem spirits and the heroes, and with sacred paintings and other rites they themselves help to increase the number of spirits.

They can do all these things because they know the myths. In ceremonial paint, and with tufts of down glued to their skins with blood, the natives merge themselves with the unseen beings of the countryside of which they, too, are part, in an atmosphere of strong, positive reverence and helpfulness. And when they regard their churingas, and sing over them, they get from these poor painted shingles a rapture and a sense of beauty such as an altar or a stained-glass window might give a Christian.

I said at the beginning of this book that religion does more than give aesthetic or spiritual satisfaction, and so it does for the Australians; it gives them community of purpose, and fortitude, which they sorely need. If you were an aborigine of Australia, would you rather face your life realistically, or some other way, that is, "religiously"? Com-

---

[3] If you have any difficulty comprehending this, reflect that everything in the Bible happened about two thousand years or more ago, but that the Kingdom of God is still imminent.

pare it to that of the Bakongo. The latter live in sizable villages of some comfort and permanence. Their principal dread in life is sickness, not hunger; as to their food, they can see it growing all around them in their gardens and livestock; they know where their next meal is coming from, and where next year's meals are coming from as well. What a miserably uncertain life is the Australian's, compared to this, when a sudden drought might send away the animals and thin out the wild yams to the danger point. The Bakongo can provide for themselves, and know it; nature is the Australian's only provider, and he has no other idea than to depend on it. Little wonder, then, that while the Bakongo ask their ancestors incessantly for children, the Australians are forced to kill a certain number of their own newborn, because they can neither burden the mother with two infants in arms at once nor burden the group with too many helpless mouths when starvation may come at any time.

So the Australians, who can in no wise control nature, take the second course and surrender to it, align themselves with it and make themselves part of it. Through totemism they understand that all nature is like them, and they like nature; nature is safe for them because they are part of it, and not a separate, embattled species of creature. Through their heroes, myths, and increase rites they express their wishes that nature and society will go on as at present, and they do their wholehearted bit to help the totemic heroes create spirits. This is the function of the cult members, and from it they draw confidence and zest. The cult also suggests some meaning in life, since they look on themselves as the embodiment of totem spirits, created in the dream time, which will after death once more go to the totem home.

Thus the Australians, like the Bakongo, expand upon the idea of souls to give them a cult worthy of their needs. The Bakongo's admirable conception of being watched over by a group of the nobler of their departed seems to accord with their more advanced society. The Australians in a different way comfort themselves by becoming one with all nature, using totem souls and a totemic system of philosophy as the threads by which the whole is woven together. Both peoples thus use souls to round out their views of the universe and to soothe their direst needs and wishes.

13

DEMONS

You would think, if you took the point of view of certain tribes, that as generation after generation died off and their souls joined up with those ahead of them, there would be standing room only in Kingdom Come, especially if the abode of the dead were near by and had the general dimensions of this living world. But no; there appears to be space in the invisible for other spirits—not ancestral souls, or any other kind of souls, but just disembodied spirits—perhaps hordes of them, having as good a right to the territory as the human people.

There are, of course, all possible kinds of such beings. Some tribes may be hazy about their connection with true souls, thinking that perhaps all spirits once were men; anthropologists of the past have also been only too eager to theorize along the same lines, but this is not a point of consequence here. On the other side, spiritual creatures may run without clear distinctions all the way from minor sprites up to mighty gods, widely adored and obeyed. What I am concerned with here, however, are the least of them: demons, hobgoblins, junior-grade devils—all those who are close to men and take some kind of interest in their doings, who may or may not be malevolent but whose prerogatives had better be respected; who are therefore attended to and propitiated but without being worshiped or having a cult addressed to them.

Heaven knows, such elves abounded in our own recent

history, crowding the paintings of the Temptation of St. Anthony, or providing us with a rich lore of leprechauns, trolls, poltergeists, and the like. Poltergeists are not simply the creation of ignorant central Europeans, for they have greatly tormented the Anglo-Saxons, and still do. They are practical pranksters, fun-loving phantoms who delight to swish through a house, blowing out all the candles at once; they intend no great harm, which means that they are not likely to kill you outright, but they have an adolescent notion of what is comic, and express their joviality in beating you up, tossing you out of bed, and above all in smashing your china. They throw your good pieces across the room against a wall (observers agree that dishes take a queer wobbly flight when pitched by a poltergeist), and will keep it up night after night, breaking really important amounts of crockery.

Mr. George Walton suffered a severe attack of these hyperphysical hoodlums in and around his house at New Castle, New Hampshire, in the spring of 1682. One night a shower of stones assailed the family outside the house, and continued to crash against the clapboard walls. Windows were "miserably and strangely battered" by stones striking the leads and casements from the *inside* and falling back into the room. "Pewter and brass began to frolick about," and the candlestick was struck from the table. The man who recorded the horseplay was "near danger of having my head broke by a mall or great hammer brushing along the top or roof of the room from the other end as I was walking in it, and lighting down by me." This man was Richard Chamberlayne, no local gull but the secretary of the province of New Hampshire, and he wrote a little pamphlet tersely entitled: "LITHOBOLIA: or, The Stone-Throwing Devil. BEING An Exact and True Account (by way of Journal) of the various Actions of Infernal Spirits, or (*Devils Incarnate*) Witches, or both; and the great Disturbance and Amazement they gave to *George Waltons* Family, at a place call'd *Great Island* in the Province of *New-Hantshire* [sic] in New-England, chiefly in Throwing about (by an Invisible hand) *Stones, Bricks,* and *Brick-bats* of all Sizes, with several other things, as *Hammers, Mauls, Iron-crows, Spits* and other Domestick Utensils, as came into their Hellish Minds and this for the space of a Quarter of a Year. By R. C. esq; who was a Sojourner in the same Family the whole Time, and an Ocular Witness of these Diabolick Inventions. The Contents hereof being manifestly known to the Inhabitants of that Province, and Persons of other Provinces, and is upon Record in His Majesties Council-Court held for that Province."

Wausau, Wisconsin, was visited in 1941 by a more restrained pixy, who tapped on the bedroom windows of a nine-year-old girl (and, oddly enough, desisted when she left the room); this went on for several nights despite a cordon of six policemen which was finally thrown around the house; and careful raking of the grounds below the windows failed to yield any footprints. One officer had this to say: "I don't believe in these supernatural stories, but this gave me the willies. It first sounded like someone beating with a pin against the window. Then like a dime was used. It continued to grow until I thought the side of the house would fall in."

This is the merest token of the subject. It is all very amusing (if it is not happening to you) but it is only what we call superstition in our culture and has no especial significance beyond the angry ascribing to conscious supernatural beings of something baffling and irritating, which is one impulse of animism. But among some folk these same spooky nuisances can take the form of a well-organized set of beliefs which affect the general attitudes and behavior of the populace to a significant degree, still without becoming, as I have said, a true cult. This is very much the case with the jinns of Moslem countries, and particularly of the somewhat backward Berber peoples of North Africa.[1]

These include the Riffians, various other large groups of Morocco and Algeria, and the Tuaregs of the Sahara, who

[1] See especially Westermarck, op. cit.

are, except for the last, ancient farmers of northwest Africa who are now Mohammedan and who have been Arabized to various degrees. Aside from their orthodox Mohammedanism they entertain an enormous amount of belief regarding sorcery, charms, the evil eye, and so on, and a lively interest in jinns, whom you have met in *The Arabian Nights*. Wherever the belief in jinns has its origins (i.e., in pre-Mohammedan times), it is countenanced by Islam, because the Prophet himself preached to them, and converted many of them to the faith. (These are now the best jinns; the worst ones are Jewish and Christian.)

Jinns were created before men and are a different kind of being, having nothing to do with ghosts (although some of the Tuaregs say they are mortals who have been dead for more than a hundred years). They die, or can be killed, but they live for centuries. They outnumber mankind because the females give birth to many young at once, and procreation takes place through the male of the species simply rubbing his thigh against that of the female. What they look like is not known, because they are invisible, but of course they can take whatever shape they wish, often disguising themselves as men and women to have dealings with humanity proper: they may even marry or seduce mortal people, which is seldom a successful arrangement for the latter. When in human form, they may be undetectable or they may have some slight oddity about them, and they may change into something else before your eyes. Often they take the form of animals, of any sort, but particularly of frogs, toads, tortoises, and snakes, which the people are therefore careful not to harm; and it is just as well not to take a stick to a dog or cat in the dark, especially a black cat. I need hardly tell an educated person that jinns can pass through a tiny crack and can travel great distances in a twinkling, taking people with them.

The Tuaregs claim that the jinns live in uninhabited parts of the Sahara, but the authoritative version elsewhere is that their home is underground. Be that as it may, they are much absorbed with the doings of men, and are always present in large numbers around earthly communities. They like to study the Koran and so they come to classes in the mosque. They also come to market for food; when prices go up, people know that the jinns are out buying in force, but at the same time jinns will not eat salt and therefore the butchers and bakers, to whom a jinn's money is as good as anybody else's, are careful to sell their meat and bread unsalted, so as not to discourage the jinn trade.

It is their personal dealings with mortals, however, which are significant. There have been cases where jinns bestowed favors on men or on their human spouses out of sheer friendliness, but this is certainly not the usual thing; on the contrary, a jinn seems to have a hair-trigger temper, and for slight causes to attack a human victim by shooting him with an arrow or entering his body, which results in illness of any description: neuralgia, convulsions, strokes, insanity, and so on; historical epidemics have been caused by an army of jinns camping right in a town and letting fly with their arrows. They may also act like poltergeists, tripping you up, knocking over the milk, making you yawn, or giving you bad dreams, but these are minor complaints. The main thing to bear in mind about a jinn is that he may take lightning offense and strike you ill.

Ordinarily jinns are like wasps, leaving the first move up to you. But with their vulgar love of intruding into human business, the jinns are never far away, and after dark they positively swarm; if they insist on being underfoot you cannot help tripping on them or bumping into them, and they are quite pushy enough to eat out of the same dish with you or get in bed with you. Fortunately there is a long list of things which are distasteful to them, and which can so be used to keep them away. One is to utter "Bismillah rahman rahim [In the name of God, the merciful and compassionate]", and indeed to sit down to eat without saying this is to invite the jinns to tuck their napkins in; it is said on every possible occasion when a jinn might be around: when going to bed, crossing a river (full of jinns), putting out the light (jinns prefer the dark), doing anything with ashes (jinns like to stay in ashes), or passing any place where jinns are particularly common, etc. Readings from the Koran are another expedient for special purposes. Jinns dislike loud noises and gunpowder, whence the lavish firing off of guns at a North African wedding. There are several kinds of herbs and gum unpleasant to jinns, which can be burned to send them off, and are thus used to a great extent in cures of sicknesses which they have caused, but the best and most usual household remedies are iron and, above all, salt. This last can be used liberally to keep the obnoxious beings away, by putting it under the pillow, on the bed, on the food, where you bury treasure, and around the place generally at childbirth and weddings; and you can simply eat it like popcorn to render your interior temporarily jinnproof.

The real menace of jinns is not so much accidental encounters or simply having them around. It is more that certain conditions or certain actions attract or annoy them, and furnish the occasion for their attacks. This should sound familiar. It is the same as being in a tabu state, exposed to danger, but here dramatized differently. And many of the same things summon jinns which are tabu in Polynesia or the Old Testament, seeming to be ritual rather than moral in their reasons.

Blood absolutely fascinates them, and it is therefore dangerous to people, bringing them in contact with jinns; a man who has killed another—has shed blood—is therefore haunted by them, while a butcher has them around in droves, keeping them at a distance with Bismillahs; butchering must be done in a careful way and blood washed off the meat (Moslems may not eat blood anyhow); even the red meat is exceedingly attractive to jinns. Childbirth is a fearful source of danger, not only because of the presence of blood but because children, particularly infants, are special targets of jinns, who also like to change their own children for human ones. Newlyweds are likewise in a state of exposure to the interest of jinns, and every precaution is taken at weddings: guns are fired, salt, knives, and needles are used, the bride wears pounds of amulets, especially silver; one of the most haunted parts of a house is the threshold, so the bride is carried over that, and as a last touch in one tribe the groom puts a pistol under the pillow.

There are many small acts which will bring on the jinns with some punishment or other. Along with certain avoidances in connection with red meat there are various things which sound like biblical prohibitions, but these merge with others which have a basis in etiquette, morals, or useful social behavior. Here is a sample list of don'ts. Do not relieve yourself with your head uncovered, or on the highway, or in water, or in the shade of a fig tree. Do not go to bed with greasy hands. Do not pick up and eat again on a bone or piece of meat you have once put down; the jinns think you were through with it and it is theirs. Do not put your slippers under the bed. Do not forget to fold your clothes up when you take them off, or jinns will dress in them. Do not get angry. Do not get frightened. Do not drink alcohol. Do not go out on Saturday night in a state of perspiration. Do not spill water on the fire; jinns live in it.

Thus, apart from the direct prohibition of certain things, the belief in jinns constantly tends to create a sense of carefulness, of circumspection, in individuals; in a roundabout way it works to produce self-discipline and at the same time propriety in behavior, both desirable qualities in members of society. This will epitomize the effect: a scholar, instead of avoiding jinns, may actually summon one and obtain from him a gift of hairs from the jinn's head, each of which on being burned will summon the jinn once more to execute a command; but the man who does this takes his life in his hands, and must be completely good and pious, saying regular prayers, fasting properly in Ramadan, never drinking alcohol, nor being unfaithful to his wife, lying, stealing, or doing any kind of wrong.

Obviously the jinns have other useful functions, which are like those of witchcraft. They give an outlet for annoyance and anxiety caused by illness and bad luck, displacing these emotions onto non-existent creatures, something even

better than human witches; and they furnish a crystalliza-
tion of malicious tendencies which can be condemned with
enthusiasm. And not only can a man enlist interested sympathy in his hard luck by saying, "Let me tell you about my
jinn"—jinns are also like magic because they provide a
"scientific" explanation of the trouble, so that it can be
treated; cures, once a jinn has actually got into a person,
are good, sound, magical measures to deal with possession.

A sense of carefulness is similarly fostered among a people of northern New Guinea who have been described by
Dr. Margaret Mead.[2] These are the Arapesh, who live between the shore and the lower reaches of the Sepik River
in the region of Aitape. They have a long list of foods which
are tabu to people of different ages and sexes, something
which acts in a disciplinary way, since the beliefs connected
with the tabus emphasize things important to Arapesh attitudes. Aside from this and the inevitable mass of lore on
magic and sorcery they are rather poor religiously. They
have no public cult with a priesthood, though they give
some recognition to their ancestral dead. Like other Melanesians, they have a secret society for men. And like other
Melanesians, they believe in local spirits of the land called,
in pidgin English of the region, marsalai. It is the marsalai
who help them to toe the line.

Marsalai are strange, if not horrifying, in appearance
(they are seldom actually seen, this being very dangerous,
perhaps deadly). They may look like a double-tailed,
double-headed lizard in bright colors, a one-legged kangaroo, a pig with bushes growing from its back, or a rat with
a phosphorescent rump. They are credited with having created many ordinary things, though the Arapesh take little
interest in origins. Marsalai are the guardians and owners
of the land, apparently in co-operation with the ancestral
spirits, but each marsalai resides particularly in a certain
place, of an inhospitable or dangerous kind, like a bog, a

[2] Margaret Mead, "The Mountain Arapesh. II. Supernaturalism," *Anthropological Papers of the American Museum of Natural History*, Vol. 37, Part III (1940).

quicksand, a deep water hole, or a sharp declivity. These places are known to the people, who also know the name and nature of the marsalai of their territory. The important character of them is, however, that, like the jinns, they are touchy bogeys and must be handled with kid gloves. When they are offended, they will attack with sickness, rheumatism, delirium, madness, and death. They are especially easily angered by women and will vent their annoyance in rape or by causing miscarriage.

So the marsalai, like jinns, are a reason for not doing certain things, things which are significant to the Arapesh philosophic system, so to speak.[3] The Arapesh (a "savage" people) in their attitudes repress personal aggressiveness, admiring and cultivating restrained, unprovocative behavior and the kind of conscientiousness toward gardening, hunting, and family life that marks the proper husband and parent; and they have an insulting name for men who do not live up to this standard, but who instead eat food which keeps them out of the secret society, and act in an exhibitionist and aggressive manner. Corresponding correctness is expected of women.

Now the Arapesh tend to allegorize all this, or express it to themselves, in terms of sex. Sexuality, in their eyes, runs a gamut from a mild, almost unsexual condition, a well-domesticated kind of atmosphere which is protective and nourishing, to a forceful and passionate power which generates dangerous, heated influences, a degree in which the two sexes reach their highest psychic and physical contrast and are most inimical to one another. Dr. Mead distinguishes these states as typifying "the aggressive specifically sexual nature and the cherishing parental sexual nature of both man and woman." Strong sexuality is felt to be bad for growth and strength. A husband and wife must leave off

---

[3] Although Dr. Mead remarks that the starting points of Arapesh thinking are affective rather than cognitive: "Two things are associated, or stand for one another, in myth or rite, not because of some logical connection, but because both are symbols of the same emotional attitude."

sleeping together after she has become definitely pregnant, and may not resume until the child can walk and talk, or the child might die. An older boy, an adolescent, must try to repress his own feelings of sexuality, because sexual indulgence would stunt his growth; these feelings make him uneasy, and his recourse is to cut his own organ of sex and let out the accumulated "bad blood." When he marries, the heat of sex is dangerous for him and his new wife, and their early indulgence in it calls for purifying ceremonies; if his wife comes from the neighboring Sepik Plains this is doubly so (for in New Guinea, as in the great world, foreign, exotic women are held to be more highly sexed than the home-towners); they cannot even sleep together for several months, and when they do he keeps an eye on his yams and his hunting, to see whether passion is still too high between them, injuring not only his husbandry but his own physical powers.

Now the marsalai are in a way identified with the male extreme of sexuality, and are represented in myths as harshly lustful, contrary to the Arapesh ideal. What is offensive to a marsalai is the other extreme, the utmost in femininity, and he is angered not only by a woman who is pregnant, or in her menses, but also by a man who has lately had intercourse with a woman, and if any such as these catches the attention of a marsalai, or above all goes near a marsalai place, there will be trouble. People in these conditions may therefore protect themselves, and live to a good age, only by being careful to observe the proper rites and tabus.

Thus do the Arapesh accentuate emotional caution as socially desirable, and thus do they modulate their lives to supernatural dictates. Like the Moroccans, and like other peoples, they feel compulsions (Reinach's "scruples") of certain kinds (and rather common kinds, like those surrounding the behavior of newlyweds), and they get together on these compulsions, and make them social in their effects, by setting up the marsalai as the lurking danger. Of course, this is all a negative business, and such demons are not the same thing as deities; they are not treated in positive ritual ways like the Bakongo's ancestors, or the Australians' totem heroes, or any accepted gods, high or low. In its sphere of feeling and operation, the whole conception is more like witchcraft or sorcery. But it acts positively, nevertheless, using the fear of misfortune, and especially of disease, to strengthen a system which, like tabu, is one of group self-control.

14

GODS

Gods, as I have indicated, come in all sizes and shapes. There are big gods and small gods, handsome gods and ugly gods, noble gods and mean gods, gods who live near by and gods who live far away, gods of one thing and gods of everything, bloody-clawed gods who relish the flesh of men and smiling gods who bend a friendly ear to anyone.

Most human groups have their own deities and ways of addressing them; these are the typical native cults I spoke of at the beginning of the book, and are what is usually first thought of as the "religion" of a people. It is a somewhat different subject from the demons of the last chapter since in these gods (as with the Bakongo ancestors) we have not only the beings of the accepted public belief but also beings who can be turned to and supplicated, privately or publicly, with confidence and in a definite approved fashion. It is also, of course, an enormous subject for sheer variety.

It is possible to make some generalizations and to select types of divinities commonly met with, such as creator gods, culture bringers, and departmental deities—those who have charge of particular functions of nature or human life—and in fact a great deal has been written along these lines,[1] but I doubt if the collecting, sorting, naming, and framing method is the useful one for our purposes. When you come

---

[1] A good book is Toy, op. cit.

down to it, you must expect the practically boundless imagination of man to give birth to a practically boundless kaleidoscope full of spiritual beings, and about all you can say is that it has happened. If you abstract and classify, you are less likely to see the gods as citizens of the culture to which they belong, and you are also apt to fall into assumptions regarding a supposed evolution or development of the idea of gods, and say, "This religion is high, that religion is low."[2] Let us therefore simply take a few societies and see what gods they have and how they get along with them.

In some regions the people have a rather diffuse notion of a realm well filled with deities of not too distant and awesome a nature. The Pueblos of the Southwest and the pagan Filipinos both recognize gods of some individuality, together with large numbers of spirits of a general kind, who tend to come in types and classes and may include the spirits of the dead. The Pueblos elevate Sun Old Man, or Iyatiku the Corn Mother, and a certain number of other such, to high importance, but they also recognize and pay homage to great collective groups like the Cloud beings (which take in the dead) and other spirits, who live around the shores of the sea surrounding the universe and in the lakes or the mountains.

The Ifugaos of Luzon,[3] wanting a favor, invoke both their ancestors and the deities applicable to the case by means of offerings, treating both types with no great evidence of reverence. These people, who are possibly a little more formal about the register of their gods than other Philippine or Indonesian groups, have about fifteen hundred distinct beings, according to an estimate by Barton, who after long acquaintance with the Ifugaos found that these gods fall into about forty or more classes and are rather specific in

[2] I do not mean to deny that *within* a given cult gods have grown from a crude to a refined conception. That is quite different.

[3] R. F. Barton, "The Religion of the Ifugaos," *Memoirs of the American Anthropological Association*, No. 65 (1946).

their individual functions, representing every kind of conception: things in nature, great ancestors, sicknesses, and the emotions of man.

Let us take the Convincers, a group of gods numbering 109 and consisting of a sort of tool kit for getting your way over the resistance of other men. In their most common employment a man will invoke a bevy of them before going out to try to collect a debt (this is a hard job in Ifugao territory, because there is no political authority charged with enforcing payment, and an Ifugao who does not want to resort to force has to rely on his tongue). After first bespeaking the ancestors, the hopeful creditor entreats the aid of the following gods: Thunder in the Skyworld, Lightning Son of Thunder, Toothed Son of Thunder, Sharp-rattling Thunderer, Like-the-Cry-of-a-Startled-Pig Thunderer, Halupe of the Skyworld, Fast Beating of the Heart from Fear, Gasp of Fear, and Fear in the Lungs. Going into operation, these will scare the debtor (to say the least), and in order that he shall not become desperate or violent the next deities called into play are to cool and soothe him: Air Coming out of a Cave, Gentleness, Cooling of Fever, etc. Then Transparency, Gentled, Rattling of the Teeth, Too Steep to Climb, Slowness, Craziness, Concession, and Leaning on Something soften the debtor up, and others, including Slamming Down Payment at Once, Agreed-on, Consolation, and Overflowing-and-Overflowing, cause him to pay fully and freely, whereupon Carried on the Forearms, Termination, et al., help the creditor to bear his booty home. To plug up any loophole, the creditor also invites the attention of Reinforcement (who will make bystanders speak up, advising the debtor to pay), of Dammed-up (who will hold back claims of other creditors while this one gets paid), and of somebody called Hanubok, who prevents the debtor from going and hiding when he sees the creditor approach. (I think this is the same Hanubok who is always letting the local bore catch me flat-footed.)

Selection and invocation of the right groups of deities in this way takes care of most Ifugao activities. It calls for sacrifice (often of chickens, perhaps of a pig) and some ritual, and the deities or ancestors come and possess the priest or priests who are making the invocation. For something of public importance, like a funeral or a head-taking expedition against the enemy, every step of the business involves a ceremony made of these elements, interspersed with simpler omen-watching of kinds I have described earlier. On a head-hunt, before and after spearing the victim, there are continual rites, major and minor, ending with a full-dress ceremony to forestall enemy vengeance, at which the following whole categories of spirits are called on: Ancestors, Messengers, Paybackables, Deceivers, Omen Deities, Gods of Reproduction, Hipag, Talisman-Activators, Flying Monsters, Harpies, Ghoul Deities, Spitters, Hunters, Mountaineers, Liver-Spearers, Baiyun, and Convincers.

This would appear to be a highly practical cult, not exactly brimming with spiritual beauty. Notice that for its devotees it functions much like magic, and for the same ends: it is a question of finding the right gods and then bribing them, and strikes us as having a less noble conception than the general supplications made by the Bakongo to their ancestors. The deities' very names, commonly expressing actions, show how the Ifugaos project their everyday hopes and anticipations into the realm of spirits. As far as the gods go, there are so many of them, and they are so specialized, as to bring them all down to a dead level of mediocrity, tending to prevent any of them from attaining grandeur and impressiveness on one hand or an appeal to general human qualities on the other.

The Gã peoples of the Gold Coast of West Africa[4] have local divinities of a more godlike nature than the above. The Gã are town and village dwellers who have established themselves on the shore and the lagoons not very long ago, and they change residence fairly freely, in individuals or groups, joining other villages or founding fresh ones. They

[4] Field, op. cit.

are like the other tribes of Negro Africa in general, and
their attitude toward their ancestors is the same as that
of the Bakongo; however, the ancestors defer in interest to
the gods; the gods furthermore benefit by the fact that the
Gã have no fetishes.

Compared to those of the Ifugaos, these gods have a
more universal, less special, quality. They have their work
to do—they are to some extent departmental, and they are
also localized, the most important ones being the gods of
the lagoons; as a matter of fact, these gods were there before the Gã themselves, who took them over from their
predecessors and still sing songs to them in a foreign, forgotten dialect. But the gods are flexible in their nature, and
obviously have their own ups and downs in popularity and
importance.

For the worship of them is free and individual, as well
as being public. Each village has its own god, supreme
there, although colonists from other towns may bring their
gods along with them, without pretending that they are
superior to that of the village. Also, there are village ceremonies for the gods all together. But anyone can privately
worship any god whom he wishes to interest in his problems. (In one village, Labadi, the gods live in the hills except for six weeks in the year, when they come right into
the town; during this time no private ceremonies may be
held, but only public ones, so as not to distract them from
town business, and anyone so heedless as to die in these
weeks commits blasphemous death, because the gods will
be intensely interested in the newly dead ghost and will
fail to attend closely to the rites being held in their honor.
Notice how this expresses in dogma an insistence that individuals shall participate in community interests during a
sort of yearly reunion.)

The gods in their own forms are horrifying, and the sight
of them would probably kill the beholder, but they can take
any shape, and do not as a rule mean to harm anyone. If
one passed you in the guise of a man you might be able
to spot him: he would seem a little queer to you, and if

you turn to take another look he will have walked almost out of sight in a few seconds. One god, indeed, saved the village of which he was the protector from an enemy attack by assuming the form of a beautiful maiden and going out to meet the hostile chieftain, whose fancy lightly turned to thoughts of a non-military nature.

Each god has a house in the village, serving as a temple, which is kept by a priest and is also attended by one or more woyei (see p. 139), female acolytes who dance at ceremonies and become possessed by the god, speaking for him to the congregation. Now the house, the priest, and the woyo are all supported by the worshipers of the god, and his popularity will be manifest by whether the house is a little hovel with a starving priest or a handsome, well-kept enclosure with several woyei attached to it. And it is plain that the passage of time has made changes in the gods. Old chants which have become fixed in form reflect an earlier picture of the pantheon, and these chants may neglect the gods who are now of prime importance, while giving great attention, and addressing as "Almighty," gods who have slipped to insignificance, and even naming gods now totally forgotten. The Gã also express events in human history by marriages or adoptions among the gods: at one town the main god is the original lagoon god; he belonged to the people ousted by the Gã, but they have nonetheless raised him to supremacy, and married their own chief goddesses to him.

Here is a godly religion of a most general kind. The gods are not great or distant lords. To the Gã they are powerful, but in actuality they are local, tribal, and tutelary in nature. At the same time they are not rigidly departmental, bound to one single function, nor are they pointless devils like the jinns, who have little to offer but trouble. They are more or less human in their outlook, which means that they are sympathetic. They are sufficiently well interrelated by myth and belief so that a public cult can exist around them all together, and they also offer individual worshipers a chance to seek out a sympathetic protector. It is not a highly organized theology, and it is not specialized. It is in simple form the same as the religions of Greece and Rome.

The Aztec pantheon shows, I think, a development of the same kind of thing among a culturally more advanced people in a state of political flux. Eight hundred years before Cortes, the Teotihuacán period came to an end in central Mexico; this had been an era of evident peace and a common cosmopolitan culture, in which temple building and the higher arts had appeared, and such famous gods as Tlaloc and Quetzalcoatl had been established; this tranquil state of affairs broke up and collapsed, and there came into the valley of Mexico several less cultured tribes, the so-called Chichimecas, who may have been responsible for the debacle. They included the Aztecs, with their tribal deity Huitzilopochtli. The barbarians adopted the classical culture, struggling for supremacy all the while, and after three centuries of fierce vicissitudes the Aztecs went to the top of the heap, with Huitzilopochtli now their ravenous war god and with a number of other principal deities borrowed from the Teotihuacán people and from their neighbor nations. Although by Spanish times these gods were all fitted into a calendar, with well-defined (and exceedingly colorful) ceremonies assigned to them, yet the pantheon gives an impression of having been recently put together, with confusion and overlapping in the characteristics and the relationships of the gods.

The gods of Polynesia[5] were among the highest philosophical achievements of a primitive people, showing the same refinement of conception as their idea of mana. The Gã look only as high as lagoon gods, but the important deities of Polynesia were gods of the universe and, while they had a departmental aspect, they were also gods of general human qualities. This was a rich and full religious development, embracing nature (like the Australians), souls (like the Bakongo), man, and gods all in a single

[5] See Handy, op. cit.

scheme: great gods, minor demons and elves of the wood, and ancestral spirits of man, all were called atua.

In the beginning, said the Polynesians, there was only intense darkness and a void. (Such an idea of starting from nothingness is extremely rare in primitive ideas of creation.) Then, in long successive eras, principles and realities appeared. These eras were something like generations, with each founded upon the last, so that the generations of gods and men came naturally out of this in sequence. Gradually, through a number of aeons, light was born, from the least flicker to full day, and after this the necessary principles of existence, like growth, thought, breathing power. Different island groups had different versions of this succession, of course, and in Tahiti and New Zealand the whole impulse was traced to a first god, a World Soul, who rested inert, contained in an eggshell, in the darkness for unmeasured time before deciding by an effort of will to cause the appearance of light and of the universe: said Io the parentless, the self-created, "that He might cease remaining inactive: 'Darkness, become a light-possessing darkness.'" But Io was so refined and holy a conception that he was a secret of the Maori priests, and unknown to the laity.

At the end of these eras concrete reality appeared, in the form of the parent gods, the Sky Father, Atea, and the Earth Mother, Papa (in this case Papa is the Mama). These two lay long in close embrace and gave birth to the great active gods of all of Polynesia: Tane, Tu, Rongo, and Tangaroa. Tane was god of light, not a sun god but a god of sunlight, the "water of life," a vivifier, god of the male principle, of generative power (which was not narrowly sexual, to the Polynesians); he was also god of trees, forests, and forest life. Tu was god of power, of war; god of the right side and the harsh nature of man, Tu-of-the-angry-eyes, to whom human sacrifices were made by some tribes in war. Tu had his peaceful arts as well, here and there, being the woodworkers' patron in Hawaii. But it was Rongo who was the god of peace and plenty; he was the god of a third kind of force, that of the fertility of nature, particularly of cultivated foods, and also of rain, a source of this fertility. Tangaroa, while being more variable in his capacities than the others (he was the World Soul in Tahiti), was generally the lord of the ocean and everything in it, a very important department in this island world, and he was, of course, the major patron of fishers.

Those were the great gods, but they were not the only children of Atea and Papa—the Maoris counted seventy gods of this union. These gods were oppressed by the darkness and lack of space, caught as they were between their parents. Some proposed to separate the parents by force, but others resisted the idea furiously; nevertheless Tane by a tremendous effort thrust them apart and let in light and space. Now, said the Maoris, Tawhiri the Tempest, outraged by this treatment of his parents, led an attack against his brothers; Tangaroa, unable to withstand him, fled into the ocean, but Tawhiri was defeated by Tu.

Thus, after many generations of creation, the world existed, and the primary gods. One of the later ones was Maui, not worshiped as a god but revered as a culture hero in a long series of myths for the benefits he got for man: he made the islands by fishing them up from the bottom of the sea with his hook and line; he made the day longer by noosing the sun and forcing it to go slower; he stole fire and brought it to man, but he lost his life in trying to conquer death by entering the womb of the goddess of death herself. There were many lesser gods as well (the Maoris had ranks and classes), going all the way down to demons, and to multitudes of woodland spirits, for whose benefit the Hawaiians danced the hula.

Now at last Tane made mankind, and in a way which establishes woman as the earthly, dark, and passive aspect of human nature; he molded a woman out of earth and brought her to life, the Earth-formed-maid, Hine-ahu-one (Woman-pile-of-sand); he took her to wife and their offspring were the first mortals, born thus of a god on the male side only. But there was no great separation between gods and men because, in addition to all the gods who ap-

peared during the creation, and never were mortal, fresh
gods arose as great chiefs, or other men, died, and their
spirits were deified. Many of the local and tribal gods of
Polynesia, or gods of crafts and occupations, were either ancestors in the chiefly line or else great leaders in the field
they patronized. So the line of succession ran down from
the first stirrings of the universe to living man, and men,
gods, and the earth itself were all brought together in one
family tree.

This feeling of unity carried over into the worship of the
gods and attitudes toward them, which were those of participation. Gods and man both possessed mana, in degrees
proportional to their standing in the scale of creation, and
in this respect they were joined together through the chief,
who was nearest the gods in both blood and mana and had
the religious duty of preserving the mana he was given.
The priests not only knew the chants that helped the gods
perform, but those who were craft priests, rather than ceremonial priests, generated mana by their own skill and per-
fection in work. The other kind of religious functionary, the
kaula or medium, actually brought the god into the midst
of the people, by being possessed (see p. 79). The gods
were in any case not far away, and at a ceremony they
were right among the people—and a great many activities,
such as building a canoe, were ceremonial. Offerings, of
course, of every kind including human beings, were made
in plenty; and the first fruits of any crop, including fish,
were proffered to the gods, or to their living vessel, the
chief. Feasts were also a form of offering, and a very satisfactory one, in which the Polynesians constantly indulged
for ritual reasons, for the gods came to table and ate heartily; the mortals were glad and the gods were glad, and
they were linked by the usual rapport of eating together.
Dancing was a kind of rite made equally engrossing: as
everyone knows, Polynesian dancing was decidedly erotic
and roused the passions of the watching gods as it did those
of the living, and so stimulated the mana of the deities,

which was generative and creative in its nature, and thus was linked to sex.

Prayers, or chants, were on the whole similarly extroverted forms of address. Some prayer was direct appeal, though cast always in eloquent and poetic phrasing, but much of it was of a more compulsive nature, depending for effectiveness on the recitation of old and formal genealogies and sections of myth, repeating the very words and actions by which the gods themselves had accomplished something, and in this way helping the gods with their work of nature and reinforcing their mana. In sympathy with the purpose, such ritual prayers were usually chanted with force and accuracy, and to make an error, ever so slight, would cause an entire festival to be abandoned, and perhaps bring disaster on the blundering priest.

Here is a religion which clearly flowered from a humbler base into a breadth of conception and a fullness of myth that equal the classical cults. Another such pantheon and faith grew up in Dahomey from an African base entirely like the Gã cult, but took a different tack from the Polynesian: instead of permeating all activity, serving as the vehicle of the state religion, of community ceremonies and private rites, it concentrated on ministering to the emotional satisfaction of individuals, and it developed churches in our own strict sense.

The kingdom of Dahomey reaches the Slave Coast of West Africa just to the east of Gã territory and extends far inland.[6] It has a striking history in recent centuries as the most powerful of a number of absolute kingships which developed in this region, many of which it conquered and incorporated; not long ago it was a totalitarian state in familiar clothing—it had secret police, it had a successful military expansion, and no man's life was safe from the king's justice. Some of its prosperity flowed from slaves, captured by the king's army and sold to Yankee traders. But it has

[6] Melville J. Herskovits, *Dahomey, an Ancient West African Kingdom* (1938).

certain progressive features: labor is organized into self-governed working guilds, and the idea of insurance existed in mutual-aid associations.

The ancestral dead form a cult of importance, as in the Congo, and the official religion of the kingdom is the worship of the king's own forebears. Each clan also holds rites for its ancestors. But the great gods are something different, forming a family having the same stature as the high gods of Polynesia; it is they who are the objects of popular worship and who came to the New World in a general form in the Voodoo religion of Haiti (which is not what you think it is at all).[7]

The first creator was the goddess Nana-Buluku, who gave birth to Lisa and Mawu, the father and mother of the rest of the high gods. But these three are not the particular gods of the churches and are very far away, particularly Nana-Buluku; Nana-Buluku has no rites to her, and only one shrine in all Dahomey, but nevertheless hers is a specially honored shrine, and in this town there is no buying and selling (and the Dahomeans are great merchants), and people who particularly love her children Lisa and Mawu make pilgrimages to her shrine. She is not offered to; she is too far away, and her own children, the other gods, should give her presents. (It is a fact that creator gods are usually not the gods of the people's interest.)

Lisa and Mawu are twins. Mawu is the moon, and she is kindly and the Dahomeans are fond of her; Lisa is the sun, more harsh and vigorous, and he makes men toil. Their children are the sky gods, of whom different churches give different numbers, but the two most important are Sagbatá and Khevioso: Sagbatá is one person and twins, and is parent of the earth gods, and Khevioso is androgynous, having both sexes within himself (or herself), and is parent of the thunder gods; the earth and thunder gods are important subfamilies, as we shall see. Other children of the family are Gu, god of iron, or rather of the principle of cutting, which

[7] Read Alfred Metraux, *Voodoo in Haiti* (1959). "Voodoo" comes from "vodun," the Dahomean name for any deity.

is in iron, and Mawu held him in her hand (he is not like
a man) when she made the world; Loko, god of trees, very
important because of the place of the souls of trees in magic
and healing; and several others, related to food, or water,
etc.

Lastly comes Legba, the joker, the trickster, a character
who is found in many other religions and seen here in all
his glory. According to myths of the Earth Cult, Mawu and
Lisa made the world in six domains and gave these, each
with a different language, to six of their seven children;
Legba was odd man out and was made the messenger of
the family (like Mercury) and given knowledge of all the
languages. Sagbatá got the earth and Khevioso got the
thunder and was jealous of Sagbatá. Legba suggested to
Khevioso that he withhold the rain; Legba likewise went
to Mawu his parent and told her that water was running
short in the sky, and Mawu therefore also ordered that
there should be no rain on earth. The people began to com-
plain, and Mawu sent Legba down to find out why. Legba
now went down to Sagbatá on earth and told him to build
a huge fire; Mawu was frightened for fear the sky would
catch the blaze, and ordered rain. For this reason the rain
is now controlled from the earth (according to the doctrine
of the Earth Cult). This is a typical story of Legba's doings,
and Mawu's sufferings from him. Once he became jealous
of her popularity with mortals and went to her with the
false report that thieves were going to rob her garden. She
said that whoever did it must die, and Legba went that
night in Mawu's own sandals to pull up her yams. Next day
he suggested that everyone's shoes be fitted to the footprints
in the garden, and when Mawu realized what had happened she became so angry that she left the region of the
earth for good, and that is why she is so far away.

There is no baseness or trickery to which Legba will not
stoop; he is the god of the admired deceit and the dirty
joke; he twists the messages of the gods for mischief, and
he is lewd beyond belief; in stories he performs heroic feats
of lasciviousness, and when he is acted in a dance he grabs

at every woman he comes near. No Dahomean would think of speaking well of him, and all of them are fond of him. When the missionaries came and heard what he was like, and what people said (not what they thought) about him, they jumped to conclusions and identified him with the Devil. They could have done nothing more calculated to establish Satan worship. For aside from his popularity as a puckish character, he sympathetically helps mortals escape grim destiny. He can change the orders of the gods, because he carries them, and he is appealed to for that; he is a court of last appeal.[8]

These are the gods, in Dahomey. You can worship them or not, as you like. From their descriptions, they sound as though they had departmental functions, but this is of little consequence, for a person may ask for what he wants—health or children—from his favorite gods, or from any of them at all; he may go to a temple of the god he selects and get the priest and his attendants to hold a small private ceremony for his purpose.

Legba is invoked at many small, open-air shrines dedicated to him, but he has no formal cult. Not so the central gods of the pantheon, around whom full-fledged churches have grown up; these are of three denominations: the sky gods (the pantheon in general), the earth gods (essentially the same, but concentrating on a group of deities presided over by Sagbatá), and the thunder gods (those under Khevioso of the thunder). Each of these cults recognizes the same general pattern of gods but differs in details of myth and dogma: for example, in thunder mythology, Khevioso was successful in withholding rain from the earth until Sagbatá had to admit defeat, so that rain is controlled by

---

[8] There is a goddess, Fa, the personification of fate and the will of the gods, who controls divination by palm nut kernels (see p. 77) and is thus a sort of oracle of the gods. She and Legba are closely connected. Whatever she ordains she may not revoke, but Legba can thwart this simply by changing her message.

the thunder pantheon, and not by the earth gods, as the Earth Cult holds. Each church has sizable temples in various parts of the country, a temple being a compound with a number of priests and priestesses in residence. The three cults can be compared to our churches, differing perhaps a little more than our denominations in belief and practice but not so much as Christianity, Judaism, and Mohammedanism. As among us, you can address yourself to any of the churches, or you may become a full-fledged member of one of them; the difference is in the fact that actual joining is a much more serious business in Dahomey and is undertaken by only about a quarter to a half of the people, mostly women.

One joins because of a boon granted by the gods, or because one's parents have promised a child for some vow, or because someone in the family always belongs, like the Colonial Dames. In the first rite, a god enters the head of the novice and he begins to dance to drum music. He enters the temple house and goes through forty-one days of secret ceremonies, following which he is "killed" by the god, and a funeral is held for him, outside; then the candidate is brought to life again by the priests, but as a new man, belonging to the gods. He now undergoes a long novitiate, secluded in the cult house, seeing no one outside, during which he learns dances and a secret language, and his skin is cut to produce a pattern of small scars to show his membership in the cult. At last he is ready to come out; he is shown how to summon a god and told to cleave to the gods of his own cult though respecting all of them, and his hair is shaved off and kept by the cult priestesses to insure future piety (the same old contagious magic). One day, when a group of initiates is ready, the gods come and "attack" them, and they rush about trying to defend themselves; they are overcome, and the priest then tells them what god has captured each; they are thereupon entered by these gods and begin to dance.

This is the end, and the devotees are now full members of the church, but they stay on in the cult house for a while for polishing and training before going home to resume their ordinary lives. Some women may remain permanently as priestesses. The rest simply observe the Sabbath every four days, saying a prayer and abstaining from work and love, and on occasion making an offering to the church and dancing in ceremonies when called upon. Membership gives a degree of social distinction. Some people join for this reason, and their possession by the gods is clearly put on, which seems to be all that is required; but others apparently have true trances, of the type which can be called a religious experience. The faculty of being possessed also has its conveniences; a lady member who has been slapped is very apt to become possessed on the spot and scream her head off, to the mortal danger of the slapper and the admiration of fellow cultists, who gather around. A cult member's soul goes immediately to the cult gods when he dies, and not to his clan ancestors.

I could not present much more of interest by going on with further examples of gods and their cults. I have tried to show the scale of the dominant deities from high to low, and also the variety of their types from the utter vagueness surrounding the spirit beings of the Crow Indians, whose one clear function is to hear requests for visions, to the fussy departmentalism of the regiments of Ifugao godkins.

The civilized, world religions are strongly moral, and except for Buddhism are highly theistic, making the good and the godly synonymous. Is such a connection present in god cults of primitive peoples? It is not easy to see. The gods worshiped in Dahomey show some preference against sin: the thunder gods kill men by lightning and the earth gods by smallpox, both for presumably fearful offenses which they do not disclose. Notice, however, that mischief is also punished both by Nzambi Mpungu, the creator god of the Bakongo, and by the jinns, the demons of Islam, neither of which are worshiped, so that the existence of a cult is not the moral element. But if gods are not greatly interested in good for good's sake, letting custom look out for morals, they are definitely interested in prosocial ideals, and there are very seldom recognized gods whose worship entails actions inimical to the community.

After everything I have said about supernatural beings it should be apparent what else they do for men. They make the people happy. They do what ancestral spirits and totem heroes do: they put order and backbone into the universe, and so into the community's existence. As to why gods should be such a satisfactory recipe for accomplishing this, Buck says of the Polynesian divinities: "They were given the supernatural power that man desired but could not himself possess. With a belief in that power, man was inspired to accomplish many things that he might otherwise not have attempted. The religious beliefs of the Polynesians were founded on faith just as much as were the tenets of the better-known religions. By faith they were able to remove the mountains of doubt and fear. Faith in their gods supplemented by innate courage and supreme daring enabled them to cross the thousands of leagues of the vast Pacific stretching between southeast Asia and South America and so to complete the most marvelous Odyssey the world has ever known."[9]

[9] Peter Henry Buck (Te Rangi Hiroa), *Anthropology and Religion* (Yale University Press, 1939).

15

THE ART OF WORSHIP

In ritual and worship we have the meat which goes on the bones of a cult's beliefs: all the work and the posturing by which the people deal with their gods, and all the behavior which each individual feels in himself and sees in others that satisfies him of the rightness of things, divine and human. If the kinds of gods and spirits believed in are myriad, then the variety of ceremonials performed for them is infinite, and descriptions of rites fill chapter upon chapter of any work upon a people's culture. I have no more intention of being encyclopedic about this than about deities, because I am trying in a short space to say what gods do for people, not what people do for gods. Therefore I shall here and there use as single words what others have used for the titles of books, and of series of books.

Strictly speaking, worship is the opposite of magic, because it recognizes deities who have the power to say yes or no, while magic, you will remember, means working a known formula to get a known result: you put a nickel in a slot and a package of gum comes out another slot—you cannot see inside the machine, but you are satisfied that there are wheels or things in it that always work the same way, and it always takes exactly a nickel and you always (obvious witticisms aside) get a package of gum. Worship, on the contrary, is filling out an application, perhaps in triplicate.

It is well to remember, however, that this is a savants'

distinction, which would have no great meaning to a cultist, for in ritual the notions of supplication and magic run very close together. In ritual, indeed, it is often obvious that people are using magic directly on the gods, to compel them or to aid them; the Egyptians worked magic to help their gods, and so do the Australians, with their increase ceremonies. And the Polynesians chanted hymns which *had mana* because of the things which they recounted and the rhythmical, forceful way in which they were recited. So we may best think of a sort of scale in the attitudes of worshipers, from magic at one end, where the devotees practically hold the whip hand over the gods themselves, running to the humblest supplication of a god of wisdom, where the petitioner does exactly what he believes his god would like, and puts himself quite into the latter's hands. Near this end we find the Bakongo, who say to the ancestors in effect: "Now look; we are your children. Surely you do not want the village to go to ruin. What about it?" But there is still a further attitude: "Thy will, not mine, be done." This is a most unusual one in primitive cults.

Like magic, ritual has a strong tendency to jell. When we think of worship, we think first of prayer, in which man in the most direct way uses his power of speech to frame a need and make it known to a deity. It can be spontaneous, and as simple as possible. It can be urgent or capricious: "Help me win this race," whether the race be with another boy or with a shark. Prayer may even be mute: in the Plains, the Indians would put a small infant (whose hold on life is still precarious) in moccasins with holes in the soles, so that the spirits, not entirely heartless, would not call on him to make a journey to the other world in poor shoes. But normally prayers become a fixed form of words, however simple, and thus they may borrow from the nature of a magician's spell. Public prayer especially is completely formal, so that it becomes a rite, and the essence of ritual is its familiarity. For only if it is familiar can ritual be socially effective, because only if its form is known can more than one person partake in it, can ceremony go smoothly, be well performed, and have the necessary artistic value. Ritual must come from somewhere, of course, but it must have establishment before it is any good. Notice that even among the Crows, where every man makes his personal interpretation of his ineffable vision, the vision-user wants something to fasten the vision itself: Gray-bull's grandfather made a bird skin, had a woman tie it in his hair, and sang a song, all as he had learned to do in his vision (see p. 28).

Let us look at the kinds of rites in general. Prayer, in its central idea, is a matter of persuasion. So are offerings and sacrifices, in one way or another, especially when they take the simple form of presents for the gods, as they usually do. Food offerings are particularly satisfactory when the god eats the soul of the meat and you eat the meat itself, where the vitamins are; this is a ceremonial feast. It is more of a sacrifice if you have to burn the food up entirely, or throw it in the river, in order to send it up above; or if you have to spill the wine on the ground, and so lose it, as the Bakongo do in their ancestors' cemetery. Some people invariably put a little of every meal out for the gods, from sheer hospitality.

Now the idea of sacrifice fascinated the older theorists in anthropology, and reams were written on its "origin," as if it had to come from a single thing; the most famous suggestion made it parallel the Eucharist, in which worshipers eat a sanctified meal together with the god, and so unite themselves with him; this was a suggestion applied especially to Australian totemites who, in the beginning of the hunting, eat a little bit of their normally tabued totem beast, and Freud borrowed the same idea and made this a remorseful commemoration of his imaginary slaughter of the imaginary patriarch of the imaginary primeval horde. This is an example of precisely the kind of thing in which I am not interested in this book, speculation which interests itself in special forms and phenomena and refers all too little to the landscape of facts. Naturally there are sacrifices, or the putting aside of offerings, for various reasons, all ritual-istic but not all for the immediate purpose of lobbying with the gods. Some animals are killed as scapegoats to carry off sin and evil, which is a sort of exorcism; a goat is killed for this reason on behalf of a novice in a Dahomean cult. Other sacrifices are propitiatory and may be required in expiating a broken tabu, as a sort of fine. First fruits in Polynesia have to be offered in order to take the surplus mana out of the rest of the crop. And of course, grave offerings or goods burned at funerals are simply "killed" so that they may go along into the next world with the dead man.

Human sacrifice has been the most exhilarating topic to cogitative pen wielders, but there is no reason why it should be especially mysterious, and it generally has counterparts in other kinds of sacrifice or ceremony. For example, human victims have been killed so that they, like the other chattels mentioned above, might go beyond the grave with a dead king. Others have been killed as an offering to gods, as the finest gift man could give—either because the gods like to dine on men or because they are flattered by this evidence of human regard. Again, some sacrificed scapegoats have been men instead of animals. The king of Dahomey in the old days used to dispatch messages to his ancestors by dispatching the messengers.

There are also the many reports of human beings killed in order to help the fertility of the crops through a blood bath, in various societies high and low; and there has been as well the slaughter of individuals who actually were supposed to represent gods incarnate. The latter may have some occasional connection with the former, and also might be related to the killing of their semidivine kings by some of the Nilotic Negroes of the White Nile, who used to do this in order that the king might die while he was still vigorous, and so pass on to his successor his sacred soul still untarnished by senility.

Now I do not like to push past whole volumes of Frazer's *Golden Bough* in a paragraph, but I think that most of the above things are merely special forms of ritual, and not of first significance in general religious development. In any case, human sacrifice is definitely not characteristic of the simplest human cultures, being a trait calling for considerable economic independence and advanced political organization. In fact, the most spectacular cases are provided by three peoples just arriving at an early stage of full civilization: the Aztecs, and the early Bronze Age dynasties of Mesopotamia and China.

Prayers and offerings appeal to a god in a rational way; they are what the god would like and appreciate if he were a man. They also include many other parts of ceremony: hymns and chants are prayers which have been put into poetry and set to music, while such things as temples, shrines, and all the decorations used in a festival may be put under the head of offerings, being things made and given to the deity for his use and delight. There is more to it than this, however. Shrines and sacred objects may have a deeper significance, like the churingas of Australia: they may be objects of power, given by the god, or closely connected with him somehow, which are to be used in ceremony, or they may be such things as idols, which represent the god and his own power and which he may temporarily inhabit and possess. (The old idea of idol worshipers is entirely in error, for primitive people do not confuse gods with images, and they do not worship images for their own sakes any more than Catholics do.)

In addition to this, many of the other things that go into ritual are connected with prayer and symbolism, but seem more and more to exist simply for the sake of complication. Dress in all its details is important.[1] A participant in a cere-

[1] Jehovah's explicit directions for constructing the Ark of the Covenant and the Tabernacle, with their fittings, consume six whole chapters of the Book of Exodus. Here, from Chapter XXVIII, is the description of Aaron's breastplate: "15 And thou shalt make the breastplate of judgment with cunning work; after the work of the ephod thou shalt make it; of gold, of blue, and of purple, and of scarlet, and of fine twined linen, shalt thou make it. 16 Foursquare it shall be being doubled; a span shall be the length thereof, and a span shall be the breadth thereof.

mony may be enacting a god, so that he is either dressed
as the god would appear, like a Hopi kachina, or made up
to symbolize him. On the other hand he may be loaded
down with paraphernalia for which the reasons are mythical
and capricious. The same applies to dancing and other action: it may be dramatic in content, or it may be done simply because that is the way the ceremony is. For a famous
example, the Todas of India have priests to tend their sacred
buffaloes, and these priests all day long dodder through the
most baffling and pointless routine while milking the cows

---

17 And thou shalt set in it settings of stones, even four rows of
stones: the first row shall be a sardius, a topaz, and a carbuncle:
this shall be the first row. 18 And the second row shall be an
emerald, a sapphire, and a diamond. . . . 21 And the stones
shall be with the names of the children of Israel, twelve, according to their names . . . 24 And thou shalt put the two
wreathen chains of gold in the two rings which are on the ends
of the breastplate. 25 And the other two ends of the two wreathen
chains thou shalt fasten in the two ouches, and put them on the
shoulderpieces of the ephod before it. 26 And thou shalt make
two rings of gold, and thou shalt put them upon the two ends
of the breastplate in the border thereof, which is in the side of
the ephod inward. 27 And two other rings of gold thou shalt
make, and shalt put them on the two sides of the ephod underneath, toward the forepart thereof, over against the other cou-
pling thereof, above the curious girdle of the ephod. 28 And
they shall bind the breastplate by the rings thereof unto the
rings of the ephod with a lace of blue, that it may be above the
curious girdle of the ephod, and that the breastplate be not
loosed from the ephod. 30 And thou shalt put in the breastplate of judgment the Urim and the Thummim; and they shall
be upon Aaron's heart, when he goeth in before the Lord: and
Aaron shall bear the judgment of the children of Israel upon
his heart before the Lord continually. 31 And thou shalt make
the robe of the ephod all of blue. 32 And there shall be an hole
in the top of it, in the midst thereof: it shall have a binding
of woven work round about the hole of it, as it were the hole
of an habergeon, that it be not rent. 33 And beneath upon the
hem of it thou shalt make pomegranates of blue, and of purple,
and of scarlet, round about the hem thereof; and bells of gold
between them round about: 34 A golden bell and a pomegranate,
a golden bell and a pomegranate, upon the hem of the robe
round about."

and working in the dairy, so that every motion is formalized, and the man must keep touching the pots, his head, this, that, and the other, surrounded all the while by a great many restrictions in conduct; the prayers and utterances accompanying this, and the lore of the priests themselves, while couched in ancient myths, make no immediate sense.

There are yet other accouterments of typical ceremonial. Perhaps it is necessary for the worshipers to be in a special state of purity, attained by fasting and washing. The time may be important, relative to the day, or the season, or the moon, or the state of a crop. At any rate the proper execution of a ceremony, with all the elements going into it, is something like the staging of a play.

The Pueblo Indians are ritual-minded to a high degree. Their ceremonies are elaborate and arranged in a calendar, running almost continuously through the year. These are not something to be left to a church and priest but call for everyone's participation. The gods are close, with many kachinas—gods come to earth—being actually in the town much of the time. Worship is in the hands of societies and clans, and the offices charged with its conduct are parceled out among the principal men, but practically everyone knows the basic rituals and is called upon to assist. Much of the procedure is strongly magical and there is a good deal of use of powerful or sacred objects that are something like fetishes.

The details entering into ceremonies are many, and characteristic of the Pueblos generally.[2] Prayer of course is prominent, used both publicly and personally, but the ideas in prayer are reinforced by offerings which are akin to prayer themselves. Prayer images convey concrete requests: doll-infants ask the favor of the birth of children, and small animal figures of wild or domestic animals make these likewise fertile, the images being scattered around the fields or buried in the corral. Prayer sticks are very important: they are carefully cut wands of wood an inch or so up to a

[2] See Elsie Clews Parsons, *Pueblo Indian Religion* (1939), who lists fifty-five types of these ritual elements.

few feet long, painted and with feathers tied to them, several sticks being sometimes tied together; both the colors and the feathers used have their symbolic or magical associations: yellow is a female color, black is associated with the dead and the kachina beings, in Acoma; and after they have been made the sticks must be prayed over. Then they are used, or offered, in any way: tucked in part of the house, buried, put on an altar or a shrine, or thrown under a tree, and this is done either in asking a favor or in meeting obligations. Ordinarily a prayer is made at the same time, but it may not be, and a prayer stick is a prayer and an offering together. Other objects are offerings of a like nature, with a feeling of compulsion in them. Feathers alone are given. Corn meal is used constantly with prayers, being dribbled on the ground, put on and around altars, and sprinkled on kachina actors, and in myriad other ways it sanctifies or lends force to actions. Food is left out for the dead and for spirits, and is offered to sacred objects like scalps, masks, sacred corn ears, etc. Beads, pigments, and tobacco are similarly used.

Shrines are places where the spirits are approached or offered to, and may be a cave or a small structure made artificially. The sipapu, the small pit in the plaza or the kiva, which is the place where the people emerged into this world from the one below, also constitutes a shrine. An altar is something different, being set up in a room or kiva (underground ceremonial chamber) in a particular way for a particular ceremony: it will have decorated panels symbolic of the spirits and other sacred objects needed in this case, like sacred images and corn ears, pigments and prayer sticks, flutes and rattles with, in front of the whole, a sand painting, and away from this a narrow line of corn meal making a spirit path, which acts to summon gods. Also obvious in ceremonial preparations is always the strong feeling of the six cardinal directions (including up and down), in relation to which altars must be laid out, and ritual actions referred; each of these directions is important in myth and has parts of the natural world associated with it, as well as colors and other symbols. Finally there are the masks, which represent the embodiments of the spirits, as kachinas, and when a man puts one on for a ceremony, to enact that god, he himself is the kachina, the god in living form. All of these masks have a dangerous quality because of their sanctity and some of them are extremely sacred.

Types of Pueblo ritual action are many, representing typically American Indian ideas. Dancing is of course important, and has a force of its own, with large numbers dancing in heavily accented rhythms, while at the same time special kachina figures, and also the clowns, use a variety of set gestures and postures to enhance the special meaning of the dance (like producing rain). Singing has a similar nature, and so has music, using flutes, rattles, or a bull-roarer (a shingle on a string which makes a buzzing when swung around). There are ritual races and games, and ritual smoking and sprinkling of water, and many other such acts, particularly ceremonial whipping, which is performed for purification and also for discipline and to initiate the children; the whipping is done by kachinas.

All these particular things and many others are familiar to a Pueblo Indian. They are put together to make up a given ceremony much as a choreographer takes the steps and forms in which a dancer is trained and puts them together into a ballet. Here follows an abridged description of the Nima'n Kachina ceremony of Walpi, a Hopi village, as seen in 1893.[3] I give it at some length as an example, though not an extreme one, of the involved nature of some ceremonials, and I think it will bore you as much is it does me.

Intiwa, the Powamu Kachina society chief, of the Parrot clan, determined the correct day in July by watching the sun, and two officials of the Horn kiva called out the Horn society's members to the kiva. On the first day of the ceremony, Intiwa set up the standard, a blue-green prayer stick

[3] From Parsons, op. cit., quoting Alexander Stephen.

with four feather pendants of eagle wing and downy yellow bird feathers, and made some other paired prayer sticks, blue and yellow, one each for the four directions and three sacred springs, as well as some prayer feathers for the nearby kachina shrines. In the late afternoon his son took all these to the proper places, with his hair hanging loose and without trousers, running as fast as he could, to signify that the Cloud beings would come quickly. Intiwa himself took other feathers for Masauwü, god of death, and two for Wind, putting the latter in a rock crevice, and Masauwü's in a shrine along with bread crumbs, tobacco, and a pinch of meal.

On the next two days Intiwa again had prayer feathers and prayer sticks put out for the directions, and in addition made a prayer feather for Spider Woman and four hawk prayer feathers for the War Brothers. Every night there was song practice in the Horn kiva. The fourth day Intiwa made more, different prayer sticks, assisted by Naka of the Parrot clan; then from his house and a cache in the Chief kiva he assembled medicine bowl, corn ears, netted gourds, mask, altar slabs, and altar cloth; on the cloth he painted Clouds, Tungwup the Whipper kachina and a dog-head kachina; he put these together into an altar, using lines of meal in the directions as a guide, using also honey and colored stones, and sprinkling pollen on certain altar objects. He and Naka got pipes ready, each prayed, and began a series of sixteen songs; after the first of these Intiwa poured water over the corn ears to wash off pollen and stones into a bowl; after the second he shook the pollen off the sprinkling brushes into the same bowl; after later songs he performed other actions, like sprinkling meal here and there. During the twelfth song Naka blew bubbles with his whistle in the water bowl and called the Cloud beings to come, four times, and sprinkled water about, also with his whistle; at the fourteenth song Intiwa rapped on the sipapu plank, twenty-four times, to call Müy'ingwa and all the chiefs of the Directions. This session ended with smoking over various of the objects.

On succeeding days this same ritual was gone through, but more officials of the society, drawn from various clans, joined in the prayer-stick making, and also brought their special kachina masks to the kivas, for redecorating. In all, 387 prayer sticks were set before an altar on the eighth day.

The dances took place on the last two days, beginning with a maskless dance before dawn. After dawn there came out a group of the Hümis kachinas, men and "women" (female kachinas danced by men). The male kachinas wore a helmet-and-tablet mask painted with cloud, rainbow, butterfly, and corn designs, a spruce-twig collar and spruce twigs stuck into blue leather armlets, a white kilt and two belts with spruce boughs in them, also a foxtail, knee bands with a rattle, and anklets; the skin of the body and limbs was made black with corn smut. (This general pattern of costume will be familiar to anyone who has seen a Pueblo dance, or a picture of one, but of course each detail is special to this kachina.) Each wore a blue yarn bandoleer and carried a rattle in the right hand and a sprig of spruce in the left. The "women" wore typical Hopi women's dress: blanket, and legging moccasins, with coiled hair and a yellow leather half mask, the mask being painted also in red and blue, with a red hair fringe falling over the face and many bunches of bluebird tail feathers attached to it.

These kachinas went to each of the dance plazas in Walpi, dancing and singing, with one special song which the women accompanied by scraping on notched sticks with deer shoulder blades. Back at the Chief kiva, Intiwa brought out the members of the Powamu society, who sprinkled the kachinas and gave them prayer sticks and meal while Naka puffed smoke on them; the kachinas then went to the kachina shrine and left the sticks there. Performances went on at intervals throughout the day, and at the last the kachinas passed out small bows and arrows and dolls to the onlookers, and the latter plucked spruce from the costumes of the kachinas, to plant in the fields.

Next day there was a smaller ceremony on the roof of the Chief kiva, with eight kachinas (two special, and different from the others), ending when one of them threw a branch of boxthorn down into the kiva entrance, and this branch (with prayer sticks and other things attached) was put on the altar. At this moment eight youths came running into town, having started from a certain spring, painted white and carrying onions, beans, chili, squash blossoms, coxcomb, and melon vines, which small girls took from them. The kachinas and society members went once more through the smoking and sprinkling rites of the day before, and as the kachinas started away the people spat on the ground, so that the kachinas would take all sickness away with them. Intiwa led them out of town to the shrine, and now the gods supposedly left the impersonators and went away to the San Francisco Mountains. At the last, all the society members underwent exorcism to rid them of dangerous effects of their contact with the deities.

Here is a tolerably complex ceremony (the above is not even a full outline) of a general and public nature, emphasizing, as the Pueblos do, correctness in minute detail and conformity to essential patterns, like the fourfold repetition of many small actions. Society ceremonies on the Northwest Coast were much freer and more dramatic in their own qualities. The Hopi ceremony occupies the attention of, and benefits, the several hundred people of a town. Below is one ceremony, out of a full calendar, celebrated on behalf of the thousands of people of the Aztec nation, as it was recorded by Father Sahagun.

"Under the first signs of the first month of the year . . . they celebrated a great festival in honor of the gods of the water which they called Tlaloques. For this they searched for a great many infants, buying them from their mothers and choosing especially those who had two twisted tufts of hair on the head and were born under a lucky sign, saying that those were a more agreeable sacrifice to the gods to make them grant water at the opportune time. They carried these infants up to the high mountains to kill, where they had made the solemn vow to offer sacrifice. There, on those mountain-tops, they tore out the hearts of some of the infants, while with others they did it in certain places in the lagune of Mexico. . . .

"Before these poor young victims were taken away to be slaughtered they adorned them with precious stones, rich plumes, and with blankets and mantles very elegantly made; with very elaborate and highly polished sandals. They furthermore put wings like angel's wings on their shoulders, and dyed their faces with ulli (gum) oil, in the middle of their cheeks they painted small white disks, and placed them in litters which were ornated with rich plumes and other precious jewels. While they bore them in these litters they played flutes and trumpets for them such as they used, and wherever they passed the people were weeping. Upon reaching an oratory close to Tepetzinco on the eastern slope . . . they stopped over night and kept watch over these infants; in order that they might not fall asleep the priests of the idols sang their songs to them. If the children cried very much when they took them to the place of sacrifice, those who were with them were glad, because they considered it as a sign that there would be abundant rain. . . .

"During this same festival they committed another cruelty, namely, they took all the captives to a temple called Yopico, belonging to the god Totec. There, after many ceremonies, they tied each one of these captives to a stone looking like a millstone with a rope long enough and in such a way that the man could walk all around the stone; then they gave them wooden swords with dull blades and a shield and put before them pieces of pine wood to throw and the same men who had captured them went to fight with them with swords [edged with obsidian] and shield, and when they had vanquished them would take them at once to the place of sacrifice, where, thrown on their backs over a stone . . . they called techtecatl, they held them, two by their feet and two by the head, while another one with a large flint-knife would cut open the chest with one stroke and, thrusting his hand through the hole, tear out the heart, which he at once offered to the sun and to the other gods, raising it in the four cardinal directions. The body was then thrown down the steps of the temple, and it would fall slowly, bumping against them until reaching the bottom. There the dead man's captor again received it, cut it to pieces, which he distributed, and these pieces were cooked and eaten."[4]

Much ceremony, particularly among such people as the Pueblos, appears to exist simply to keep the gods content and the calendar running smoothly. But rituals do tend to have definite purposes: note that in the Hopi dance the onlookers spit to get rid of illness as the kachinas leave town, and other Pueblo ceremonies are concerned entirely with weather or curing; there exist whole societies which simply perform curing rites, and which the recovered patient is himself obliged to join. I have described how specific in purpose are the invocations of the Ifugaos, and Barton says that they incline to make almost any ritual a shotgun affair —they are at no pains to hide the motives in their piety. Nevertheless even the Ifugaos feel a certain compulsion to perform their rites with regularity, having for example a series of eighteen which must be performed at successive stages of rice growing and storing.

There is a class of rites of very great importance, and so universal that they may or may not be connected with a cult of gods, since they can exist as more or less magical procedures. These are the "rites of passage," when an individual steps from one state into another: through birth into life, from boyhood into manhood, from bachelorhood into marriage, or from life into death. Such rites are half public, half private, because these changes are significant to the people of a group as well as to the person going through them. I have already dealt with death rites and their meaning. These are one of the two most important types; the other comprises rites of adolescence, or cere-

---

[4] Fray Bernadino de Sahagun, *A History of Ancient Mexico*, translated by Fanny R. Bandelier (Fisk University Press, 1932).

monies of initiation into the tribe, which I touched on in describing Australian totemism.

These initiation rites for boys, and very commonly for girls as well, find some expression in almost every culture. The initiation into one of the Dahomean churches is of course allied to this, but in other parts of Negro Africa the pattern is much like the Australian. In South Africa boys enter "schools" in which they undergo circumcision and a long period of privation, secluded from the community, in which they are both hazed and taught by the older men; they may have to collect food for their instructors and then stand for hours in the cold river watching the instructors cook and eat; at other times they have to resist sleep for six days, have their fingers squeezed in a special finger squeezer, or be whipped by other boys for irregularities. (Privations and whipping are also characteristic of American Indian initiation.) Girls will be taking a similar curriculum, getting lectured, ducked in the river, being made to walk in a crouch or wiggle on their stomachs, and carry heavy stones or hot ashes in their hands.[5] Now of course all of this is strongly social and psychological, since they are learning conformity and all the fabric of custom, and since a naturally emotional and impressionable period of life is being taken advantage of. But the religious elements, though variable, are vital: secrets and sacred lore are imparted to the youths, making them feel their responsibilities as men and recompensing them for all the discipline and pain, and heightening greatly the impact of the whole thing on them. There is often the idea of the boys dying and being recreated, and the feeling of the whole group that they are successfully carrying out something which must be done, in thus finding new, fully developed members of the tribe. There is also a kind of aura of specialness, a tabu quality of difficulty or danger, which clings to times of passage and gives the rites their general importance. This appears particularly well among some peoples whose actual

[5] H. A. Stayt, *The Bavenda* (1931).

rites are not overly complicated, like the people of the Andaman Islands in the Bay of Bengal.

The natives here are one group of the far-flung Negritos, or pygmy Negroes. They are hunters and fishers but their food is plentiful; they have bows and canoes; and are only seasonally nomadic, living in semipermanent villages of well-built, raised sheds.[6] But their bands are small and organized extremely weakly; there are men who act as leaders simply because they have the qualities of leadership, without other authority, and there are also shamans of a sort; but if there is trouble or crime, society usually reacts by taking to the hills and letting the parties concerned settle the matter unattended.

Now the Andamanese do not segregate the youths of either sex in adolescence, but they do mark the occasion, as they do other rites of passage, by making the individual highly conspicuous and deflecting his life out of the ordinary by putting him under food tabus. At marriage, for example, this conspicuousness rises to a point of hideous embarrassment: the young couple are made to sit together on a mat while the elders lecture them on proper marital behavior and duties, and their relatives weep—loudly, copiously, but quite falsely (some Andamanese once wept convincingly for Radcliffe-Brown upon his request for a demonstration). The boy is usually so mortified that he tries to run away, but his friends know he will do this and promptly catch him, and his desire to be swallowed by the earth is then crowned by his being made publicly to sit on the bride's lap. Next day, still before the newlyweds can bring themselves to look at one another, they are both painted with white clay by the others in the wedding party.

But before this, when a girl reaches puberty she notifies her parents, who immediately *burst into tears*, as above, and for three days she must sit motionless in a hut, going

[6] A. R. Radcliffe-Brown, *The Andaman Islanders* (1922). I use the present tense, but the original natives of Great Andaman, the main island, have since become virtually extinct, though tribes survive on other islands of the group.

only to bathe in the morning; her arms are folded and her feet tucked beneath her, and she can stretch but one limb at a time, and she may eat with only one hand, using a skewer so as not to touch the food. This ordeal may have no stated meaning, but it is something she will not forget in a hurry. When it is over she remains only under certain food and name tabus.

A boy's adolescence is celebrated by a dance, followed by the cutting of three rows of cuts in his back with a pig arrow. Now he, like the girl, must not eat some of the important foods of the group, taking these prohibitions in rotation for a number of years. In one tribe, for example, the boy or girl for a long time must avoid turtle, dugong, or porpoise, along with certain other subsidiary foods, and then, after release from these tabus, must abstain from pork and a series of other foods. This first period is brought to an end in a full ceremony, at which the boy sits and has turtle fat rubbed on his body by an older man in charge, and is finally given some turtle to eat. All the while his relatives *weep*. During the ceremony the boy must sit silent and still with his arms folded, and use a skewer to eat, while an instructor tells him what foods he may now eat or not eat; he cannot sleep for two days, and on the third he is given a special belt and necklace and is painted red and white; on the fourth day he leaves his hut to take part in a strenuous song and dance, and on returning to it resumes his cramped position, but he can now talk to friends; on two more days the dance is repeated, and then the youth is free to take up his ordinary life (tabus excepted), although for some weeks he is felt to be in an abnormal condition.

Radcliffe-Brown has his explanations of the function of the above rituals, of which more later. Let us look more closely at this sense of being in an abnormal condition at life changes. The Hottentots have a name for it: "!nau."[7]

[7] The Hottentots and Bushmen of South Africa speak click languages, meaning that they begin some words with consonants made as you take your breath in, instead of on the exhale, as we make all our sounds. "!" stands for one of these clicks, and

In this condition a person is suspended, and is dangerous to himself and to others, and must leave the tasks of ordinary life alone[8]; he has left a previous state and is in transition to a new one. In some cases only persons already in this new state may have anything to do with him, and may "vaccinate" him into the new state by rubbing dirt from their own skins into cuts in his; his clothes have become !nau, and when he is through being cleansed they must be got rid of (usually given to the official who is helping him). Then he is ceremoniously reintroduced to all his old pursuits—food, hunting, etc.—as though he were a new person. When a child is born, he is introduced to water, in the first rain. And so is his mother. Boys, and particularly girls, are !nau at puberty, and girls are highly dangerous. The girl must sit walled off in a part of the hut, not exposed to wind or sun or cold water and going out only when guarded by old women, for two weeks, after which she is cleansed, re-clothed, and reintroduced to everyone and everything. Even a widow or widower who remarries passes through this state, though ordinary Hottentot marriages escape it.

Now we are here, obviously, back at the idea of tabu, expressed as a ritual condition; we have a sense of impurity, and rites for getting rid of it, which are common enough to earn the designation of purification rites, or lustral rites. But it is simpler for our purposes to consider the whole thing as a question of ritual badness or ritual goodness: in the latter, the world and the people are in harmony and everything, in salty lingo, is squared away, and satisfaction and contentment reign; in the former something is amiss, perhaps slight, perhaps serious, which will fester in the public peace, causing apprehension while it is there; it cannot be left alone and must be dealt with.

This brings us at last to the true functions of ritual (as distinguished from its alleged purposes). The effects are

---

about all I can do to describe it is to say that it is like the sound of "t" pronounced backward.

[8] I. Schapera, *The Khoisan Peoples of South Africa* (1930).

powerful, because ritual is what people actually do, and do together, in their cults. Also, the functions are varied, because ritual itself is so varied and makes up such a large part of all religious activity. But taken all together, ritual (with its book of directions, myth) works like a sheepdog to keep society from wandering aimlessly and disjointedly. To change the metaphor, ritual not only pilots society back whenever it drifts or is blown from the channel of certainty and cohesion, but also at all times works at deepening, widening, and straightening the channel itself.[9]

In the first place, ritual allays anxiety. The anxiety may be the creeping kind, accumulating from the worries and disappointments of everyday life, which I described in connection with witchcraft. Here ritual replaces the witchcraft belief; a periodic ceremony can wipe out this anxiety (which may be interpreted as ritual badness) both because it is an emotional cleansing and because it is an acceptable positive action to keep life normal.

Anxiety may otherwise arise because of worry over some definite emergency, like too much rain. This heightens tension, in a situation which the people cannot relieve by practical means. There is a familiar, not to say trite, scene in plays and movies, in which several people are awaiting the outcome of an offstage crisis; there is much putting out of half-smoked cigarettes and rubbing together of sweaty palms, and at last one of the characters screams: "I can't stand it, do you hear? I can't stand it!" and has to be slapped in the face by a more hairy-chested type. In the play the author resolves the crisis; in real life the rain eventually stops but in the meanwhile ritual may resolve the tension, which is disorganizing the life of the village, by

[9] Many writers have contributed to this kind of interpretation, and I would be unable to assign credit correctly everywhere. Of special interest are: Durkheim, op. cit.; Radcliffe-Brown, *The Andaman Islanders*, and *Taboo*; Clyde Kluckhohn, "Myths and Rituals: a General Theory," *Harvard Theological Review*, Vol. 35 (1942); George C. Homans, "Anxiety and Ritual: the Theories of Malinowski and Radcliffe-Brown," *American Anthropologist*, Vol. 43 (1941).

focusing the attention of everyone together on some positive and trusted action.

Thus ritual in many ways is an alternative to magic, as you will see if you will look back in Chapter 4. The same is true in many smaller actions: an Ifugao setting forth to dun a debtor after having put the 109 Convincers in motion has simply been spading the ground in a way that someone in another tribe might do with magic. Dr. Mead has also pointed out[10] how the Arapesh of New Guinea use both magic and ritual measures for the same ends: they will have charms against high wind and rain, but will also beat slit gongs and shout to drive away the marsalai who caused it, or they will aid their yams to grow both by magic and by carefully observing all the sex tabus. But ritual is in many ways superior to magic, simply because it takes in more people; it is more a group affair and magic is more private.

There you have the advantage of ritual, in its wider effect. It helps society by dealing with the individuals who make it up, but treats them more as a whole group than as individuals; they are like a tangled head of hair, and ritual is the comb; when the Bakongo clan elder charges the ancestors: "Be like the hairs of a dog, Rest all smoothed out together," he is surely making a wish that the clan itself might be like this. And with the people reinforcing one another, ritual heartens and cheers them. It is based on myth, something they firmly believe. It is familiar, which gives a feeling of safety, making the future like the past; this is very important. The Australians give an example of it, deriving their ceremonies from myths which tell of the doings of totem heroes in the dream time. Also, ritual is a vehicle for art: music and dancing, drama and poetry, painting and sculpture; and good art, of course, has a restful, quieting influence, by exciting the emotions and then "smoothing them all out together." I am willing to guess that we may not always have seen the full effect of the purely artistic side of rites, because of the strangeness of

[10] Op. cit.

style among many people, but Elkin certainly has appreciated the strength of feeling the Australians have about their churingas, and their totem representations, drawn on the ground at ceremonies.

All the above has to do mainly with helping society to handle unusual conditions. But there are other theories regarding the place of ritual in society's normal functioning. Man is and certainly always has been a highly social animal, and Durkheim long ago suggested that individuals derive an indescribable feeling of strength and support from being part of a group. Using the Australians for material, he believed that these feelings are particularly lively when a large group is gathered for tribal ceremonies, that these ceremonies heighten the feelings, and that ritual and ritual objects, like churingas, reawaken these sentiments, and sustain them, in between major ceremonies. Elkin,[11] also talking about the Australians, puts the matter more generally and simply. The ceremonies, he says, "preserve and inculcate the historical traditions and social sanctions (or authority) of the tribe and thereby strengthen the social sentiments; in the second place they enable the members of the assembled group or groups to express and feel their unity and common life—a life which in the ritual wells up from the past and becomes available for the future.

"Such means of maintaining the social sanctions and ideals, and of strengthening the common life is essential for the Aborigines if not for all mankind."

In other words these general rites, these communal religious actions, are a potent force to unify society. Radcliffe-Brown takes the same idea, but frames it slightly differently: as I recorded in connection with tabu, he feels that a society needs what he calls "ritual values," that it must find symbols for its sense of unity and then defer to these symbols in a religious way, either through tabu or through ritual. In this fashion it imposes a sort of discipline upon its members which in turn rewards them with solidarity. I

[11] Op. cit.

talked about this in connection with death rites—how the living are expected to show grief as much for the sake of group sentiment as for the sake of mourning itself—and Radcliffe-Brown particularly cites rites of passage as being those which show his point.

Let us say that many rites allay anxiety, and that there is some reason to be anxious at times of passage. Radcliffe-Brown thinks it goes further: that rites of passage actually create anxiety, while at the same time handling it safely, simply in order to draw society's attention to symbols of its own demands for stability. The Andamanese must for long periods abstain from their leading foods; this, says Radcliffe-Brown, imposes respect for food—so important in this primitive culture—and also for the social effort and organization required to get it. Others would turn it around and point out that food—so important to anyone, anywhere—by being forbidden to the individuals underscores the heavy significance of the rites, and I think they are correct. (I said earlier that the fear of disease probably has this effect also.) But the point is the same: society wordlessly establishes its dominance over its members and trains them in compliance. They signify this by feeling a degree of emotion brought on by the rites, or at least by making some response. The Andaman Islanders weep at a child's puberty or marriage, when they ought to be glad and have certainly no reason to be sorry; in these rites the people most concerned must register their special ritual state in some visible fashion, and this exaggerated blubbering is what custom has settled upon. The form itself does not matter much. Come the Fourth of July, we glory in our independence not by cheering nor by solemnity; instead we risk fingers and eyebrows to make loud noises all the day.[12] Come their daughter's wedding, the Andamanese weep.

Some feel that Radcliffe-Brown's theory is a little special. As long as this is largely in the realm of theory anyhow, a single pattern makes a simpler hypothesis. Let us suppose

---

[12] These wonderful rituals are now illegal in most states.

that ritual and myth ordinarily serve to keep society on an even keel—in a state of ritual goodness—and thus to defeat uncertainty and insecurity, and that certain conditions bring on ritual badness which are breaches in this system and have to be dealt with by reassuring rites of passage or purification (Homans practically suggests that rites of passage *are* rites of purification; if he doesn't suggest it, I do.) This would still allow Radcliffe-Brown's point, that society may seize on such occasions to stress the spiritual values which bind it together. We can thus, as I have said, look on ritual and worship as discipline—not punishment but merely the kind of common action and thinking which makes soldiers out of a mob. In its very simplest usefulness it is like this: fifty people who are used to doing particular things because they are expected to, who all understand much of the thought and feeling of one another, and who know where they will turn in an emergency, are certainly a more effective half hundred than fifty people, each of whom thinks only his own thoughts and has no bridge to those of others.

All this seems so close to the core of basic religious forms that the reader may be wondering how these actions come into being. There is no answer based on fact. They cannot, of course, grow out of the ground like daisies. And, in spite of all the above talk about "society" doing this or that, as if it had arms and legs, never forget that society is an abstraction, just as the species Homo sapiens is an abstraction: both are made up of individuals. And so it is from individuals that rites must derive.

Marrett[13] and Hartland[14] believed that a wish or an anxiety felt forcefully enough would be expressed in some almost involuntary action like shaking a spear, or in uttering the wish itself, and because it gave a sense of satisfaction would be repeated, becoming either magical or ritual according to the belief which would be associated with it. Kluckhohn suggests (and you should remember here how

[13] Op. cit.
[14] E. S. Hartland, *Ritual and Belief: Studies in the History of Religion* (1914).

widespread are such things as the feeling of strangeness at life crises) that rites spring from automatic actions of the sort we all know: "The basic psychological mechanisms [like those by which] individuals . . . construct private rituals or carry out private divination—e.g. counting and guessing before the clock strikes, trying to get to a given point (a traffic light, for instance) before something else happens . . ." and he submits that when these common tricks, though personal, strike a congenial note because of conditions in the culture, they become accepted ritual. Do not forget how many children feel compelled to skip the cracks in the sidewalk.

Wherever rites may find their ultimate origin—and I certainly do not know—I should think that both the above kinds of impulse, merely emotional or slightly neurotic, would find satisfaction in ritual action and thus lend strength to the latter. In any case ceremony has a strong tendency to expand and become more elaborate, from its inherent desire to be careful and correct, and it does this through the agency of an important personage, the priest. He is the specialist in ritual. He may be simply the leader of the cult, like the older men who conduct the totem ceremonies in Australia, or he may be a full-time professional supported entirely by the people and living a life of purity and celibacy. But it is he who makes worship into an art, because he is practiced at it, like the skilled worker in other fields; he is the religious philosopher who dwells on the beliefs and the ceremonies, turning them over in his mind, trying to make them fit together better, little by little trimming here and adding there as he recites the myths or passes them on to his juniors, and so giving more definite form to the cult.[15]

It was undoubtedly in this way, for example, that something similar to the loose, unco-ordinated belief regarding

[15] See Paul Radin, *Primitive Religion, Its Nature and Origin* (1937). This book is devoted to the thesis that religion owes its development to the changing social role of the priest-thinker.

the vague and changeable gods of the Gã-speaking people
was taken in hand and developed into the far grander family of the gods who rule Dahomey. Certainly this was the
state of things in Polynesia. On Ra'iatea in the Society Islands there was at the temple of Taputapu-atea a religious
seminary of great importance, and it is believed to have
been the priests at this seminary who settled the form of
the Polynesian pantheon by putting the major gods together
in one family, born of the sky and earth.[16] And in New Zealand another priestly college existed, the Whare Wananga,
and it was here that there grew up the refined idea of the
first god, Io the Self-Created, which was an advanced intellectual achievement and a cult considered so holy and
secret that, as I have said, it was not even imparted to the
lay public, but conducted solely by the priests themselves.[17]

Priests, of course, in their nature reflect the societies in
which they are found. Properly speaking, priests are servi-
tors of gods, and thus are distinguished from the two religious specialists we have already met, the magician and
the shaman; for typical magicians ignore gods or spirits, and
typical shamans try to bullyrag them. In simple cultures
priest, shaman, and magician are apt to be rolled all into
one—cults being absent or ill defined—and this one will be
only a part-time functionary at that. As you go up the scale
distinctions appear, and the priest tends always to win out
over the other two, first the shaman and then the magician.
The shaman, who deals directly with spirits and is more or
less able to coerce them, would seem to be in a good position, but he is only a big frog in a small puddle: his spirits
and his carryings-on are not an adequate conception for a
complex society, and as greater gods appear so does the
power of their servant the priest rise, even though he as-
sumes a humble and subordinate attitude. Shamans, espe-

16 Buck, op. cit.
17 Ibid. and Handy, op. cit. Handy thinks the belief in Io is
very ancient and traceable in other parts of Polynesia; Buck believes it recent and native to New Zealand.

cially in North America, actually compete with one another; priests co-operate and organize.

As to the magician, he may be distinct from the priest even while both are primitive. The Australians have magicians quite different from the elders of the totem groups, and the same difference is found in the Bakongo, between the ancestor priests and the fetish workers and diviners. The magician is no pushover, having survived nicely up into our own society, particularly in his divinatory capacities. But the priest has all the advantages. For one thing the magician lacks a monopoly. Priests can also work magic all they care to, and do so to great effect: even the perfected Maya calendar and time count were worked out for reasons of divination, in connection with the gods, and not, in spite of their exactness, for any love of mathematics and astronomy. For another thing, the magician has nothing to build on, in spite of being a tenacious form of life, while the priest has all the majesty of his church behind him, and is doing things for the populace as a whole which are beyond the capacity of the medicine man.

The priest may have his personal discomforts; he is a marked man and for the good of all may have to live in ritual purity. A priest of Mexico, who entered this life in boyhood, even had to offer his own blood daily, almost as often as a Catholic might cross himself, by piercing his ear with a maguey spine or running a thorny string through a hole in his tongue. But priests attain a position of high importance, great enough in some cultures to dictate the expenditure of much of the people's surplus energy, as in the building of the Maya ceremonial cities. Such things are historically important, for through the co-ordination of effort and the necessity of trade that goes with these ceremonial developments, whole nations have been built.[18]

[18] For this kind of thing in the foundations of our own civilization, see Gordon Childe, *What Happened in History* (1943).

16

THE RISE AND FALL OF A RELIGION

A favorite adjective of Sunday-supplement anthropology is
"age-old," applied especially to custom and ritual. It suggests that people with an ancient and primitive culture have
similarly unchanging and imperishable cults, lighting for us
the trail of religion's development. This is nothing but an
assumption, and probably a wrong one. Cultures may be
old, yes, in the sense that a hunting life cramps material
change and invention, as in Australia, but even here tribes
exist who lack totemism as I described it, and there is also
indirect evidence that certain Australian social and religious ideas, like types of marriage groupings, or the mutila-
tions of boys in initiation ceremonies, have been spreading
and displacing one another throughout the continent in relatively recent years. What I mean, therefore, is this: that the
religions seen among modern primitive peoples are mentally and psychologically characteristic of the modern type
of man, Homo sapiens; that these cults have the same bases
as civilized religions; and that they are definitely not a collection of inbred race memories from a day when our great
toes stuck out from our feet, and our foreheads were not,
and our speech was "Ugh," "Guggle" and "Glok."

I think this is an important notion, because it means that
religious conceptions can be more sensitive to the needs of
a group if they are flexible rather than unchanging, and can
thus meet new conditions and accommodate themselves to
advancing, more complex societies. We might look at it

thus: a given culture is continually choosing and adapting religious ideas out of an arsenal of typical forms, and is not simply caught in the grip of a set of fossilized customs. So, while certain general patterns may be very old, and may even have characterized particular areas for many thousand years—it is probable that shamanism in northeast Asia and North America is a case—it is likely that specific cults or complexes of religious elements have flourished and decayed in shorter periods, changing at least as easily as we know human languages must have changed.

Doubtless we get an impression of fixity in religion from what we know about the past of the great cults, like Judaism or Hinduism, whose antiquity is impressive. But these, like the others, have been fixed by written scriptures and bolstered by well-organized churches and priesthoods. Native cults lack those very things almost entirely, which permits them to be modified from generation to generation, in the purely spoken literature which is their existence. This also, of course, makes it difficult to tell much about the age or the speed of development of a cult, although sometimes we can use collateral evidence. We have seen, as an example of minor change, how among the Gã people ancient chants, like an old newspaper, reveal which gods have since risen or fallen in importance. Archaeology helps: as I have said, certain of the high Aztec gods such as Tlaloc or Quetzalcoatl can be traced back into the Teotihuacán archaeological period, which began about the time of Christ, but these gods disappear in the underlying "Formative Cultures."

As a further example we can conjecture a good deal about the Crow Indians. First of all we know, from archaeology again, that the typical, highly nomadic life of the Plains Indians is something recent, and that shortly before Europeans came the Plains were occupied by a more settled, village-using culture. Also, the Crow idea of seeking visions for power is doubtless derived from a general North American pattern of shamanism and guardian spirits, which was here given a new vehicle for expression in the exhibitionist warrior society which developed. Furthermore, other Plains tribes like the Blackfoot had further worked out the Crow belief, and had come to embody the "power" from a vision in a medicine bundle containing feathers, furs, grass, arrows, and so on, much like an African fetish. These bundles had ceremonies connected with them to call forth the power, and they could be sold by the man who had the vision originally, so that the power was not restricted to the visionary, as it was among the Crows. All of this indicates that here was a new religious development (using old material, of course), very recent and following the appearance of Plains nomadism, with the Crow version of it being perhaps its first and simplest stage. The great Plains ceremony of the Sun Dance shows the same general thing. It was analyzed carefully, by Wissler, Lowie, et al., and the distribution of the many elements that go to make it up was plotted among the tribes; this indicated that it had one general geographical center of development, and spread out from there; it was still spreading at the end of the last century.

Better than anywhere, we can make some deductions about the whole development and collapse of the native cult in Polynesia, because of a combination of lucky factors but particularly because of their prodigious efforts to remember what they considered to be their history. You will recall that the priests got long training in chants recounting the past, and there was also a vast body of historical lore in chiefly families, with a dominant theme of heroes who made great ocean voyages in canoes. Furthermore the Polynesians kept their personal genealogies straight, remembering and reciting the generations from the living back to the gods: mothers in well-born families even taught the children, by tossing balls with them and reciting a generation with every toss instead of saying, "Ibitty bibitty sibitty sab." Much of this has been salvaged, and a comparison of accounts from different island groups shows that, in spite of the legendary aura, they are consistent in some detail and therefore have something to tell in actuality.

That is, if you find a long recitation of generations in New Zealand you might accept the last half dozen, representing perhaps two centuries, and discard the rest as beyond reliable memory. But when you find that the early parts of the New Zealand account name the same ancestors and tell the same stories as the tales from the Cook Islands, and elsewhere, you must conclude that both places are remembering common lore and common origins, and that the point at which the genealogies become different is the point at which, in this case, the Maoris left the others and went to New Zealand. The matching of the various genealogies, and actual dates determined from archaeological remains by the method of radioactive carbon, demonstrate that the Polynesians were spreading into the eastern Pacific several centuries before the birth of Christ. The following is what probably took place.[1]

Their epics tell of sailing from great lands in the west, from Hawaiki (Java?). And so they must have, for they brought foods typical of the ancient Indies, and their language is closely related to Malay and the other tongues of Indonesia. They came to the eastern islands, the first men with the navigating skill and the sailing canoes necessary to cross open ocean, and arrived in the central islands, probably Samoa, Tonga, and the Society group; from here, impelled now by a powerful tradition of venturing and a high confidence, they sailed out again in all directions and eventually populated all the islands which would support them, not excepting the astronomically remote Easter Island. Like younger sons going out to seek their fortunes, this was done by the junior branches of a leading family, partly because of population pressure, and so this conformed to the Polynesian pattern of rank and feudalism in general. Such voy-

---

[1] The problem of Polynesian origins, and of details of their dispersion, is a very complex one; it has been attacked through legends, culture, language, and physical type, and the literature swarms with differing hypotheses. I am giving only the gist, and neglecting entirely the less pertinent and more controversial details.

ages continued back and forth, partly to keep up ancient connections and for ceremonial reasons, and partly for war and conquest.

Now the gods, naturally, reflected this order of things. In Indonesia the typical cults recognized vague deities, high and low, and also ancestral spirits. From such a base as this—there can be no certainty—the Polynesian system may have grown up. At any rate the gods of local significance were deified ancestors, who might be only the gods of a large family, but who might, depending on their antiquity and the power of the group which worshiped them, grow into a district or tribal god, and finally into a god important throughout a major island group.

Such gods were known ancestors, but it is entirely likely that the gods of the great pantheon—Tane, Tu, Rongo, and Tangaroa—were also not simply mythical ancestors (Tane and the Earth-formed-maid) but very remote real ones, leaders of the great pioneer voyages; and Maui, too, who fished up the islands from the ocean floor, might be traceable to a navigator of the second generation, who led in the discovery of outlying groups after the first settlement had been made. Of course such personages would have gone through some two thousand years of legendizing at the hands of the priests, so that in order to win heaven they had lost any correct connection with places or lineages on earth. But the whole process would be congruous with the rest of Polynesian religious development. In any case, whatever their origin, the highest gods seem to be native to Polynesia. They are found practically throughout the area, showing that their origins probably go back to the time before the colonization of the outer groups (Hawaii, New Zealand, Marquesas, Easter) from the original center where the Polynesians established themselves. But at the same time they have not been traced in any form, separately or as a pantheon, to the Indies or the rest of Asia, and it is therefore unlikely that they were brought by the pioneers. So it appears that we can envisage a whole religious development (away from a system like the Indonesian?) in less than two thousand years, growing up into a rich and well-formed system of gods throughout the great area, capped off with a highly refined notion of mana and the occasional appearance of another refined conception, that of an original World Soul, existing before matter.

Professor Peter Buck (who is himself half Maori) was a principal advocate of the above interpretation and, in *Anthropology and Religion*, a brief summary of the whole subject, he also described the collapse of the Polynesian cult through the example of one island, Mangaia in the Cook group. Now, tied as they were to their worshipers, and their worshipers' fortunes, the gods might undergo changes in relative importance, and in fact different members of the pantheon were looked on as chief god in different parts. In Mangaia, for example, Rongo took first place because, Buck believed, the Mangaians wanted to repudiate something in their past. Everything in tradition and culture indicates that they came originally from another important island in the Cooks, Rarotonga. There they probably had some ignominious position, possibly as slaves, because they later seem to have doctored their myths to hide the past and change it. According to them, the island of Mangaia rose from the ocean with the first Mangaians already on it; and these were descended directly from Rongo, and not from Tane and the Earth-formed-maid. In Rarotonga, Tangaroa was chief god, but the Mangaians eased him out of office with a typical Old Testament trick: when Atea, the Sky Father, proposed to give all edible foods to his first-born son Tangaroa, the Earth Mother Papa persuaded him instead to give Tangaroa only the foods which were red, the divine and chiefly color, and to let Rongo, the second son, have the rest. Rongo got far the larger amount by this, and Tangaroa, said the Mangaians, left the family in a rage.

But all such changes took place within the Polynesian system, which was not true of the changes wrought by Europeans. In 1800 the native life was flourishing, in a complicated equilibrium which it had reached after its long growth. There were thirteen tribes on the island, each with its own tribal god, temple, and priest, and these priests were important hereditary officials of considerable power. Over all ruled Rongo, with two great temples, one inland and one on the shore, each presided over by a high priest of great rank and sanctity. The political control, unlike the religious, was a shifting matter, somewhere between the two-party system and that of the Latin-American republics: the chief of one tribe held universal power, officially, until another tribe could overthrow the first by force. When this happened, the new dictator was ceremonially installed by each of the two high priests of Rongo, who stood above the conflict. A human sacrifice was made to Rongo, the high priests sanctioned the new local appointments made by the new ruler, and a procession with drums—the drum beater was another fixed official—announced the end of fighting and amnesty for the defeated tribe. However, the winning tribe enjoyed all the privileges of the good lands, and the losers took the worst, waiting for a day when they could organize and win again. This may not have been the best system in the world, but it was the one which the Mangaians had reached by trial and error, and it had precisely the same kind of strength and vigor as our own national life, with the added fact that the religious side was knit completely to the economic, without conflict or confusion.

Then came the Europeans, with their impressive ships and with material possessions which the alert-minded Polynesians at once appreciated and desired, and naturally the force of new ideas was bound to affect Polynesian life in every way. In 1798 the London Missionary Society sent the ship *Duff* to Tahiti with missionaries who, with their successors, worked seventeen years on one small chieftain before converting him. This man, Pomare, after long considering whether Jehovah might not be more effective in battle than his own gods, took his followers to a Christian service one Sunday morning. In the course of it, his enemies were seen advancing in force to attack. Pomare ordered the service finished (from the Polynesian horror of a bungled ritual, not from a sudden access of piety, as one missionary writer, Ellis, hopefully concluded), and then went forth to his first successful battle in years, the enemy chief being killed by a musket shot. The god of the Christians having acquitted himself so spectacularly well, all Tahiti accepted conversion.

Native Tahitian missionaries landed on Mangaia in 1823, and were so rudely received that they had to swim back to their boat. But the Mangaians then had an epidemic of dysentery and attributed it to the anger of the gods of the missionaries, and when further Tahitian Christians landed next year the Mangaians were willing to let them set up shop. Mangaian politics were in a state of upset at the moment: a government had been overthrown, and the high priest of Rongo's shore temple, instead of keeping impartial, sided with the losers and vacated his office, preventing the new ruler from being ceremonially inducted at that temple; then this new ruler died, leaving as the only person of national consequence the high priest of the inland temple.

The perseverance of the missionaries began to make converts among the party in power—for one thing, Christianity preached peace and condemned fighting, and to the recent winners this meant an indefinite prolongation of the status quo—and at last the heads of the tribes in power turned Christian, desecrated the old gods, and burned the temples down. At these outrages the opposition gathered its forces to attack in desperation, and there was a clear-cut battle between the old faith and the new, with the enemy priest invoking his tribal god Te A'ia on the far side, and the missionary Davida, just back of the Christian lines, continuously on his knees imploring Jehovah to grant victory to the converts, which He did.

This, which sounds like the happy ending, was only the entering wedge. Circumstances, a Polynesian willingness to recognize power in other gods, and the prestige of Europeans generally, had led to Christianity's adoption, which must have seemed as practical a move to the Mangaians as it did to the Tahitians. But the old ceremonial, pointless enough on the surface, was woven into native life in many subtle ways. Much of the stability and authority attached to the rulership had been based on sanctification at the temples of Rongo, by priests who, like the King of England, were above politics. These men thus were figures of consequence and symbols of stability—strong points in the social order—as were the other priests, and Christianity could not replace these whole conceptions in a twinkling; furthermore, the conversion did away entirely with other such symbols of the establishment of order as the human sacrifice and the drum beating. Various craftsmen who had social status (like vestrymen) because they were builders or keepers of the temples lost both status and employment. A birth ceremony of cutting the umbilical cord conferred distinction on those whose parents were entitled to it or could afford it, as a regular upper-class custom, but the baptism which replaced it made no distinctions in social rating. Now Mangaia may have been aristocratic and un-American, but this was their system, by which they lived. Many other such things were abolished as heathen, irrespective of their underlying significance. The regulation of life, no longer something automatic under an established system, fell largely into the hands of the missionaries. They, of course, were acting quite properly by the lights of the early 1800s but a little tyrannously by ours: they broke up existing polygamous families; they took the arrangement of marriages out of parental hands and sanctioned only love matches, which weakened parental and family authority; and they instituted codes of behavior, especially relative to sex (a people to whom amours were pleasant trifles were now fined heavily for putting an arm around a girl in the dark), which the natives had no training to respect, leading to an opéra bouffe police situation very like our own prohibition era.

All this is an illustration of one part of the process by which most Polynesian populations have been gradually reduced from self-reliant societies with a gleam in their eyes to relatively listless remnants. Now I do not wish to emphasize the destruction of Mangaian native life—historically speaking, nothing could have been done about it, and as a matter of fact the Mangaians got off easily. I am only trying to reveal how a naturally evolved religion fits into the life of a people by showing what happens when it is amputated. When the missionaries put a stop to something Polynesian they did not replace it with something else Polynesian but with something non-Polynesian, so that soon the religion which was part of the culture was not there any more. Now a three-legged stool with one leg taken off is not a two-legged stool—it is no stool at all. That is why the life in fact disintegrated.

To put it more abstractly, people must have lives which are wholes; they must live by a philosophy, which is a system of values or ideals. Ritual, we have seen, expresses and preserves values, putting them in religious terms which are familiar and meaningful to the people. But ritual, patterns of culture, and properly fitted lives all grow up gradually, and new religions and rituals will not convey as much to a whole people as old ones to which they are used. Decline and decay, on the other hand, especially with outside help, can be much more rapid. And when values and ideals have little left to represent them, and the people have no way of being communally aware of them, their life will most certainly become disorganized and apathetic.

However, values have a grip of their own, and are not as readily upset as the single example of Polynesia seems to indicate. How people cling to them, and depend on them for confidence and self-respect, has often been evident in another phenomenon: when a tribe's life and religion, instead of simply being uprooted, is put under very great pressure, this is apt to lead to explosive manifestations like revivalist cults. These have appeared in various primitive cultures under civilized control, but most spectacularly in the celebrated Ghost Dances of 1870 and 1890.[2]

[2] Cora Du Bois, "The 1870 Ghost Dance," *Anthropological Records*, Vol. 3, No. 1 (1939). James Mooney, "The Ghost-Dance Religion," extract from the *Fourteenth Annual Report of the Bureau of Ethnology* (1896).

Often in American history the Indians tried to stand up against the tide of the Whites, recognizing what it meant for them, and, seeing the true danger, they sometimes formed confederations of normally warring nations. More than once a prophet lent help to these movements by telling of a vision which promised that the Indians' turn had come at last. But they were always wrong; crushed and sick with dismay, the Indians saw the Whites pass right through them to the Pacific. Their most desperate efforts did them no good, and they could not be sure of anything ahead of them; whatever the Whites wanted they managed to take, keeping only a fraction of the promises they gave in return.

The Indians along the Pacific, especially in California, belonged to a large number of tribes speaking different languages, but the religious pattern was a general one and strongly shamanistic: the shamans were dreamers who traveled in trances and saw spirits and retrieved souls, and did spectacular things like raising the dead, along with sleight of hand. Combined with this were ceremonial societies with rites and dances, like the Pueblo societies but much less formalized and much influenced by the shamans. Now the American rush to the West unsettled Indian life badly. By 1870 a large proportion of the Indians in the North had been put on reservations, cutting old roots; general white infiltration cut other roots, and so this was a period of widespread tribal disorganization, with intertribal movements and the introduction of powerful American ideas, not omitting the symbols and beliefs of Christianity. Except for the Modoc War the Indians gave little trouble, but it was a time of Indian maladjustment and excitement.

The Union Pacific line was completed in 1869. In the same year, apparently, near Walker Lake in western Nevada, a Paiute shaman named Wodziwob went into a trance and had a vision, which he reported. He is said to have prophesied that all the dead Indians would come back and that dancing would bring this about, but what he actually said is a matter of doubt. He preached his vision in a few places, but he did not leave the Paiutes, and the Paiutes did not become greatly excited. Two years later, however, another Paiute shaman became his missionary. This man went to the Washo at Carson City, and then up to the Klamath reservation in southern Oregon, saying that he had talked with the dead Indians who were coming back, and that people who believed, and danced, would see their relatives again and that those who did not believe would turn to stone. This was going to happen very soon—a few years—and when the dead arrived, all the white people would disappear.

It was wonderful news, of course. It is true that at least two of the groups he visited were skeptical, and sent observers to Wodziwob himself to check up on the accuracy of the report; Wodziwob struck them as a second-rate prestidigitator and they went home to call their dancing off. But elsewhere the doctrine seemed better at third hand than at first hand, and it ran like a powder train. All in the year 1871 it was carried down into California and up into other reservations in Oregon and down from them into still other parts of California; different messengers also carried it from Nevada directly across California to the Wintun Indians, where another prophet received a fresh inspiration as a result of it, and formed a new variation along the same lines, the Earth Lodge Cult. The Indians were dancing with fervor, and other shamans in these tribes were dreaming in confirmation of the belief, and getting new songs for the dance. As it traveled, it appears that the tribes which took up the cult most hungrily were those suffering the greatest deterioration in their former ways of life, while those which were lukewarm or flatly rejected the dance were the ones who had had the least disturbance.

The original Ghost Dance was not complex, consisting usually of outdoor dancing in a circle and singing, and of bathing. Promising return of the dead, and boding no good for the Whites, it nevertheless did not preach any action but dancing, since the Whites were to be removed by other means. The Earth Lodge Cult was similar, except that it predicted the end of the world through fire, wind, or flood, from which the Indians could save themselves by gathering in semiunderground earth lodges (typical of the Californian Indians), leaving the Whites to their fate. But the dead Indians were also supposed to come back.

Hardly had this variant formed than, in 1872, it in turn stimulated another cult, the Bole-Maru, a little farther south. This also spread north in California. It likewise had its origin in dreams, and was danced, in a dance house, but it differed from the other two in striking ways; it was triggered, so to speak, by them, but it consisted of a mixture of Indian and Christian ideas. The leaders were dreamers inspired by God, who preached their own revelations and were highly moral, forbidding drinking, stealing, and other evil behavior, and exhorting everyone to believe and dance. Each leader dreamed a flag and a uniform for his flock, as well. This uniform was not Indian in type, but consisted of simple American dress of the period, specified as to color of cloth and as to certain appliquéd ornaments like hearts or triangles. The reward of belief was heaven, and not the return of the dead. Now, when the millennium failed to appear the Ghost Dance and the Earth Lodge petered out, but the Bole-Maru still exists (or did in 1934). The other two cults were anguished protests against the falling apart of Indian life, but the Bole-Maru was a first compromise, to keep what could be kept. Starting as something mainly Indian, it became gradually more like American cults, so that in the end it brought together shamanism and Christian revivalism, and made it possible for such churches as the Indian Shakers, the Four Square Gospel, and the Pentecostal to come in and take its place.

After the Ghost Dance and its offshoots were abandoned, whatever manifestations arose remained local. Doubtless the fever of 1871 had immunized most of the tribes, and for twenty years nothing of national consequence happened. Then there was another conflagration and it started, incredibly enough, in exactly the same place as the first, among the Northern Paiutes at Walker Lake in Nevada. Here a shaman, a "dreamer," had a vision and organized a dance. His name was Wovoka, or Jack Wilson, and he was the son of a shaman who had actually been associated with Wodziwob, the 1870 prophet; however, though undoubtedly he had the logical background for a new prophet, he does not seem to have been as deliberate in the creation of his dance as this would suggest. For one thing, he made no attempt to spread his doctrine widely, and never left his own valley; he was personally unpretentious, and no fanatic. Mooney talked with him in 1892 (he died in 1932) and found him pleasant and agreeable, and apparently straightforward as far as he wished to go in talking about his affairs with a white man; he was definitely a weather-working shaman and knew sleight of hand, but this is quite appropriate in Indian culture and not a sign of double-dealing; and he made no claim to be Christ, as was widely reported, but only to have had a revelation from God. He had when young been cared for by a white farmer named Wilson, and he wore European clothes and averred that the Indians would be better off in adopting the ways of the Whites.

During the solar eclipse of January 1, 1889, amid the excitement which this caused his fellow Paiutes, Wilson went into a trance. He was taken up to heaven, he said, where he saw God, who showed him all the dead, playing their old games in a land of plenty, all happy and all young. God commanded him to go back and preach to his people, telling them to live in peace with one another and the Whites, to work hard, and to avoid lying, stealing, and war (this last suggestion was still a new note to Indians). This would bring them after death to the beautiful other world, and God gave him a dance for the people to perform, which would take them to heaven more surely and quickly. God also showed him how to manage the weather. So Wilson told Mooney, but in a letter to the Arapaho and Cheyenne he said that the reunion with the dead would be on earth, not in heaven, that the dead were even now alive again, and that everyone would become young; and, whatever happened to the Whites, they would apparently not interfere with the Indians any more. The dance would bring this about; he also once said that dancing would *move the dead*, the old feeling of the power in dancing. Now here, in Wilson's message, was a promise of salvation and a chance for all Indians to feel that they could yet combine and save themselves; the ban on war was no pious smoke screen for the benefit of the Whites, because in the same letter saying "Do right always," he also said "Do not tell the white people about this."

Wilson came back to earth, and in January 1889 he held a Paiute dance and at once attracted much attention among the Paiutes and neighboring tribes. Everything was obviously orderly here, for two years later, at a time when Eastern newspapers were screaming Indian insurrection, the Indian agent of the district, certainly a stupid man, did not know Wilson's right name, asserted there were no ghost songs or dances around his agency, and that they wouldn't be allowed anyhow. But the dance spread quickly both through Paiute missionaries and through visitors from distant tribes who had heard of the prophecy. It traveled into related nations, and down into southern California, and it flickered into northern California and part of Oregon, but this territory had been burned over in 1871 and it took no hold among the tribes who had reacted most strongly before. It was carried down by Paiutes directly to the Navahos, who laughed it away; the Navahos were then at the peak of their prosperity, being rich in livestock and not yet feeling the modern pinch of overgrazing and overpopulation, and so they were not having the troubles and discontents of the Northern Indians. It had no effect on the self-contained Pueblos, whose life and religious ideas have proved the most imperturbable of all; though it is known to have been reported back by Hopi tourists, it left the Hopi cold. But it crossed over the Rockies to the east, and in the Plains it ran wild. In Oklahoma the Cheyenne and the Arapaho fell to dancing with a passion; when Mooney visited them after seeing Wilson himself, people of these tribes crowded around him, trembling with excitement, and all, after grasping his hand, prayed aloud earnestly that they, too, might through this contact see visions of the time to come. The Ghost Dance seems to have missed the Crows. But it struck the Sioux, and there was an explosion.

The Sioux were then the largest and most intransigent of the tribes, but in 1890 they were suffering both privation and the misery of seeing their way of life strangled. In 1868 they had agreed to stay on a reservation which was most of South Dakota, in return for food, cows, doctors, teachers, and other benefits. Then gold miners rushed into the Black Hills on the reservation, the Indians reacted, Custer made his Last Stand, and the government in the ensuing "agreement" took a third of the reservation away. Then the government took half of what was left, and the best half. The buffaloes having vanished, it was also trying to make farmers out of the Sioux, no easy task, but in the summer of 1889 it had the men come in to the agency for a meeting lasting a month, during which their cattle destroyed their corn. At the same time there were epidemics of measles, grippe, and whooping cough in quick succession, and next year the crops failed independently of the government. Then Congress, over the protests of those who had to care for the Indians, drastically cut the food rations which had been promised in all the treaties in return for land, and on which the Indians at this moment depended for life—it is a move against a people in our own borders that recalls Russia's starving of her balking peasants in 1933.

The Sioux were not starving, but they were certainly hungry. They had grounds for complaint, and they complained. Though they had so recently given up their independence they had on the whole co-operated well with the Indian agents, who were good men; on the other side, however, they were under the influence of a few white-hating leaders, above all the great irreconcilables, the chief Red Cloud at Pine Ridge in the south, and the medicine man Sitting Bull, a veteran of the Custer affair, at Standing Rock in the North.

Word of the Ghost Dance came in 1889, and the Sioux

sent a delegation of about a dozen men to see Jack Wilson himself. These returned in March 1890 deeply impressed; Wilson probably told them nothing new, and even advised them to go to work and to send their children to school, but in their eagerness they believed in all his powers, and reported that he had actually conjured up a vision of the returning dead before their very eyes. (There is nothing strange in this; such religious experiences are not confined to Christians.) The Sioux were greatly excited and, responding to the preaching of one of the delegates, Short Bull, organized dances on the Rosebud reservation at once. The dance itself took a more virulent form: faithful dancing was necessary, and would cause not only the return of the dead, and of great herds of buffalo, but also the absolute annihilation of the Whites, through a great landslide which would cover them up forever. In dancing, while the Indians were to carry no arms, nor any metal, they were to wear "ghost shirts," dance shirts cut in Indian style, which were believed to be bulletproof.

The agent at Rosebud did not like the look of things, and ordered Short Bull to stop the dances, and the Indians obeyed. But the dance was the very flame of new hope to the Sioux, and probably nothing could have kept it from spreading. In June a large dance was held, with ghost shirts, on adjoining Pine Ridge reservation. Red Cloud had announced his belief in the Ghost Dance and urged his people to take it up. In August two thousand Indians met for another dance. The Pine Ridge agent went out to stop them, but they took up their guns and said they would fight with their lives for their new religion. Back on the Rosebud reservation the dance broke out once more in September, again under Short Bull; again the agent managed to stop it, but when he had to leave for a short while, dancing burst forth anew. The dance was carried in October up to Standing Rock, on Sitting Bull's invitation; here also the reservation agent tried to stop it, but Sitting Bull declared flatly that he would keep the dances going.

So the Indians were asserting themselves in their right to

dance the Ghost Dance, and it is not hard to see how, on top of their other difficulties, they felt that the Whites were interfering unjustly. But there was no revolt; the Indians were not out of control, and the agents on the whole were certain that the excitement would lead to nothing they and their Indian police could not cope with. But in the meanwhile the Indians were not getting their rations; at Pine Ridge the agent was delivered less than half the treaty allotment of meat, and the Indians demonstrated.

Finding that he could make no impression on Washington, the agent resigned and in his stead there was appointed a real incompetent. This man let his Indians get entirely out of control in less than two weeks, reported that three thousand of them were dancing, and asked for military aid. The experienced General Miles passed through, talked to the Pine Ridge Sioux, advised them to stop dancing, and gave it as his opinion that the craze would die down by itself. But the agent went into a panic and in the middle of November was telegraphing daily for help, saying the Indians were wild and crazy. They knew their man, of course. Short Bull was calling for larger gatherings, and saying that he would bring the millennium within a month. The Rosebud Sioux, just to the east, were now inflamed also, and out of hand, and on November 17 troops from Nebraska were called out.

Now the Indians took fright, and large numbers of those who had been dancing in the southern reservations, Pine Ridge and Rosebud, fled from their homes northwestward into the protection of the Bad Lands, taking many government cattle with them. The troops met this by stationing themselves on the far side in order to push the Indians home. There was no flight from the Northern reservations, but nevertheless, at Standing Rock, Sitting Bull had broken his peace pipe, had been keeping up the Ghost Dance, talking bitterly and denouncing those who wanted quiet and would not dance. Since Sitting Bull was now the center of trouble outside the Bad Lands his arrest was ordered, and Indian police went to his camp to fetch him.

After first assenting to capture, Sitting Bull precipitated a fight; Sitting Bull and several other Indians and police were shot to death. Part of his band took this calmly but part, in fear of the troops, fled south into the Cheyenne River reservation and joined the band of Big Foot. These had also been dancing the Ghost Dance and Big Foot was considered dangerous; it was feared that he and Sitting Bull's followers would join the other refugees in the Bad Lands to make worse trouble, and troops went after him to stop him. Big Foot, however, agreed to do whatever was wanted of him, and with some effort managed to get his whole band to come down to Pine Ridge, where, before going into the agency itself, they camped on Wounded Knee Creek. At the same time all the Sioux in the Bad Lands had agreed to come back, and were camped elsewhere around the agency.

On December 29, surrounded on all sides by soldiers, Big Foot's people at Wounded Knee were asked to turn over their arms. They did not do this willingly or promptly, and soldiers started searching the tipis, causing confusion and nervousness among the Indians. What actually started the affair at Wounded Knee has never been decided; the following is Mooney's account. A medicine man, Yellow Bird, began urging the warriors (in Sioux) to resist, reminding them that their ghost shirts made them invulnerable. At last an Indian brought a rifle from under his blanket and fired a shot, and immediately there was a violent toe-to-toe battle, with the government troops using two-pound shells; in a very few minutes sixty soldiers and almost all the Indian men were killed, and the soldiers, who were raw, shot down many women and children who were trying to run from the scene; about two hundred and twenty Sioux were later found dead on the field.

The other groups of Indians encamped around the agency heard the firing and saw fugitives, and thought the whole massacre was deliberate; they could understand it only as war and they attacked the agency. They remained hostile until January 16, 1891, when General Miles was able once more to persuade them of good intentions (by hypnosis, I should think) and of the hopelessness of their own situation, whereat they all surrendered, and even the leaders like Short Bull, who were asked to come into custody for the time being, did so readily. What is remarkable is not that the trouble occurred, but that it was no worse, which was due to the fact that the leaders on both sides were mainly good and honest men. At any rate, this hideous tragedy was over, a winter of great suffering behind and many Indians dead, and among the Sioux the Ghost Dance was ended.

Then the government increased the Indians' rations.

Now the Ghost Dance was not the main cause of the outburst, though it had much to do with bringing things to a head. The Indian commissioner, in fact, named it as eleventh in a list of twelve factors, putting his finger squarely on the first one as follows: "A feeling of unrest and apprehension in the mind of the Indians has naturally grown out of the rapid advance in civilization and the great changes which this advance has necessitated in their habits and mode of life." The important lesson is therefore that the Ghost Dance was the religious expression of a social hysteria, a desperate infatuation unlike the solid marriages of secure peoples with their religions (see how the Pueblos spurned it). Such cults need not be quite so ephemeral, but in this case, of course, the fate of the Ghost Dance depended on the fate of the Sioux. In any event the Ghost Dance represented, as Dr. Cora Du Bois says, the last attempt to establish or retrieve native values—to save, not the form of the religion, but the feeling of the culture itself.

The Plains have since been obsessed by another cult, which is milder and is carried on by societies, and not the tribe itself. It centers around the chewing of the peyote cactus of Mexico, which gives feelings of exhilaration, hallucinations, and color visions; the Mexican Indians use it for divination or for formal ceremonies but in North America it has fallen into the characteristic vision-seeking, shamanistic pattern, and consists of all-night sings around an altar, and the use of peyote and tobacco. Like the Bole-Maru, the cult is adorned with Christian trappings, and in fact is established as a sect, the Native American Church. In this way it seems to be a transition, an acceptably Indianized Christianity (or the reverse). It spread north through the Plains between 1910 and 1920 and has invaded Canada.

Things like the Ghost Dance can happen anywhere. New Guinea had a harmless but very similar attack, in the Vailala Madness of late 1919, which sprang up among the natives at the mouth of the Vailala River and affected a stretch of the coast of the Gulf of Papua,[3] where most certainly nobody had ever heard of the Paiute prophet Jack Wilson. How it began is not known, but it is believed that it was started by a native shaman or prophet of prominence; at any rate it was carried on by such persons, known by the magnificent pidgin English name of head-he-go-round men. Shamanism here consists of possession, of a semiviolent kind, with the prophet tottering and swaying, rolling his eyes, and declaiming unintelligibly (though the shamans probably use foreign dialects), and the subjects run the usual gamut from men who go easily into proper trances or fits to those who fake the whole thing.

When these men first began to announce visions and be possessed, entire villages would be seized sympathetically with the same hysterical state. Later the people simply watched with awe and absorption while the head-he-go-round men themselves prophesied. Like the many local dreamers among ghost-dancing Indians, the Papuan proph-

[3] F. E. Williams, "The Vailala Madness and the Destruction of Native Ceremonies in the Gulf Division," *Anthropology Report No. 4, Territory of Papua* (1923); "The Vailala Madness in Retrospect," in *Essays Presented to C. G. Seligman* (1934). This was repeated in several other localities, so that the outbreaks are now all referred to as Cargo Cults. I learn from Dr. John Useem of still another which flourished just after World War II on Palau, in Micronesia. Similar in nature and many details to the Madness and the Ghost Dance, it is called Modekngei (coming together again).

ets all saw visions having to do with one general theme, that of the original prophecy, and the theme was, as in the Ghost Dance, the ancestors. Interest in the dead is native to the region, but in the Madness it was mingled with garbled Christianity: the head-he-go-round men saw visions of heaven, which looked very much like a dressed-up New Guinea and contained such figures as Ihova, Noa, Atamu, and Eva, whom I leave it to you to identify. The central idea of the cult was that the dead ancestors were about to come back to the villages on a steamer, loaded with presents for the people. The head-he-go-round men saw them, and reported that the ancestors were white, and dressed like white men—possibly an old belief about the color of the dead, possibly simply assimilation of the prestige of the governing Whites of New Guinea.

Otherwise the doctrines of the cult were ethical in nature, and established by the prophets, who showed some tendency to combine and agree in their teachings. The usual varieties of sin were frowned upon, and equality of women was preached. There seems to have been little that was in any way anti-white in the doctrine, and instead of helping to revive native ceremonies, it tended to replace and dishonor them. The cult itself lapsed after a few years—sooner in Kerewa, where the steamer was so definitely expected that the people arranged a great reception and were badly let down when no boat came. Missionaries and plantation managers helped repress the meetings, for pious and economic reasons respectively. But instead of ending in wide disillusion and shamefacedness it simply faded, and people years later looked on it as a glamorous time, and legends have even grown up that some of the dead actually did rise, and the steamers came after all. But it is only a memory, not a cult.

The Gulf Papuans have probably not felt the same pressures as the American Indians, and the reasons for the Vailala Madness would seem to have been slighter than those for the Ghost Dance. Williams believes the Madness was founded in a sense of inferiority induced by white control and supremacy in many things, and that it was a compensation for a fall in excitement and satisfaction in their own social and ceremonial lives. It is hard to say exactly what such phenomena represent, or when they may lead to something more lasting. Our own frontier sects, from Mormonism through Holy Rollers and the like to Snake Handlers, have had plenty of vitality. Remember that Christianity itself began as a faith of the oppressed and not as the ruling religion, and that it was akin in many ways to the cults I have described: it called forth prophets, and it used much old material, and in its idea of resurrection for all it offered a new light of blinding brilliance. Certainly such cults are characteristic of a people in stress, who have found their old beliefs out of adjustment with harsher needs and who are trying to re-express to themselves their own sense of integrity and to reinterpret their understanding of what life is all about.

17

ORIGINS AND CONCLUSIONS

If the reader by this time feels thoroughly lectured to, let me assure him he has not heard the half of it. I have selected and omitted. I have cut down and simplified, always dangerous. I have left out things of interest and importance —myths, for example. I have made nice blackboard distinctions that the Polynesians might ignore. I have bit my tongue and held back, when I might have run on about the ins and outs of tabu or ritual for pages more. I have still not gone far enough in demonstrating how completely and deeply religion is mortised into social life.[1] What I have tried to do is to choose the main landmarks on the map of religion and to concentrate on them—to spotlight them —letting the less definite types and the many variations go.

What have we found? We have found a number of striking and well-marked beliefs which turn up over and over again in the small societies of the world's still primitive people: such things as magic, totemism, witch beliefs, types of gods, shamanism, and ideas of souls. But while tribes tend to have these several beliefs, they may not have all of them, and in fact may differ a good deal in the number

[1] For this, read Ruth Benedict, *Patterns of Culture* (1934). Taking as examples the Melanesians of Dobu, the Pueblos, and the Kwakiutls of the Northwest Coast, she shows how all the aspects of a society move together like a ballet, around some central theme. This is an outstanding book in anthropology for the lay reader.

which they entertain. Magic and the idea of souls exist literally everywhere, but there are groups who pay no attention to gods even if they believe in them.

The Bakongo of equatorial Africa and the Arapesh of north central New Guinea are both truck farmers with well-organized social lives. The Bakongo are industrious fetish workers and use other magic as well; they have magicians who are diviners rather than fetishers, and they once used the poison ordeal regularly to try charges of witchcraft. The witch idea flourishes, and most deaths are set down to witches; the Bakongo can tell you of long rites which dastardly men go through in order to be able to turn into spiders and eat the souls of others. And they also believe in beast-men (werewolves), who can use fetishes to turn themselves into leopards or crocodiles. They have a great secret society, revived about once a generation to dispel accumulated troubles, into which large numbers are initiated in rites which formerly took four years; it is something like an exaggeration of the Dahomey churches, but the spirits who rule it are not gods or the ancestors. Then, of course, their central cult is that of the ancestors, to whom they pray and offer food, and on whom they depend as their fathers. They do not pray to the great creator, Nzambi Mpungu, but they respect him and obey his commands to be moral, and they remember that he made everything and gave them their fetishes, without which, they frankly say, they could not survive. And beyond all the above there are the other spirits, of the demon variety, nature spirits or souls of violently killed or evil men, whom of course the Bakongo do not worship, but which they try to capture to put in a fetish, as the force to make it work.

Now the Arapesh get along with no such panoply of religious forms. They have plenty of magic, and food tabus are important, and it is on this that their rites of passage and some other ceremonies are based. They have a club-house and society for the men, which also has some magical ceremonies connected with it. They fear sorcery, through magic, but witches to them are a matter of fable, somewhat as they are to us. They have some slight concern with ghosts of the dead. But they have no gods, and no worship, and no explanations for sun, moon, stars, earth, and life; they are, as Dr. Mead says, cultless. Their one significant spiritual belief is in the brutal local demons, the marsalai, who regulate Arapesh behavior simply through menace. So these, and the varieties of magic, are the only real working elements in Arapesh religion. (Dr. Mead therefore will not even call it religion—she calls it supernaturalism.) Yet, bear it in mind, the Arapesh are not a very primitive people.

Going behind the plain facts, what else have we seen? You can draw your own conclusions. But I think we have seen that there is not much difference in the basic ways in which people imagine, behave, and formalize, either between the Indians and the Polynesians and the Africans, or between any of them and ourselves. There seems everywhere to be a sort of compulsion to act in a "religious" way, or ways, and these ways are all of a piece with the rest of a tribe's life. They may not be quite the same in different places, but whatever they are, they are good enough for the people there.

And I think we can see that the tribes in this book have not been squandering their energies and emotions on false gods and idle fancies, things empty of meaning for human beings. In the Western world certain things are considered sacred, true, and valuable, like the New Testament, or prayer, or the lives of the saints, or our souls in life or in death; and we think of other things like foretelling the future, or using charms, or believing in witches or poltergeists, or dealing with mediums and ghosts, as superstitious or evil. But simpler societies show us that the plain scientific truth about any of these things does not matter; if they are believed in they are true, and they work for the people. Certain philosophers and some of the religious debunkers fail to see the forest for the trees when they lament that, in all its history, religion has been the custodian of barbarity: human sacrifice, unbridled orgy, and bondage to error and superstition. Of course these things are wrong, and of course we have had to put them away; we, now, can no more afford human sacrifice, or the hunting of witches, or the blinkers of ancient, unquestioned dogma, than we can afford slavery. But the debunkers fail to see that things like this, or magic, or absurd rituals, have done hard work for their societies and are not chance tyrants. Rituals may be time-wasting and laborious, marsalai are repellent creatures, and it is not good to be hanged or poisoned for a witch; all that is true. But you do not get something for nothing in this world, and if eternal vigilance is the price of liberty, then the price of order has usually been wholehearted submission to some common beliefs, however unbelievable.

Those primitive people who still have their own cults in good working condition may be living in a fool's paradise, but they are probably lucky. Even if they are doomed to feel the disquieting breath of civilization before long, they may find it cooler than in the old days. Whether or not it listens to them, our government, like the British, sends its own anthropologists among the uncivilized people of whom it has charge. And, while I have not read any mission reports on the subject, I think the day is past when missionaries opened their ministrations to a subject people by immediately burning and banning those things which the people had through centuries developed as the religious embodiment of their common life. There are safer, less destructive ways of merging native ideals with those of Christianity, which missionaries like Father van Wing and anthropologists like Professor Elkin have pointed out.

So much for the struggling savages of the globe. What is the significance of primitive religion for us, the civilized? Now the difficulties that religion is having today are a matter for theologians, philosophers, and sociologists, and the evidence in this book is mainly to serve as a beginning point: by presenting the ideas which mankind has put into play many times over, it shows the base which underlies everything higher. Nonetheless I think there are some facts sufficiently general to shed light on what confronts Christianity and the Western world.

In the first place, in order to exert some social control and guidance, a religion should be social in its nature. So typical cults are; we have seen repeatedly how they fit into the social structure of a people. Compared, however, to small communities living in some isolation, it is naturally difficult for huge and rapidly changing nations to find common, dominant religious expressions; at the same time we do not know whether they need the prop of religious unity any the less. Yet Western religion is fragmented. Church attendance has been getting more ragged and less meaningful. And, though we are still impelled in common ways by the momentum of Christian tradition, we increasingly cherish the ideal of depending on ourselves, as reasoning individuals.

In the second place a religion, to keep its effectiveness, must be believed in implicitly. Judging from primitive cults, once belief is well undermined it becomes outworn supernaturalism and dies away, and can no more be restored than Humpty Dumpty. Furthermore, everything religious has been founded upon the supernatural, the unseen. Now our whole culture fights tooth and nail every weekday to see the unseen, to drive the supernatural and the mystical back at every point. This can have only one effect, which is to gnaw away religious belief. Philosophers and others try desperately to hush up this conflict of science and religion, and suggest various kinds of adjustments and refurbishments of belief, but these are not promising because they are generally reduced to a set of ethics and a highly abstract idea of the divine, and could hardly serve as a religion that people at large could get their teeth into.

There is the dilemma. Can civilization retain enough of the supernatural to constitute a base for religion? In the past, and among primitive peoples, the area of the supernatural was enormous, but it is a question whether, in the skeptical atmosphere which is the essence of scientific inquiry, the supernatural can be extended far enough ahead

of modern man. I do not for an instant imply that skepticism
is scorn; that scientific men all have a callow insouciance
about the very things that lie before them: the baffling origins of matter and its laws, and the stimulating grandeur
of life and the evolution of living things, to say nothing of
the fearful practical problems of present humanity. And
this whole book should show that the atheist's victory is
everybody's defeat. It is simply that religion today finds itself under unusual pressure in a changing society and, as
it stands, is losing out.

The distant future of religion can hardly be forecast. It
is the more obscure because we can tell less about the past
than you might think. We have been examining the simplest religious ideas we could find, including some which
are extinct in Christianity today. But what we have seen is
forms, and not origins, which remain a mystery.

It is not that nobody has tried to give an answer. Tylor
sought it in the belief in souls—animism—suggesting that
this gave birth to higher and higher gods; and Spencer
agreed, emphasizing ancestor worship. Marrett thought
mana was the simplest notion, and probably the earliest
impulse both to action and to belief. Frazer saw the same
thing in magic, supposing that man, after a long apprentice-
ship in which he thought magic would suffice to control his
world, at last perceived that magic was a sham and that
there must exist greater powers yet, in the gods, to whom
man thereupon began to address himself. Durkheim held
totemism to be the first kind of cult (he did not count magic
as religious), founded on the feeling of society's own force,
out of which all other cults in time arose. In these and many
other theories there is a general supposition of the progress
from rustic religions of local spirits up through higher forms
to monotheism at the top. Father Schmidt of Vienna (following Lang) reversed this, believing that the very most
primitive living cultures always recognized a single creator
god, and that this showed that, early in time, mankind had
been given a primitive revelation and a true monotheistic

idea, which only primitive tribes have kept, with more progressive peoples gradually developing secondary ideas of other gods and cults, which are, he says, a degeneration from the original revelation, and a pollution of it.

Only one of the above theories can be the right one, if any. And they have other shortcomings. Most of them suppose man carefully thought out his religion; if that were so, religion would be a luxury, not a necessity. More important, these schemes are all evolutionary. (Father Schmidt's is not, but it is easily the most suppositious of those mentioned and is embedded in a theory of culture history which is as evolutionary as any.)

Now the essence of evolution is that something has appeared from a continuous line of development, depending on all its antecedents for its existence. This is well enough for forms of animal life, but it has been taken by social scientists and used as a cooky cutter to turn out theories of every sort. If it seems correct, in any given region, to trace highly developed gods from simpler ones, or some of the polytheistic cults from ancestor worship, this still does not warrant piling all departments of religion, like mana and magic, into one single ascending column, nor does it force us to think that every society must have passed through totemism, let us say, to get anywhere else.[2] Also, as human culture in the past progressed, and society became more complex, so did religious cults grow into higher and more polished forms; but this is a natural development, and is not like organic evolution; religion does not grow up on its

[2] The wide appearance of totemism, and its common inclusion of the same things—tabu, exogamy, etc.—have aided this hypothesis, doubtless, but those facts are no more surprising than the wide appearance of witches, with their night riding, their soul eating, and their cats, and no one has suggested that the witch belief is a necessary step in religion, or that it was carried all over the world at a given stage in the history of culture. The anthropologists who are skeptical of rigid evolution and of the universal diffusion of ideas from a single center believe that such things are examples of "psychic unity," or the likelihood that the human mind will invent certain ideas more than once.

own stem, independent of society. These points of view easily become confused: Radin,[3] for example, espouses the simple, more or less functional, idea when he says very positively that the kind of spirits a tribe believes in is closely related to the tribe's economic level, but he goes entirely evolutionary on other pages, talking in general terms about a "period in man's existence" or "layers of man's religious evolution."

Have we the slightest excuse to reconstruct the first phases of religion? I think not. We have no evidence. We know absolutely nothing about ancient man, throughout most of the Ice Age, beyond his bones, his stone tools, and a little about what he ate and where he lived.[4] The bones show that he was then a different animal, and not like us. So we have absolutely no justification for making assumptions as to what went on in his head, or which of the foregoing chapters would have sounded most familiar to him. I may add that we also have no business supposing, as some have done, that we might recreate the mind of an adult Pithecanthropus erectus by listening to the ideas of a juvenile Homo sapiens.

The matter might be made clearer by comparing it with what we know about language. Primitive people do not speak primitive languages; they may lack words for abstract ideas, and for things their culture does not contain, but the languages themselves are fully formed and complex. None can be placed on a lower plane than others. And so we cannot possibly know what the first form of human language was, and whether the first words were nouns or verbs, or such particulars. We will never recover this.

All we know is that men did start to speak. Now the evolutionary-minded might suppose that in a dumb hu-

---

[3] Op. cit.

[4] Toward the end of the Lower Paleolithic we have Neanderthal man with his grave offerings and his bear-skull shrines, but these do not prove that the afterlife, or animal souls, were the first supernatural ideas; they only indicate he held beliefs found also among American Indians.

manity a particularly brilliant specimen, after long cogitating about the fire, or the sun, or something, finally could not contain himself in silence any more and erupted like Old Faithful, bringing forth the first word. Or sudden and acute necessity might have given accidental birth to a common noun: "B-b-b-bear!" Thus encouraged, the people took up other simple words and taught themselves to speak, by the Berlitz method of pointing and pronouncing. Of course I am being silly; the above is unknowable, and in any event improbable. If early man was anything like his anthropoid relatives, he was in fact a jabbering fellow who made well-nigh incessant sounds on all occasions, and somewhere along the way his sounds very gradually adopted grammatical habit and meaning. But the actual steps between his original babble and the completely inflected, complicated languages of the Australian natives are something lost forever.

If you can transfer this viewpoint from language to religion I think you will see why we must look on evolutionary reconstructions of religion with some suspicion. Religion has a history, of course. But this does not mean that every tribe has had the same religious history, with no returns, or fresh starts, or special developments. It does not mean that totemism was invented only once. It does not mean that religion started with some definite thing, as when man first perceived the vastness of the universe. (Always read through narrowed lids a sentence which begins "When man first . . .") And it does not mean that a group of modern children—civilized or not—somehow stripped of language and culture and put off in a hospitable land to live an Old Stone Age life and grow up and propagate, would have to wait many thousand years before they were again speaking definite languages and forming religions like those of present-day savages. And I am not saying that religion and language would have become inbred in them, either; I mean rather that language would probably appear fairly rapidly as a natural function of the modern noisy, brainy animal, and I mean to suggest something rather like this for religion.

Notice that all the evidence we have reviewed has dealt with types of religious ideas and their functions, and none of it has pointed to religious beginnings. We have been more successful in seeing what primitive religion does than what it is.

Certainly we have seen it as something indispensable in primitive life. It rounds out the techniques of existence, whether these are material or social. The Bakongo hunt and kill the game of the forest, for example. Socially they strengthen themselves by uniting in clans under clan heads. Now these latter cannot work directly on the game, to make it more plentiful, but they can work through the ancestors, and make a rainbow around to the sources of the game in that way, closing the circle, so to speak, and thus they rid themselves of the fear that the needed game will not be there when they hunt it. So the ancestors fill a gap, a weak point, in Kongo life. Magic does the same thing, and so, in other ways, does tabu. If you take the adult dosage, "Religion [is] a culmination of this basic tendency of organisms to react in a configurational way to situations. We must resolve conflicts and disturbing puzzles by closing some sort of a configuration, and the religious urge appears to be a primitive tendency, possessing biological survival value, to unify our environment so that we can cope with it."[5]

But we have seen religion doing more than that. It is not merely wish fulfillment and reassurance of security and regularity. It is an emotional release, relief from anxiety and frustration (shamanism, witches, demons). It provides comforting patterns of behavior (tabu, ritual) and in this way helps co-ordinate community life and effort. It gives

[5] Hudson Hoagland, "Some Comments on Science and Faith," a conference paper, quoted by Clyde Kluckhohn, "Myths and Rituals: a General Theory," *Harvard Theological Review*, Vol. 35 (1942).

usable explanations of the universe (totemism, myth). And it guards against precise fears, like death and disease.

Perhaps the difficulty has always been in trying to recognize religion as a thing by itself, instead of as a characteristic of man and his culture. If writers have been able to see it in so many guises, give it so many definitions, and find for it so many possible origins, surely it cannot be a single thing. It is as various as the aspects of human life; it is still a puzzle, but it is human in its nature and human in its origins.

More than anything, it seems to reflect the refusal of man's whole being, physical and psychic, to accept a block to his aspirations or a menace to his peace of mind. You could feed certain facts and figures into a thinking machine, and it would return you the answer that such-and-such a man, of such an occupation and such an age, would probably die at the end of so many years, and that that would be the end of him, forever, body and soul. A thinking machine could reach no other conclusion, and there it would stop. Or you might feed it a great mass of weather records and figures on animal and human populations, and it would conclude that a given Australian tribe would go on living its frighteningly precarious existence, that every so many years it would suffer from famine and lose half its members, and that the chances were one in ten, let us say, that it would perish entirely on one of those occasions. A thinking machine would be satisfied with this.

Not so the human psyche, with its capacity for weaving a garment of religion, glamorously colored, to protect and adorn its tender self. It has found us a belief in souls, to promise us eternal life. It has promised the Australians eternal life. Have they not survived already ever since the distant dream time? And did not the totem heroes work to make things safe for living men, and are not the heroes here and everywhere, even now?

INDEX

Aaron, 38; breastplate, 228 *n.*

Adolescence: Andamanese ritual, 239–41; Australian ceremony, 191

African tribes: Azande, 46, 48, 57, 69, 71, 73, 75–77, 109, 113–19, 133; Bakongo, 60, 124, 166–77, 194–95, 225, 274; BakXatla, 64; Bangala, 82, 153–54; Bantu, 52, 72–73, 86, 94; Bavenda, 149; Berbers, 154, 198; Bushmen, 52, 70, 90, 158, 240 *n.*; Dahomey, 181, 217, 227; Dinka, 181; Gã, 93, 96, 110–13, 121, 139, 150–51, 158, 210–12, 213, 251; Hottentots, 158, 240, 240 *n.*; Kikuyu, 41; Masai, 154; Nandi, 53, 69, 181; Tuaregs, 80, 198, 199; Zulus, 80, 87

Aglernaktok, 41

Aglirktok, 41

Ainus of Japan, 179

Alectoromancy, 71

Algeria, demons, 198

Algonquins, 25

Altar, Pueblo, 231

Altjira, 192

America. *See* Indians, American; North America

Ancestor-heroes, 192

Ancestor worship, 165–77; Bakongo, 169, 177, 274; Bakulu, 170, 171; Congo, 167 *et seq.;* Dahomean, 217; Gã, 210–11; Feast of Dead, 173 *et seq.;* Polynesian, 165–66

Andamanese: food tabus, 245; ritual, 239–40, 245–46

Angina pectoris, developed from fear, 100

Animal gods, 179

Animals: omens, 70–72; tabu food, 95–96; totemism, 179 *et seq.*

Animism, 19, 178, 278. *See also* Totemism

Ant hill, medical treatment, 94

Anthropological approach to religion, 3

Anxiety, 122–23, 242, 245

Apothecaries, 89; prescription, 57–58, 89

Arabia, ordeals, 81

Arapaho Indians, 263, 264

Medicine (*cont'd*)
95–96; trepanning, 92, 98;
unicorn, 58, 89; women
drive out devils, 93–94

Medicine bundles, Plains Indians, 60, 252

Medicine man, 57, 100; drugs
used, 97; Sumatra, 157. *See
also* Magicians; Shaman;
Witch Doctor

Melanesia: Arapesh, 203 *et
seq.*; burial customs, 156;
divination in, 82; Fiji, 153;
magic, 52; mana, 24, 32;
mourning customs, 160;
New Guinea, 160, 203 *et
seq.*, 270–71; New Hebrides,
156; Vailala Madness, 270–
71

Mencken, H. L., on religion, 19

Menomini Indians: funeral customs, 159; mourning customs, 160; soul, concept of,
153

Mental illness, 91

Menzere (medicinal plant), 46

Metraux, Alfred, 218 *n.*

Mexico: Aztec ceremony, 235–
37; gods, 213, 235; human
sacrifice, 236–37; Spanish
conquest, 67; priestly ritual,
249

Mexico City, Aztec founding,
70

Micronesia, Palau, 270 *n.*

Mirrors, magic use of, 53–54

Modekngei, 270 *n.*

Mohammedanism, jinns, 199 *et
seq.*; use of magic, 55

Montezuma, 67

Montreal, Canada, black magic
in, 65

Moon gods, 218

Mooney, James, 259 *n.*; on
Ghost Dance, 264, 265

Moral laws, 40

Morocco, 198

Moses, 37, 78; laws of, 40

Moslems: baraka, 31; jinns (demons), 198

Mourning: customs, 159–60;
dress, 160–61; self-mutilation, 161

Mummification, 89, 155

Mummy dust, as magic medicine, 89

Murder: by use of images, 50;
divination, 82

Murngin, 162, 187; white
magic, 64

Murray, Margaret, 105 *n.*

Music: chants, 212, 216, 225,
228, 252; drumming, 221,
256; Pueblo, 232; singing by
shaman, 129–30

Mythology. *See* Gods

Nana-Buluku, 218

Nandi: magic, 53; omens, 69;
totemism, 181

Narcotics, 97

Native American Church, 270

!Nau, 240

Navahos: fear of disease, 85;
funeral customs, 162; Ghost
Dance, 264; sweat baths, 93;
witchcraft, 109, 119–24

Ndoki, 124

Neanderthal man: burial customs, 280 *n.*; religion, 8

Necromancy, 79

New Britain, trepanning, 98